KIDS!

Indigo Children & Cheeky Monkeys

A Practical Guide for the Modern Parent

SCOTT ALEXANDER KING

& DR. RALPH BALLARD MBBS

BLUE ANGEL GALLERY
AUSTRALIA

KIDS! Indigo Children & Cheeky Monkeys
A Practical Guide for the Modern Parent

Published by Blue Angel Gallery, Australia
80 Glen Tower Drive, Glen Waverley
Victoria, Australia 3150
Phone: +61 3 9574 7776
Fax: +61 3 9574 7772
E-mail: tonicarmine@optusnet.com.au
Website: www.blueangelonline.com

Cover photograph supplied by iStock Photo
Monkey illustrations by Karen Branchflower
Edited by Annie Cruse
Design & layout Copyright © 2008 Blue Angel Gallery

ISBN: 978-0-9803983-5-9

1. Parenting 2. Alternative Health

In loving memory of brothers
Travis and Anthony Hall

'Indigo Warriors, both'

Acknowledgements

Scott Alexander King:

To Trudy – my angel, the love of my life and the mother of my two Nature Children, Rosie and Kaleb.

To my beautiful nieces and nephews: Jake, Charley, Demi and Dylan, who I love as my own, and Cousin Nick and his new baby sister, Ava May: a child sent in response to a prayer.

This book was written in honour of the kids that I have had the privilege of working with and knowing over the years — most of whom are now young adults making good in the world. I feel privileged to know you all as friends, in particular Joshua, Blake, Luke and Danika Campbell; Beau, Ayla, Jazz and Jamahli; Paul Jenkin; Christian Alexander; Morgan and Bentley Oliver; Anthony and Jane Branchflower; Adam Schmidt; Daniel Long; Bianca Namaste Jordan; Jay Wilson; Taisen Eruvelil; Mollie, Meg, Sean, Scott and Mark; Jacqui Boyd; Lauren Andrews; Jae Stone; Adam, Tahla and Jade Dale; Maya Rain and Adam and Damien Carr. If I have forgotten to list anyone, please forgive me. You know what you mean to me. You are like family to me. You have taught me so much, and for that I thank you.

I would also like to honour Mark, Adam and Sarah for offering their stories and giving me permission to share them in the body of this book.

With special thanks to my publishers, Blue Angel Gallery: Toni Carmine Salerno, his beautiful wife, Martine, Michael and Tanya, for giving me the chance to present this work to you. To Leanne, for introducing me to the Indigo Phenomenon and for encouraging and supporting me as I developed my early seminars that became the foundation of this book. To Judy Garrecht, for helping identify the five primary Monkeys. And, finally, to Ralph Ballard and his wife, Sushie, for their friendship, support and awe-inspiring wisdom that forms a large part of this work.

Dr. Ralph Ballard:

To the spiritual warrior who shares my life — my beloved wife Sushie. And to all the other warriors who have shared with me over the years. Thank you.

This is a book for you — the parent with a child affected by ADD, ADHD or autism, or who has a difficult 'problem child', or who has a child who seems special or gifted. It is also a book for those who want to understand and appreciate what these children are on about. And this book might even be for some of you 'new children' who feel so very different to what society expects of you, but who are not sure what to do about it all.

The book has lots of interesting ideas, insights and experiences that Scott and I have developed over the years working with these kids. It also contains a brief overview of some of the current medical and natural therapy approaches available to these children. But most of all it is a guide to assisting these so-called 'Five Monkey' children to heal their difficulties and develop into the amazing people they can potentially be. I hope you get as much excitement and interest out of reading this book as Scott and I have shared in the writing of it.

And most of all I hope this book makes a real positive contribution to helping us all honour and encourage this next generation of children to become the new 'earth shakers' which they seem so obviously to embody; all in the service of becoming better people, and in becoming a society living in conscious harmony with Mother Earth.

Contents

A human being is part of the whole called by us 'Universe', a part limited in time and space. He experiences himself, his thoughts and feelings as something separated from the rest, a kind of optical delusion of his consciousness. This delusion is a kind of prison for us, restricting us to our personal desires and to affection for a few persons nearest to us. Our task must be to free ourselves from this prison by widening our circle of compassion to embrace all living creatures and the whole of nature in its beauty.

Albert Einstein

Preface

'The greatest discovery of all time is that a person can change his future by merely changing his attitude. Do the one thing you think you cannot do. Fail at it. Try again. Do better the second time. The only people who never tumble are those who never mount the high wire. This is your moment. Own it.'

- Oprah Winfrey -

We are all children of the Earth Mother – born with equal aptitude and prospect. With this in mind, I have written this book as a way of encouraging everyone to identify and embrace their strengths and weaknesses equally, and do what needs to be done to honour them to their fullest potential. We must all improve our attitudes and our behaviour. In doing so, our kids will have admirable mentors to look up to and worthy examples to follow. Only as 'a people' can we hope to bring our planet back to a place of balance and harmony. We need to look at our diet, the products we use to clean our homes and the lifestyles we lead, and go back to the self-sufficient approaches adopted by our ancestors and the natural remedies gifted to us at the beginning of time by the Earth Mother herself. We all need to be held accountable – as a united tribe – for the poverty, pollution, tyranny, corruption and fear gripping our beautiful world and agree wholeheartedly to reject them forever. And, most importantly, we need to see our children for what they are – reflections of our own fears, errors and vulnerabilities. What if our kids are not spiritual saviours, emerging en masse to bring peace back to the land, for example? What if we have simply reached critical mass? What if all the pollutants we have been pumping into the atmosphere; the preservatives we have been lacing our food with; the hormones and growth supplements we have been force-feeding our beef, lamb and chicken to make them grow bigger and faster; the chemicals used to enhance the look and taste of our food and the toxic materials used to make our shampoos, soaps and house-cleaning liquids – what if all these impurities that have been damaging our environment for years have finally raised their ugly heads within our children? What if, like the Osprey, whose young are negatively affected forever or killed before they hatch by the pollutant-laden fish they consume over generations, our kids are paying for the sins of their fathers? If this is the case, then I feel pretty confident when I say we are fast approaching a global breaking point. So, rather than continuing to dance with the devil as we are now, I urge you to join me in my bid to show accountability by changing how we live and how we treat the Earth and each other by doing what we can to reverse the process.

Introduction

People ask me all the time, "If you are not an Indigo, Crystal or Rainbow Child, what are you? What is your purpose if you aren't one of these types of people?" They also ask, "So my kid is an Indigo ... I get that, but what can I do to support them? What can I do to make their life more meaningful and whole? And what can I do to make living with them easier for me and the other members of our family?"

This book lists five types of people, with Indigos being just one. It lists the five categories that encompass ALL people. I urge you to take the time to discover which category you fit into and then make a pact to do what you can to support your fellow man, woman and child – be they Indigo or not. Don't be surprised, though, if you resonate to more than one type. You might like to look at them as your yin and yang aspects, for example, your potential and your shadow, your up and your down, or what you have been and where you are heading. You may find, for instance, that if you connect with the qualities of the Peacekeeper Child, you might also feel a bond to the Crystal or Nature Children, and if you feel connected to the Warrior or Indigo Child's traits, you might also feel a bond to the qualities of the Winter Child. This is because the Peacekeeper Children (who resonate to the air element and spring) and the Nature Children (who resonate to the water element and autumn) are polar opposites on an elemental level, as are the Winter Children (who resonate to the earth element and winter) and the Warrior Children (who resonate to the fire element and summer). The Golden or Rainbow Children, the type that corresponds to the element of Spirit or Aether, embraces all the elements and the four seasons as one, so a connection to all or any other 'type' of child is both common and acceptable.

Warrior Children

Element: Fire

Season: Summer

Nature Children	**Golden Children**	**Peacekeeper Children**
Element: Water	Element: Spirit / Aether	Element: Air
Season: Autumn	Season: All or any	Season: Spring

Winter Children

Element: Earth

Season: Winter

I write this book as an invitation to you to take some time to get to know your children by first getting to know yourself better. In order to offer the soundest ideas and most workable suggestions, in compiling this guide, I have consulted the ways and traditions of some of the most ancient philosophies in the world. I was both honoured and thrilled, therefore, when Dr. Ralph Ballard, an integrative holistic doctor, natural therapist and keeper of a wealth of esoteric knowledge, well-versed in the ways of Traditional Chinese Medicine, Homeopathy, Ayurvedic wisdom and more, agreed to help me compile a meaningful and accurate compendium of approaches; a compilation best viewed as a list of 'prompts' or ideas, to be adopted only if they appeal. While some of the suggestions listed will appeal to your child (and you), others will not. Despite the fact that these suggestions were made in relation to each child's 'type', there will always be exceptions. There will always be those who resonate to more than one approach, or those whose personality seems to demonstrate the characteristics of more than one 'type'. So, glean what you think appropriate from the advice listed, the suggestions you feel are most appropriate to you, and by all means, abandon the rest. So long as you are truly endeavouring to do what is best for you and your child, how can you make a mistake?

My Journey from Alone to One

I am sure I am not alone when I describe my childhood as one of emotional deprivation, solitude and personal uncertainty. I am sure many of you will recognise as your own my feelings of isolation, separation and total forsakenness. As a young person I truly believed that life was a case of 'me against the world'; that everyone was 'only in it for himself or herself' and that the only person I could completely trust was me. I had no reason to doubt my belief, either, with the prominent people in my life constantly confirming and anchoring my rather limited and tainted view of life. And so it was until that fated night in January 1995, when my world was rocked by a severe trauma – an accident that tragically took the life of two kids I looked upon as my brothers. My world literally came crashing down around me, sending me, my values, beliefs and my life as a whole into a veritable vortex of confusion and despair; a whirlpool that promised to either break or make me. As if instructed by a force beyond my conscious understanding, however, I instinctively (and immediately) chose the latter, thus unwittingly establishing the spiritual foundation that had nurtured me since the day I was born and which continues to sustain me to this day.

As strange as it might sound, the night my 'old life' ended was when I first realised that I was not alone. That night part of me died, but in many ways, all of me was reborn. I lost, on a tangible level, something I will never, ever, get back. I lost something that had filled my heart with hope and purpose, making my past more bearable, if only superficially. On losing the boys, though, I discovered (over time) that I had actually gained more than I could ever have hoped for. In receiving the lesson of loss I simultaneously gained the gift of oneness. As I mourned the loss of the boys, I came to realise that their essence had returned to The Void. They had returned to Spirit, to be reunited with the source of all life. In leaving me on a tangible level, what I had lost was quickly returned in a way that inspired connectedness to all people and all things of nature. Although I could no longer see them in the physical sense, I could feel them everywhere. I suddenly felt an alliance with the world that I had never really believed existed before, let alone ever hoped to experience first hand. I realised that although I was still alone in the physical sense, on a spiritual level, I was surrounded by Spirit — a realisation that 'woke me up' on all levels. It helped me reclaim my purpose and welcome back my soul essence.

As a child I believed my feelings of aloofness were only aimed at the external world, but, as I healed and grew (on all levels), I came to realise that I had also been living my life completely detached from myself. The gift hidden within the lesson of 'loss' helped me to see that in order to be embraced by the world around me, I first had to embrace myself; that how I felt about myself determined how the world responded to me. When you feel isolated, you will be, especially when you have not welcomed yourself 'home'. If you have an issue with living in your own skin, how can you expect yourself to feel comfortable living anywhere? And most importantly, how can you expect others to feel comfortable living with you?

So, in order to welcome myself home, I journeyed back to the earliest negative experience I could consciously remember, and I forced myself to relive it – in minute detail. I forced myself to feel every emotion, ask every question and to witness every aspect. I was literally there, in the midst, as if it were taking place in the present. I cried and cried and cried. I felt my heart being ripped out all over again. I felt it break, and break again. And then I screamed at Spirit. I yelled and cursed and swore... and I meant every word. I figured that if Spirit had put me through all that, then there had to be a reason – a really good reason. They must have known what they were doing. It must have been planned and they must have considered me worthy, if you like. I decided that if I could go back to that first experience, that moment as a small child when I was 'put in a box' and labelled as 'damaged', and if I reviewed it for flaws, I might find the reason why Spirit would put me through such a thing. I decided I would view that first experience like a pebble and that if I threw that pebble into the emotional pool that was my life, the ripples that fanned out would help me address every other incident that had happened since that first one. Like dominoes, I assumed, one would affect the next. So I took that pebble and threw it with all my might and, in reliving the experience, I realised that I hadn't consciously 'done' anything to deserve it, so I asked Spirit, "Why would I need to experience that?" and I was 'told' that it was part of my spiritual training – my apprenticeship. It was the beginning of a learning from which powerful experience would be gleaned, experience that would offer me wisdom in my future, so long as I took the time to learn the lesson hidden within it now. And so I did. I honoured my sacred learning and then understood that I had to do the same with every aspect of my life, and above all, with my most recent loss. With greater confidence and desperate to heal, I painfully reviewed that, and over time, found the lesson. And it was then that I felt Spirit. And with the feeling came the realisation of the true beauty that Spirit represents.

I had always believed that God lived 'out there' and that to be close to God was almost impossible. God had always been out of reach, unobtainable and was to be feared. But I had misunderstood. I had placed God 'out there'. I had pushed God away and separated myself from what God represented, not the other way around. The day I realised this was the day I found oneness. I had been using the wrong words and looking at what God represented from the wrong perspective. I had believed what I had read and what I had been told, and I had listened to people who had been doing the same thing. So I stopped using the word God and I began using the word Spirit. I felt a stronger connection to that word because it symbolised something I had found deep within myself. When I said the word Spirit, I felt it at my core. I felt it. And that brought tears to my eyes. When I said the word God, though, the tears that emerged were triggered by other more negative emotions. So God became Spirit, and with Spirit as my ally, I marched out into the world and found myself. I found my place and I found the people, and for the first time in conscious memory I knew I was at one with the people, no longer the one to stand apart, lost to myself and alone.

Self-Realisation

In 2004 I was given the chance to attend Doreen Virtue's three-day Angel Intuitive Course. Not being someone to miss an opportunity to deepen my relationship with Spirit, I jumped at the chance and, today, am very pleased that I did.

During the workshop, Doreen spoke several times of the Indigo Children. Although I had a vague understanding of what Indigo Children were before the course, I had never really given much credence to their significance. I thought it was just another label; a name offered to further pigeonhole our kids or a term that gave permission for the kids to act up and for their parents to drug them into submission. As a retired classroom and art specialist primary school teacher, I have met many children labelled as having ADD (Attention Deficit Disorder) and ADHD (Attention Deficit Hyperactivity Disorder) and have had many an argument (within the school community and outside it) defending these kids, because even though many continually displayed violent 'anti-social' behaviour and clearly shunned fear-based authority, I refused to accept that incapacitating prescription drugs were the answer.

So, as you can imagine, it came as a great shock (and relief) to find that what Doreen said not only made sense and confirmed my observations as a teacher, but more amazingly, described me (seamlessly) as a child! At one point, Doreen asked the participants who thought they were Indigo Children to stand up. I am quite a reserved person (believe it or not), so it took some courage for me to do so. I cannot tell you why I stood up, except that the description offered by Doreen seemed to fit me like a glove, and because of that perhaps, it lifted a huge weight off my shoulders. Well when I stood up, Doreen looked at me and said, "I knew you were an Indigo, Scott," and I nearly fainted with shock. But how did she know? I wondered. Was it something I had said?

I spent a lot of time feeling resentful as a child, but instead of displaying aggression and insolence as a means of expressing my suppressed anger like a lot of the kids that I have met over the years, I went within. I shut down. I was very emotional and generally very quiet. But Doreen knew nothing of this. So how was she able to say so confidently that I was an Indigo? Apparently, the answer lay in the indigo-toned aura that encircled my body. On hearing this, a penny dropped; a penny that took the form of a Capuchin Monkey.

During my years as a teacher, my work with kids proved very rewarding. I loved being a teacher, particularly the time I got to spend with kids labelled as 'trouble'. These kids and I usually clicked straight away, I think because I recognised the anger they had pent up inside them and they recognised mine. To me their anger was a cry for help, but everyone else saw it as disruptive behaviour – behaviour that had to be stopped, punished or suppressed at any cost. As a teacher, I quickly realised that I was particularly good with the kids the system had given up on. These were generally the kids who had been diagnosed as having ADD and ADHD; the kids the schools put up with year after year in the hope that they would eventually leave and become someone else's problem. I believe that all kids are the same inside and that there is no such thing as a 'bad' kid. All kids need attention, praise and to be made to feel special. I found that by speaking to these kids (rather than at them), about things that interested them and in a way that showed that what they had to say mattered, the 'trouble' kids were actually more responsive than the 'good' kids. Most of these so-called 'trouble' kids craved one thing – attention – and it did not matter to most of them whether it was positive attention or not, so long as they got some. Negative attention was better than no attention at all, it seemed. So, sitting with these kids and listening to them share their dreams and aspirations (yes, even 'trouble' kids have hopes and dreams) as well as their fears and concerns (emotions that often dominate these kids' worlds), gave many of them permission to speak, often for the first time, from the heart. The shock that someone was actually taking time out just for them with no expectation, demand or pressure was so great that they immediately opened their hearts and spilled the beans on everything. They were so grateful for the opportunity to speak about what was in their hearts, their perception of the world and their place within it, that their 'tough guy' personas shrivelled to reveal the Spiritual Warriors they truly were. Being able to open their hearts in that way was like freeing their souls. It gave them permission to celebrate who they were and what they had to offer. It allowed them space in which to demonstrate their abilities (which often included those considered extra-sensory abilities) and to harness their personal power.

And now, after all these years, I realise that these kids were Indigo Children. And why, despite my previous lack of experience with Indigo Children, am I so sure that these kids are Indigo Children? Because, although at the time I took no notice, I could see a small black and white Monkey sitting on the left shoulder of each of them; a Monkey that harnesses exactly the vibrational qualities, it seems, as the colour indigo.

Capuchins are small Monkeys from South America. Although there are several species of Capuchin, the most frequently recognised is the White-shouldered Capuchin. The Capuchin Monkey takes its name from the Capuchin Monk, whose cowl the Monkeys' head colouring resembles. Considered the most intelligent of the 'new world' Monkeys, the Capuchin's brain is highly developed and quite large in proportion to the size of the animal itself. These Monkeys are bred as aids for the physically disabled and are regularly employed as animal actors in Hollywood movies due to their imagination, aptitude, self-pride, nimbleness and inquisitive personality – traits identical to those found in the children they represent. I have always seen the Capuchin Monkey with these particular children, but as I have intuitively seen animals with all people my whole life, I initially took little notice! I never realised the connection or the significance. I never made the link between Indigo Children and the Monkeys I saw sitting on their shoulders. Like all people, no kid wants to be told what to do, not without good reason at least, but obviously no kid can be expected to just know what to do, either. They have to see that we are prepared to guide them, to show them, to walk with them while demonstrating how to live impeccable lives and how to walk in beauty. They have to see the world as being an authentic place, where no one is innately perfect and where everyone experiences bouts of vulnerability. They need to be shown how to embrace their intrinsic beauty, how to nurture it and how to present it to the people as a true representation of their soul.

Although I endorse the acumen of the animals and the ancient wisdom of the Earth Mother with everything I do, the vision I hold for my future work involves integrating the knowledge I have acquired as a teacher, parent and Indigo Child. In doing so, I hope to facilitate greater awareness of our kids so that they might regain control of their lives, find reverence for themselves within themselves and, in turn, regain the global respect that they deserve. The kids today are not the problem — it is the society in which we expect them to live. It is the society we, as their parents and teachers, have created for them; a world that moves too fast for us, let alone for our kids; a world where kids are beginning to look to drugs and alcohol to slow things down. We need to unite and take responsibility for our kids. We need to stop drugging them up so that they may fit in. We have to rebuild society and its view of our kids by remodelling the perception we have of one another.

We have to value our kids and begin honouring them as the leaders of tomorrow and as the Spiritual Warriors they have always been. But we can only do this if we are prepared to take responsibility for our own lives and rebuild the view and belief we hold of ourselves. All kids are precious. We must encourage them, support them and ensure that they become all that they were meant to be. If we don't, we run the risk of missing out on something quite miraculous, something, it seems, the Capuchin Monkey has known about for centuries!

PART ONE

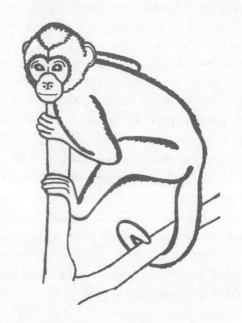

1

Today's Children

Few would argue that today's children *are* different. It is safe to say they are more aware, outspoken and defiant – completely different to what *we* were like when *we* were kids. The kids we see today appear rebellious, angry and resentful ... but when their behaviour or attitude is questioned, the kids themselves are not really sure why they feel or behave as they do. They just do. And this is the problem. Today's kids are frustrated with something larger than their conscious mind can put into words. It is right there, on the tip of their tongue, but they cannot find the words; there is nothing for them to compare their emotions with and nothing to weigh it against. They just are. And with every probing question and trip to the psychologist, our kids are getting angrier and more frustrated. They don't know what the problem is – no one does, but they do know what it *isn't*. They know it *isn't them*. They initially take the challenging questions, suggestions and the disapproving looks in their stride, until one day they snap. Their shadow side, often fed by years of confused emotion and suppressed feelings of inadequacy (feelings reinforced by those who are supposed to inspire and guide them: teachers, doctors and – sadly – sometimes even parents), eventually bursts out and runs rampant, and with a sigh of relief we label them ADD (Attention Deficit Disorder) or ADHD (Attention Deficit Hyperactivity Disorder) and drug them out to make them 'normal'. At least then we have something to blame.

The point I am trying to make is there is nothing to blame. Honest. There is nothing 'wrong' with our kids. Sure, there will *always* be the occasional kid who is different in a negative way. There have always been individuals who stand out as being a little out of the nine dots, but these cases were (and still are) rare. Today's kids *are* different. But their difference is special. There is nothing *wrong* with today's kids. In fact, today's kids are very much 'okay'. They are here for a reason and, if we were completely honest with ourselves, we would admit that we are the ones who are experiencing the resentment and the anger. We are the ones creating the communication blocks, the disruption and the defiance we see in our children. We spend so much time trying to put our kids into boxes that we so desperately wanted to escape from when we were young, that we have forgotten to ask ourselves why. We try so hard to find labels for our kids and reasons for their behaviour that we have forgotten to look at ourselves. We become angry with our children for speaking up, having opinions and for pointing out the inadequacies in our society because we see it as criticism of our ability to parent well, and in turn disloyal to the efforts we witnessed in our parents. We see it as a slap in the face, a sign that we have not loved deeply enough or participated effectively enough in their lives. We see it as a spotlight that insinuates our role as being defective or lacking in some way. We become defensive because society says that children should be seen and not heard and we superficially believe it. What we fail to feel is pride and excitement. We fail to feel these emotions because we are afraid; afraid to remember our own desire to make a difference, bring about change and to scream from the bottom of our very soul 'What about me?' A plea that echoes back over countless generations, I assure you.

Our communities are like volcanoes ready to erupt, threatening to burst apart unless we take responsibility and start listening to and communicating with our kids instead of talking *at* them and telling them how they should be acting. I am sure the riots that tore through Sydney in early 2005 were of great concern to most Australians and I am also confident that many people watching these outbursts on television were asking why. Why are our kids acting like this? The answer: frustration ... mixed with relief. The kids involved took the first excuse as the final straw and ran with it. They aimed their frustration at the most prominent representation of authority (the police) and vented their anger and resentment on them with force and passion. The kids involved probably lost sight of the trigger early on, the single incident that ignited this wildfire of emotion, and were reacting purely on adrenalin and the misguided sense of power afforded them by the realisation that they were finally being heard. What parents need to be made aware of is that many children, although sitting silently watching the riots on television, were subconsciously right there beside their peers, cheering them on.

Today's children are special. They are sacred and they are the balancing force we have been calling to for years. And now that they are here, we don't know how to handle them. Today's children are the Indigo Children, Spiritual Warriors destined to initiate great change for our planet so long as we create the forum for them to do their work. Indigo Children hate being lied to. They know immediately when someone is not telling the truth, and it angers them beyond description. Today's children cannot abide hypocrisy, arrogance or ignorance, but they are inherently forgiving, accepting and loving. Sure, they fire up quickly, speak their mind and sometimes act out violently, but they only do so in response to our being unforgiving, judgemental or selfish. The kids we see today are like walking highlighter pens, indicating society's weak spots, pitfalls and sore areas, but as with all healing, they are aware that nothing global can take place until we clean up our own back yard. So they target their elders and immediate 'superiors' — their teachers, principals, parents and other figures of authority. If the truth were told, today's children are not suffering from ADD or ADHD — we are. We are the ones not paying attention. We are the ones bucking the (new) system. We are the ones defying change. We are the ones resisting our very evolution. The angry children we see today are the result of our struggle to comply with the greater scheme of things and their desire to see us wake up.

I heard many people at the time say that the kids who rioted in Sydney (and in Perth a little while later) were probably high on drugs, most likely bought with money stolen from their parents or paid for with pilfered goods. The truth is many of these kids probably *were* 'high' on drugs, but not the sort bought in seedy back streets or nightclubs. No, many of the kids probably had the residual influence of drugs given to them by their parents, doctors and teachers running through their veins. Drugs prescribed in response to the diagnosis of ADD and ADHD. Ask yourself this question: Would you give your child a line of cocaine each morning before sending him or her off to school? No, seriously, would you? Well, Ritalin, the drug most commonly used to 'treat' ADD and ADHD is a powerful, mind-altering drug that effectively anaesthetises our children, rendering them unable to productively interact with their peers and their environment by numbing them to emotion, imaginative thought and natural creativity. Otherwise known as methylphenidate, Ritalin is a stimulant with properties similar to other amphetamine drugs. Ritalin is a CNS (Central Nervous System) stimulant that affords its users a 'high' similar to that of a slow-release cocaine hit. Ritalin, or 'Vitamin R' or 'R-Ball' (as it is known on the streets) is recognised as a possible stepping stone to harder drugs: drugs such as marijuana, cocaine and heroin and is listed among the 'Top 10' controlled drugs most likely to be stolen from doctor's surgeries and pharmacies (according to the US FDA — Food and Drug Administration). What are we thinking by allowing this to continue? Why are we trying to silence our children? What does this say about us?

Indigo Children innately know they are here on a mission. They know they have a purpose. The Indigo Children are here to bring integrity back to humanity. Indigos know it is up to them to bring legitimacy back to our governments, balance back to our relationships and equality back to our communities. They are here to instruct us in the ways of truth and honesty. They are here to coach us in clear communication, impeccability and unconditional love. Today's children say things as they are. They do not mince words, pull punches or tell you what they think you want to hear. They cut to the chase and call a spade a spade. They do so to get to the core of the issue. They do not believe in beating around the bush, compromising, or selling themselves short. Their purpose is to help us realise that we have been living a lie for years, with each generation erroneously verifying the false beliefs and values of those prior, thus effectively creating an unbroken cycle of ineptitude, and they are frustrated by our inability to see it. They are even more frustrated by our determination to deny possibility, thus preventing them from realising their purpose. The more we resist them and their mission the more they will taunt us and flaunt our obvious lack of accountability like dirty laundry, hanging it out for all to see.

So, how do we reverse the conditioning we have all fallen prey to? How do we say 'no' to the desire to believe in the diagnosis of ADD or ADHD – letters that, in a twisted way, seem to spell 'rescuer' to our exhausted, stressed ears? Well, try talking *to* your kids. Try asking them to share their dreams, their fears and their view of the world and share yours with them. Take time off from work so that you might spend some time with your kids. Set aside your weekends for them. Ask them for their suggestions and act upon them by integrating them into your daily routine. Make your kids a productive part of your life instead of expecting them to comply with pointless rules and empty promises that you wouldn't (and don't) comply with yourself. Do not say one thing and then promptly do the opposite, and don't expect your kids to fall for the obsolete 'do as I say and not as I do' rule. And how do I know this to be true … because I am an Indigo Child myself and I am confident enough to say that if you have read this introduction, and it has resonated well with you, then you are probably one too or you have one living in your home right now. If that is the case, though, I want it made perfectly clear that by identifying you or yours as an Indigo does not afford you the excuse to act up or to allow your children to intentionally make the lives of those around them miserable. With the title of Indigo comes responsibility – to the self and to one's purpose. You must see yourself as the next sacred step in the evolution of humanity, a role that affords you a position of authority and wisdom to be espoused in a gentle way that invites others to follow suit, and with this realisation comes a humbling relief that is sure to bring you to tears. Am I right?

A Brief History:
Highly Sensitive People

Before we separated them and gave them their own list of qualities and traits, Indigos, Crystals and Rainbows were collectively referred to as 'Highly Sensitive People' or HSPs.

We have all had an HSP in our family, or have known one either through school, work or socially. They were the 'strange' or 'weird' ones in our family history: the nerds, black sheep, wallflowers or the one always shunned as the odd one out.

In ancient times, these individuals may have been celebrated as seers, shamans and witches; the sensitive outcasts of society revered as wise women, medicine men or healers. These people had frequently known great suffering (more so than others) due to illness or personal circumstance, and were forced to withdraw from society as a result. Because of this, many found themselves forced to tap into a higher, more refined truth in order to survive; a truth that had to be lived uncompromisingly so as to reap the unique gifts of knowledge and power that came with living such a life.

Today, HSPs are people who have difficulty coping with the world around them and often include those suffering from:

- Chronic Fatigue Syndrome / CFS / ME
- Fibro myalgia / RSI
- Multiple Food and Chemical Sensitivities
- Depression
- ADD
- Autism
- Asperger's Syndrome

This is the story of a typical HSP, who has asked that her identity be kept anonymous:

I have only in the last five years discovered that there are a percentage of people who are more sensitive than what is considered the norm. Such people are not recognised by society as being of a special breed of human, but as dysfunctional by their current social standards.

For me, the world was a scary place. Going to school was not a pleasant experience for me as a young child. Every morning I would feel sick with anxiety and dread. I could not face breakfast or leaving my dear mother for the day. Getting to school was the hardest part of the day. Once I was there I would resign myself to the lack of quiet space that was my heart's desire. The other children were too noisy and out of control for me. They would often travel in herds creating chaos wherever they could. I would disappear into a quiet corner and just concentrate on my work. As a result I had excellent grades and was often the class captain and teacher's pet. I have found out that this is typical of highly sensitive people. They are conscientious and considerate of others. But this was also my way of coping with a world I couldn't really relate to, I would block out everything around me including my own needs if I had to, in order to cope with all the chaos around me. It was hard to sit in a boring classroom all day trying to absorb information that, in my mind, was not useful. I wanted to be sitting outside under the trees enjoying the sunshine. Why couldn't we take classes there?

I was always tired after school, particularly during my teens. This developed into daily migraines, which usually started an hour after lunch and just kept getting worse. I barely survived the bus ride home with a bunch of noisy kids screaming endlessly the whole journey. I wished that I could have gone home at lunchtime and not had to deal with afternoons. I think I started to burn out in my mid-teens. None of my family realised I was silently suffering. I looked pale with dark rings around my eyes; maybe an iron supplement would fix that, they thought. I would often sit in the garden or listen to music on the radio after school in my early high school years, but later I was too tired to even do that. I would just go to bed until dinnertime.

I disliked crowds and often felt very anxious. My family were somewhat amused by this and it was suggested I take a tranquilizer to make it easier. I gave myself a hard time for not being more robust and functional. I wasn't really coping and I had no idea that I had special needs. I needed a quiet environment in which to function, but felt like everybody expected me to be sociable and out there.

This was tested to another level when I entered university. I found life at university (my grades were now mediocre) very challenging. Peer group pressure to go out and socialise, or get involved with various causes did not suit me. My self-esteem began to plummet rapidly as I could not see a niche for me in the social model that was presented to me. I lost interest in my studies and dropped out, much to the dismay of my parents. I could not understand why people were so motivated to study such boring stuff.

Deep down, I felt at odds with the expectations of my family and general society. Getting married, having children and a career held no particular meaning as the ideal life path. I was in a daze and became depressed.

After a failed marriage and several years of anorexia and depression I decided to do a secretarial course and get a job. I was top of the class and landed the first interview I got. Things coasted for a couple of years, but there was still a feeling of emptiness within. My health declined again, and this time I was diagnosed as having Chronic Fatigue Syndrome. I became even more sensitive to noise, food, crowds, bright lights (especially fluorescents), radiation from computers and TV screens and mobile phones would give me instant pain in my head. Even people with negative emotions would drain me. I began to resent the human world. I became increasingly bedridden. I took time off for this condition but, as I have since discovered, there is no real cure.

A complete change in lifestyle and environment were the only effective answers. Leaving the smoky, dirty and noisy city environment to live in the mountains where there is more oxygen and clean water and more peace and harmony with the natural world has restored some of my vitality. And being with other sensitive people as we nurture each other's souls and honour each other's innate abilities has been very healing.

I am forever grateful to a healer friend of mine who suggested a book on sensitive people by Elaine N. Aron, *The Highly Sensitive Person*. This book has helped me to understand my journey and my struggles. According to Elaine Aron, one out of five people are born with this extra sensitive trait. Their nervous systems are actually different from the rest of humans. These HSPs are gifted, highly intelligent and were once valued as advisors to the royal classes. They are able to see and sense what ordinary humans do not. They are easily overwhelmed by society and its complexities. Unfortunately, these days, HSPs are seen as weak and needing medication.

Elaine N. Aron's book gives valuable insight into the raising of sensitive children as well as a detailed and very astute understanding of HSPs. I sincerely believe that sensitives need to be seen and heard more than ever. There seems to be more and more of these people emerging with each generation, so it is extremely important that their needs are understood.

As a sensitive I have been able to pick up some catastrophic events in the world before they happened. I did not know how to deal with this ability although this is not unusual for some sensitives. I am also concerned at how oblivious most people seem to be at the state of their environment and how they live. Their long hours under artificial lights with little oxygen do not nourish their brains. I am concerned for their children, that they are exposed to so many chemicals in the air and in the water, and to ideals which do not seem to lead to harmony and peace within society.

My needs are special: I need a lot of quiet time in nature, foods that are fresh and grown without added chemicals, and the company of people who honour my gifts. But in saying this, every one of you also has special gifts and innate abilities if only you would stop and feel your depths within the silence. I believe that the destiny of the human race is to become more sensitive and some of us are just showing you the way. Perhaps your children will be such teachers for you.

The 'Star-borne'

In 1989, an author known as Solara wrote about a special breed of children in her book, *Star-borne: A Remembrance for the Awakened Ones*. In it she describes children of the 'first and second wave'. The 'first wavers' were apparently those who arrived on Earth during the initial colonisation of the planet from the stars. Better known as 'the ancient ones', they were the ones originally revered as gods and goddesses, but who, after their subsequent descent into a state of matter, retained memory of their higher purpose. Ever since then, they have continued to work in harmony with the Earth, dedicating themselves to the service of others, while erroneously believing themselves to be alone in their quest to bring humanity to a place of completion, fulfilment and, more importantly, oneness. Following the first wavers, according to Solara, and long after the planet was created and everything had found its place, the 'second wavers' began to emerge. The second wavers are said to be impatient, energetic, enthusiastic and bursting with ideas to help return the planet to a state of oneness. The book goes on to suggest that, if they remain dedicated to fulfilling their purpose, those of the second wave are capable of manifesting to their heart's desire.

Since the mid 1970s, Solara proposes a new wave of children has been populating the planet: an influx 'from the stars'; a flood of kids affectionately referred to as 'Starchildren'. Starchildren, she advocates, are typically born with clear memories of earlier incarnations, plus more. They are protected by innocence and are of high integrity, born into families best equipped to offer them the most powerful of life experience. They are here to renew and reinstate our connection 'to the stars'. Identified by their sweet dispositions, Starchildren are overwhelmingly pure, have clear auras and bright, starry eyes. They have trouble interacting with other 'third dimensional' kids and fitting in to mainstream schools. Solara urges her readers to not only share our wisdom with the Starchildren, but to take every opportunity to learn from them. She says they benefit greatly from being taken to quiet places in nature and of having their time in front of television sets kept to a minimum. She says they need time spent alone and in quiet. They respond best when shown the utmost of respect, and when afforded deep love and tender regulation. They strongly resist authority and deliberate domination (due to the fact they are so enlightened), but respond well to negotiated boundaries and gentle direction.

Despite the fact that most of what Solara writes in her book sounds too vague and 'out there' to be plausible, she does seem to have identified the core essence of the kids celebrated today as Indigo and Crystal Children. Whether or not our planet was pioneered by beings that once inhabited the stars remains to be seen; the fact is, however, the children that Solara refers to in her book sound a lot like those described in more recent writings by Doreen Virtue and other well respected authors, to the point where the emergence dates seem to match those suggested by them as well. I personally, however, do not subscribe to Solara's new age theory of evolution, nor do I agree with the suggested time frames in which they purportedly first began to appear, but I do strongly champion (be it in a more practical, grounded way) the existence of the children she refers to.

Indigo Children

Nancy Ann Tapp first identified Indigo Children in her book *Understanding Your Life Through Colour*. She claimed to be able to see a distinct indigo sheen in the aura of these children. This individual colour led to the tag, Indigo Children. Indigo Children, as a model, was later explored in depth by Lee Carroll and Jan Tober in their book *The Indigo Children*, Doreen Virtue in her book *The Care and Feeding of Indigo Children* and then again by James Twyman in his movie *Indigo* and his documentary *The Indigo Evolution*.

Despite being celebrated by some as psychic power-houses sent to save the planet, the (Indigo) children we see today are, more often than not, kids in trouble – with many misdiagnosed as being ADD, ADHD and a plethora of other conditions. ADD and ADHD are both diagnoses given to describe children who display behaviour such as disorganisation, hyperactivity and impulsivity; behaviour that makes it near impossible for them to be integrated into the current system without assistance. ADD and ADHD are two of the most commonly 'diagnosed' neurobehavioral disorders affecting children today. Many adults are said to suffer from it too.

Other 'symptoms' may include: insomnia, fluctuating emotions (emotional lability) and difficulty with problem solving and conduct. One must be careful in the diagnosis, however, because other conditions often mimic the symptoms of ADD / ADHD, such as epilepsy, foetal alcohol syndrome, lead poisoning, sleep apnoea and thyroid abnormalities.

If one were to make a list of the typical traits of an Indigo, it would be fair to say that:

- They carry an innate anger and a resistance to *the system*.
- They suffer constant frustration, restlessness and impatience.
- They usually carry the 'disruptive child and nuisance' reputation in school.
- They don't like rules, are usually late and refuse to wear uniforms (they will find ways to incorporate street clothes into their school attire, for example).

- They are easily bored and need clear and purposeful explanation when told to do things they see no reason for.
- They have little respect for authority and often test the resolve of their teachers, parents, police and other authority figures.
- They need and want boundaries, but only ever respond favourably to them when they are fair, consistent and negotiated with the Indigo personally.
- They show disrespect for those who use fear-based discipline or hollow threats.
- They show disrespect for those who do not 'walk their talk' or who follow the 'do as I say not as I do' adage.
- They can easily detect lies, hypocrisy and falsity – traits they abhor.
- They say things as they see them.
- They do not pull punches.
- They question *everything* — a trait often confused with arguing or a resistance to suggestion.
- They are very social and talk constantly — and loudly.
- They often have a wicked (and sarcastic) sense of humour.
- They are inherently connected to nature, love animals and are excellent gardeners.
- They are usually highly intuitive and often demonstrate awareness of esoteric knowledge not readily available or understood by other children (or adults for that matter).
- They are generally highly intelligent, displaying academic ability beyond their years.
- They often have difficulty integrating their higher understandings into their everyday lives with balance between what they see as truth and what is demonstrated by society as truth causing innate conflict and confusion. This disharmony is often manifests itself in negative behaviour.
- They are usually very creative and love participating in drama, dance and song.
- They are always on the go.
- They respond well to sports.
- Many are better channelled into non-competitive activity such as horse riding, cycling, canoeing, etc. Often their intolerant natures prevent cooperative interaction on the sports field.

- They are often diagnosed as ADD or ADHD, but not all Indigos are ADD or ADHD and not all ADD or ADHD children are Indigo
- Indigos respond well to positive reinforcement, purposeful compliments and constructive criticism. They simply need their existence to be affirmed in a positive way and they generally respond accordingly.
- They march to a different drumbeat to most other children.
- They are not easily impressed with pomp and ceremony, but are quickly intrigued by those who speak the truth and walk their talk.
- It is not uncommon for Indigo Children to have experienced pain, illness, neglect, abuse, grief or hardship early in life, or for them to have considered suicide as a viable alternative to life.
- Indigos will often fall victim to alcohol, drug and tobacco abuse as a means of helping them deal with the world in which they live (but then again, so will any child raised on drugs like those used to 'treat' ADD and ADHD).

It has been said that Indigo Children are here to bring balance back to the world and integrity back to the system. They are apparently here to question the ways of the people and to reawaken truth and impeccability within their hearts. Some even say they are the next evolutionary phase of humanity ... Spiritual Warriors sent by Spirit to demonstrate resolve, offer direction and to reinstate hope and inspiration within the consciousness of all people; here to heal the planet, inspire and to reintroduce us to the wisdom of the Earth Mother. It is their mission (according to the anecdotes I have read), to force all parents to break with outworn tradition, to move away from indoctrination and to shun fear.

Attention Deficit Disorder
and Attention Deficit Hyperactivity Disorder

The scary thing is that Attention Deficit Disorder and Attention Deficit Hyperactivity Disorder are only labels, they are not true medical conditions. These names simply describe a set of symptoms – a syndrome. There is no underlying medical illness which has yet been identified. On occasion there are other medical problems such as brain damage underlying these labels of ADD and ADHD. However this is very uncommon. The fact is that these labels apply to a set of symptoms which create problems within our society – problems in families, behavioural problems at school, difficulties learning from the standard school curriculum, problems fitting in, and a general lack of regard for the accepted society norms. However, this not a medical illness. There are no objective medical pathology tests which will diagnose ADD or ADHD. In reality the current so-called epidemic of ADD/ADHD is simply the manifestation of a big upsurge of children who have a different way of viewing our world and responding to it. These kids are not sick, they are just different. So you could say that as a general rule of thumb, ADD and ADHD only exist in the eye of the beholder.

To diagnose ADD or ADHD, symptoms are said to present themselves before the age of seven and cause impairment in social, academic or occupational functioning, and must be present in two or more settings (i.e., at school and at home) before the child can be officially labelled as being either ADD or ADHD.

For the 'Inattentive' type, at least six of the following symptoms must have persisted for at least six months:

- Lack of attention to details / careless mistakes
- Lack of sustained attention
- Poor listener
- Failure to follow through on tasks
- Poor organisation
- Avoids tasks requiring sustained mental effort
- Loses things
- Easily distracted
- Forgetful

For the 'Hyperactive-Impulsive' type, at least six of the following symptoms must have persisted for at least six months:

- Fidgeting/squirming
- Leaving their seat

- Inappropriate running/climbing
- Difficulty with quiet activities
- 'On the go'
- Excessive talking
- Blurting answers
- Can't wait turn
- Intrusive

The 'Combined' types require both *inattentive* and *hyperactive-impulsive* criteria to be met.

(Source: The attachment to the FDA Approval Letter for NDA 21-284 [Ritalin LA])

Both these lists describe kids in general, if you ask me, kids with healthy, inquisitive minds; kids that are both 'normal' and developing appropriately, but forced to exist in a system that is both archaic and unsuitable in today's world.

I ask you, is it normal for a young child to sit in a plastic chair behind a plastic desk for five hours a day? Is it even healthy to ask a child to suppress their natural tendency to talk, ask questions, run, explore and shift from one activity to the next sporadically? Is it a good thing that we expect our children to eat an adequate lunch in the ten minutes allocated before being *made* to 'go outside and play'? Are they getting the nourishment a child needs in that short amount of time to not only sustain an hour long, outdoor play session, but also a further two hours of indoor study? I don't think so. That's assuming, too, that all the children present have a packed lunch to eat (many don't) and suitable clothing to protect them against the elements when they're ushered out the door ...

As an ex-primary school teacher, I know how easy it is to fall into the trap of labelling children as disruptive, rude, insolent or inappropriately aggressive, fidgety or impatient. What we fail to consider, in most cases, is the child's home life. We rarely consider the fact that the child may not be dressed appropriately for the day's weather conditions; that they may not have had breakfast or enough sleep. We do not consider the possibility that the child may be experiencing things at home that the other children in the class are innocent to – domestic violence, abuse or neglect. We never ask if they are carrying burdens or responsibilities that far exceed accepted levels. We do not ask if they have alcoholic or drug dependent parents or if their parents are even there to tuck them into bed at night. Instead we label them as ADD or ADHD and urge their parents to medicate them.

And this has to stop.

Medication

Assistance offered to 'sufferers' of ADD or ADHD generally comes in the form of medication, which is typically psychotropic in nature. Adderall and Ritalin or Methylphenidate, among others, are the most commonly prescribed drugs. What few parents realise, however, is that Ritalin is a CNS (Central Nervous System) stimulant; a mind altering drug that effectively anaesthetises the child, rendering them unable to productively interact with their peers and their environment by numbing them to emotion, imaginative thought and natural creativity.

Sure, it forces them to comply and to 'fit in', but very little learning can take place when the child is under its influence. It works so favourably because it affords the child a 'high' similar to that of slow-release cocaine hit, delivering them into a state that makes them more compliant and easier to control. Other drugs commonly prescribed include Dexedrine, Cylert, Tofranil, Norpramin, Prozac and Paxil. Adverse effects to the use of these anti-depressants as a treatment for ADD or ADHD, however, include excessive sedation and rebound hypertension during withdrawal, as well as frequent disturbance in concentration and memory.

It should also be noted that on the packaging of the drug Ritalin, a suggestion is made that is often overlooked or ignored: *Ritalin is indicated as an integral part of a total treatment program which typically includes other remedial measures (psychological, educational, social) for a stabilising affect in children with behavioural syndrome … adequate diagnosis requires the use not only of medical but of special psychological, educational, social resources.*

What are the possible side effects of these medications?

Children often express difficulty swallowing their prescribed medication, with some describing the experience as physically painful. The medication has a tranquillising effect often causing the child to fall asleep during their classes.

The drugs can have a detrimental (and permanent) effect on the organ systems, the cardiovascular system, the central nervous system, the gastrointestinal and endocrine/ metabolic systems, often resulting in any one or a combination of the following symptoms:

- Night sweats or night terrors
- Palpitations
- Tachycardia
- Increased blood pressure
- Central nervous system stimulation
- Psychosis
- Dizziness
- Insomnia
- Headaches
- Nervousness
- Irritability
- Anorexia
- Nausea
- Vomiting
- Stomach aches, cramps or pain
- Dry mouth
- Weight loss
- Growth suppression
- Hypersensitivity reaction

- Blurred vision
- Jaundice
- Anaemia
- Elevated liver enzymes
- A diminished sense of intuition, creativity and involvement
- An overall 'no care' attitude to life

It is quite ironic when you consider the fact that we have a government that, on one hand, tells our kids 'don't do drugs' (and in some cases punishes them quite severely for possessing them), while on the other hand, encourages parents and teachers to 'medicate' them with drugs of similar ilk. Ritalin, for example, is a CNS (Central Nervous System) stimulant with properties similar to those of cocaine and heroin and other amphetamine drugs. Who's to say, therefore, that the most devastating 'side effect' of the drugs used to treat ADD and ADHD won't be the conceiving of a generation of drug-dependent kids who may, some day, prove even more reliant on government help than they ever were before?

Why are Indigo Children often diagnosed as ADD or ADHD?

Indigo Children are a different breed of children to the ones many of us knew when we were growing up. They are less tolerant, louder and often more aggressive. They have a quick, dry humour and are very sarcastic. Their humour is often used as a protective device or as a weapon, which usually leads to them being labelled as the class clown, rude or disrespectful. They are more difficult to reason with and need to be offered reasons for why they must act in a certain way and have these reasons explained clearly and see them demonstrated in meaningful ways. They can tell when someone is lying to them and they will retaliate accordingly. They don't like being told what to do, unless a fair and reasonable explanation can be offered. They respond badly to fear based discipline and hollow threats and they do not suffer fools lightly. They taunt those who abuse their power, intentionally pushing the limits until an emotional outburst is experienced. Much satisfaction is gained, for example, by seeing a teacher or principal 'lose the plot', burst into tears or show extreme frustration. Victory is theirs when they have identified a weakness or a cancer in the system that must be removed, and they rarely ease up until something is done about it.

Most Indigo Children respond poorly to authority when it is not fair or acknowledged universally. The 'one rule for you and another for me' adage has never been acceptable to the Indigo, who quickly refuses to comply. They can't stand it when the person telling them to act in a certain way does not act that way himself or herself. They get bored easily and often display restless, disruptive behaviour. They cannot stay put for long; instead they wander around the room allowing peripheral things to attract their attention instead of focusing on the allocated tasks at hand. And they are *always* late.

To them it is not natural to want to sit in a confined space for hours on end when they could be exploring the broader world in a tangible, purposeful way, so they question everything and will shamelessly argue their point in the hope that they may actually be heard. They view the world from clearer and completely different perspectives from others and, as a result, are generally labelled as disruptive and disrespectful. Indigos are often accused of intentionally trying to make their teachers look foolish, when in fact they see it as trying to broaden their teacher's range of understanding. They have an innate understanding of what is right and what is wrong and it frustrates them when no one else sees things from their perspective. They are outspoken and persistent in their views and respond poorly when their views are not heard or acknowledged. They can become aggressive when they are wrongly accused or when confusion, anger and fear envelop them and no one responds to their calls for help. They are usually highly intelligent and intuitive, expressing knowledge in a way far beyond their years. Such knowledge often frightens their teachers and parents to shame. Because of this, few fit into the system and, as a result, try to alter it so that it fits them.

Having their say ...

The following are personal accounts as told by three Indigo Children who have gone through things most people would never dream of, how they dealt with their experiences and the choices they made to become whole, healthy individuals (with and without the 'support' of prescribed medication).

My name is Sarah. I am 17 years of age and a Sagittarius.

My life is a very interesting one that follows the same path as a roller coaster. It has been up and down forever. Life, for me, started in Sunbury, Australia. I lived with my mum, dad and older sister. I don't know much about my life in those early years except that Mum and Dad broke up when I was 18 months old. The fact that, unlike all my friends, I came from a broken marriage tore me up inside throughout all of my years. I didn't necessarily want them to be together, and this may not make sense, but I just wanted a family.

In my younger years Dad met Kerry who had a son one month older than me, named Brendan. In the beginning of our 'family merge' all three kids got along. I forgot to mention that Dad won the custody battle and my sister Jess and I lived with him. Brendan and I started primary school together. From a young age I started creating conflict, within myself, my peers and even my family! I have extremely curly hair and already at the age of six I had very low self-confidence. All the other girls had pretty hair, but I felt like a boy. It was from this age that I began to wonder and become paranoid about what kids were thinking about my personality and appearance. I was intimidated by the pretty girls, who quickly became the popular girls. I remained in the middle of the year with regard to popularity. I wasn't a loser but I wasn't far from it either. Brendan was popular. He played soccer and football on the oval, and he made friends with the popular girls who chatted to the sporty boys at lunchtime. From an early age I began analysing why things happened and came to the conclusion that because Brendan didn't want to play with me at school (which is understandable) I could not have possibly hung out with those girls, and when I tried I was pushed away. You see I have always been intimidated by most girls, I have never been able to defend myself very well and after having held this attitude for many years, I knew no different. I accepted anybody who would talk to me as a friend and didn't dare approach the popular girls. So I put my head down and found school fairly easy. I became slack in subjects that I had no interest in and always felt like I knew one more thing than everyone that I spoke to. I found faults in everything and I loved voicing my opinion. I believed and still believe that the education system has many holes in it. I cannot understand why most schools tolerate, at least to a degree, bullying. It happens before their eyes and yet it is often dismissed. Do these people know the pupils are sensitive and that even little things over time build up and can turn into issues such as depression, anxiety, low self-esteem and defencelessness!

At home I began comparing myself to Brendan, because he was popular at school and I was not. I felt like a loser and this personality followed me home too. I quickly saw Kerry the same way as I saw the other girls and even when she would talk to me the same way she did to the other two kids I had a feeling that she was trying to intimidate me. It was all in my head and through no fault of her own, this way of thinking kick-started conflict between Kerry and I, not mutual conflict, just an argumentative brat who would call black white just to have something to disagree about.

I began to develop some fairly serious self-confidence issues for myself. This led to the depression that I currently suffer from. I repetitively tormented myself over the years. It was in the form of self-disgust whether that be frowning upon the scales for their truth or gazing in the mirror dissatisfied at my smile, eyes, nose — you name it, I hate it. This made me wonder what everyone was secretly thinking about me. (This, mind you, has since turned into paranoia and I'm now taking anti-psychotic tablets to deal with it). If I could notice all of these things wrong with me, imagine what everyone else was thinking? I became self-conscious and rather rude toward, well, anyone.

I grew up with these problems, which seemed to become bigger every day. On top of growing up, I had to face these 'inside me' issues every day. I got so caught up in them that I knew no other way of being. I never really had the opportunity to meet 'me' or become the Sarah that I dreamed of being. I would watch other people and try to adopt their personality traits. I ended up a very messed-up person, being both confused and angry at the world. If I ever meet up with a genie in a bottle I would not ask for a mansion, or world peace, I'd devote all three wishes toward giving every being inner satisfaction. I so desperately wanted to feel at peace and I felt that the conflict going on inside me could eventually kill me.

If I were to really follow my heart I would reconstruct the entire way of doing things in schools. I am so angry at the education system and the way it let me down. Entering high school was the most difficult part of my life. You see I was trying to deal with and manage problems at home and face bullies at school without any self-confidence. I was a very fragile person and because I had no trust or care for those around me, at that stage I became very sceptical. I learnt that you could tell white lies to create whatever history you wanted to have and this gave me the ability to become very argumentative and convincing. I joined the school debating team and proved to myself and everyone around me that despite the argument and how I truly felt about it I could bullshit my way through a speech to prove anyone wrong. Even if I didn't agree with myself! Because I had adopted this personality trait, I continued analysing the people around me and wondered if they were doing the same thing. And so I became very untrusting and found relationships difficult. Throughout high school my depression escalated because Brendan remained popular, whilst I crawled beneath my sister's protective wing and kept away from the people in my own year level that I had hidden anxiety toward. I never had to study hard and often daydreamed during classes. Because I didn't find homework or essays very difficult I found that when I paid a lot of attention and tried really hard I came across as a nerd. I paid special attention to the way that the education system worked and found many faults within it. I found that I had a gift for talking — or dare I say bullshitting — my way out of trouble, whether it be detention or just in a day-to-day argument with one of the teachers. I became a smart arse and brought home this attitude too.

Meanwhile at home I was juggling my life and holding my precious heart from a thread. As my sister and I were bounced from Mum's house to Dad's house every second weekend I grew yet another complex. I began to wonder about my mum; who she really was and who she was to me and if in fact I actually needed her. I found fault in the legal system at this age, which just enlarged my hatred toward any kind of system. How or why somebody who does not know the family possibly should be qualified to determine where the kids should live! How can a degree offer such a delicate privilege! Which brings me to something else I hate about our world: the people who are very switched on but not 'educated' will never be smiled upon the same way in society compared to those who are 'qualified to have an opinion'! I could not understand how a bill or legal document could possibly decide where a loved one should live or who they should live with. At that age I wanted to become a lawyer, partially because I loved copying my sister who also wanted to be a lawyer but also partially because I thought that I knew everything and I wanted to change the system and I desperately believed in what I was telling myself, which was that I could make a difference. This stride and sense of strong character was soon to fade away as I became quite withdrawn and full of self-hatred and I learnt to not believe in me. It was almost like I had adopted the same hatred toward myself as my bullies had for me. As I desperately tried to soldier on though this period of time I found it emotionally tiring. As it stabbed my brain and heart each night, I became a bore at school as I sort of carried my problems around with me on a chain as if they were a pet. Not literally. Being the person that I am now I have come to realise that all this was just one big meaning for 'playing the victim' which took much self discipline and a hard road to snap out of. I am very grateful for these tough times; they make me unique and have helped me to own a very understanding and broad personality.

Back to the subject of school, I began to understand my inner feelings and so with self-acceptance that shone through became a part of a much bigger social crowd. It changed me as a person, into a girl who had been introduced to a bad world, a spoilt world. I ran away from home in search of a better life, of a different life, one with my mother. I believe that I ran to her house with an inquisitive mind as I had never lived with her before. Working and attending school in a different area to my new home proved too difficult, so eventually I changed schools. I forgot to mention that prior to this occasion I had moved into Mum's once before for the same reasons, however I moved back to dad's at the start of year nine as I faced my worst fears when I enrolled in another college. The kids there urinated on me, threw up on me, put my head in toilet water and your imagination would best describe what I went through. This was the experience that gave me the courage to go back to a school that was not as horrible as I had initially thought. At the old school I got along with the kids so well.

Despite how well things were going at school I started locking horns with mum, because I had grown up in a noisy environment full of humbling murmur and havoc I could not bear living in her silent, spotless place called 'home'. I became rebellious and let my mean argumentative side be her enemy. After six months I turned to marijuana and began renting my own place after she had kicked me out. This was a fairly depressive stage in my life as I experienced a lot that I wasn't ready for.

During my time renting I was involved in a serious relationship with Dave, a boyfriend who my mum despised and yet my heart was stuck to him like glue. He was *very cruel at his worst. At his worst he would ignore my feelings by promising to call and wouldn't, which was fairly difficult for me to go through on my own as I had no family around me and at the time I was renting on my own, so I had next to no money. I was unable to call him because I could not afford to so I depended heavily on his word, and had my heart broken many times when he was not understanding of my reasoning. Being involved with him was some of the worst and some of the best times of my life. It was like a separate roller coaster than my real life. It was a pretend life that I would not have dared living in the care of Dad and Kerry. Some of the time I spent with him was amazing and is way too precious to put a price upon, on the other hand, my having a relationship sunk me deeper into drugs, it taught me a lot about the street, and me. I did a lot of thinking for other people when I was around Dave and when I took a step out of myself I began to appreciate who I was and how much experience had dominated my personality.*

It is a scary thought that without these twists and turns our lives could have turned out very different. I cherish every memory and lesson, good, bad or indifferent that I have taken part in and would not want to be anyone else. My experiences are my history and they are what make me.

After having rented for a while I began to take control of my life and learn from some fairly valuable lessons, many housemates that I subleased to put me in financial crises. I decided that life and family is too precious to be thrown away on something petty and in doing so dedicated a lot of time and emotional effort into repairing my relationship with Mum. I had to find a job to pull myself out of these tough times, being that part of my resolution was to cancel my Centrelink (social security) benefits and solely support myself for a challenge. It made me feel as though I had the right to practise what I preached and this made me feel as though I had earned that right. Once finally on my feet I cleaned up my whole life and world. I moved out of the rundown unit that I had been renting for nearly ten months and began residing in share house accommodation.

This experience led to where I am at today. It began well but ended in more life lessons, more cruelty (toward my heart and its fragile beat) and both a physical and mental breakdown. During my time at the share house I went through a brand new way of life and this was brought upon by sharing with a 36-year-old truck driver and a 24-year-old plasterer. Both men were a bit rough around the edges and despite our fairly large age differences the house was generally a happy place to be. I became a lot more sociable and life couldn't have been better. I started a relationship with Simon a great mechanic who is still a friend of mine. He taught me a lot about myself. Along with my housemate he taught me how to be honest with myself, which has also played a major part in getting me to where I am at today as I always try to be honest with myself. This theory creates balance and a clear perspective on life for you as a person, so I have learnt. After having lived there for months, things began to roll downhill yet again, which led me to fairly severe depression. You see after having been so happy I found that all good things must come to an end; something I felt difficult to come to terms with. I had a job in central Melbourne and it began to wear me down. As I began to feel increasing pressure to behave within my environment in a certain manner that I couldn't cope with, life became fairly difficult for me as I had become very good at playing the victim and throwing in the towel when times got tough. For me the solution was suicide.

One dreary night Simon gave me the break up speech and that on top of other pressures I was facing led me to fall into one thousand pieces. I broke slowly, beginning with running away from him, then coming back to the house to scream at him because after I had finished being sad I got very angry driven by hurt. This led to my roommate giving me two weeks' notice to vacate, despite the situation. All of this mess gave me a feeling of desperation. I overdosed on antidepressants, for attention or as a suicide attempt. I was kept overnight in hospital and sent into an adolescent inpatient unit the next day.

I have been residing there ever since and from my time at the hospital I have gained and developed invaluable lessons, which I believe brought me closer to wellbeing and the key to open a new door to my life. It has given me a golden opportunity to end my dreary years and lead me to the journey I am now travelling upon. A positive one that I am choosing to dedicate my heart and soul toward young people who are experiencing difficulty — not to be in charge of them but to be an extra set of ears or an eye-opener. You may even call the profession I am entering 'light to dark situations'. Being in the hospital has given me the chance to experience what life at its worst is actually like. For example, I now know much about suicide, depression, anxiety, etc. all from personal experience and from within a system. I desperately want to escape the system and give my strength to someone else, if not many people. That would be fantastic!

To me, being an Indigo is taking the experiences of my life and being challenged — it was never enough for me to just imagine what it was like — I had to know *and experience beyond my vivid imagination. For me being an Indigo is never really agreeing with any sort of structure, limit or system and desperately screaming for attention or an attentive ear that also had the authority to take on board what I had to say and do something about it. To my surprise I have only just began noticing bright colours or auras around some children, I communicate with angels and am fairly spiritually connected. The best advice I would give someone (especially an Indigo) is it is very easy to play the victim and fall into the trap of 'poor me', however you will come out better then perfect if you decide to build a bridge and get through it all. I believe in anyone with a spirit, which means we all have the ability to move forward, you just need to be walking on the right path.*

The world that we live in is so cruel. It is judgmental and everything that you want is very hard to get your hands on. The only way to rip through it to reach the top is by soul searching on your own and then chasing your dreams. Systems see society in black and white, which is why it is so easy to depict faults. That is, they will always be wrong because life is also full of shades of grey …

My name is Mark. I am 16 years old and feel different to others.

Before I can remember I have always felt different from everyone else. I have always just wanted to grow up and skip everything till I turned 18 so I could have my own house, car and be totally independent and rely on no one.

I spent most of primary school daydreaming and couldn't stay focused on what they wanted; I was more concerned about what was happening for me. Not doing my homework was something I was always getting into trouble for and I didn't really care too much about what they thought.

Secondary school was a pain in the arse because I had to change from private to public school, which was a massive change and from the second I walked into the new school I knew it wasn't exactly going to be the time of my life. The discipline certainly seemed to be non-existent compared to the private school. I guess after a while I started to lose my sense of discipline too. That's when I really started getting into trouble at school. I didn't look at teachers as authority figures or somebody who should be respected just because they were a school teacher. They are just human beings like me or you. I am not against teachers I am just against those that think they are it and a bit just because they are a teacher.

No matter whom I was speaking to at school, be it a teacher, a co-ordinator or even the principal, I always just spoke my mind. I learned very quickly that teachers don't like students speaking their mind. But I did anyway. Because I wanted to show them that I wasn't scared of them and they wouldn't get away with treating me unjustly.

I have had a strong sense of justice ever since I can remember and I react angrily to situations that cause me to feel I am not being fairly treated. Ever since I started high school I have been bullied. I spoke to teachers and co-ordinators on several occasions about the bullying. Every time they said they would fix it up but nothing ever happened until one day I got fed up with it all and retaliated. That consequently got me into a lot of trouble with the teachers. Now, where is the justice in that? I got suspended.

Another incident happened where I was treated unfairly. One day we had a curriculum day and I was with a mate at his house when some kids from another school (a primary school at that) were throwing rocks and sticks at us. We thought it would be funny if we threw pies and sausage rolls back at them. I went to school the next day and found myself speaking to my co-ordinator about the incident when she asked me to pick up rubbish around the school as punishment for the previous day. I said to her, "Who are you to punish me for what I did on my day off?" I found myself suspended once again.

I have always hated school and since I started high school all I ever wanted to do was to leave!

I had my first bong in year eight and for the next couple of years I was smoking quite a lot of weed. My mates were kind enough to supply my needs and I couldn't see anything wrong with a little chill-out time. In fact, whilst I was going through that stage Mum actually kept telling me how good I had been with keeping my attitude under control and not fighting too much with the rest of the family. I now realise it was the drugs that were altering my moods to give a false sense of who I was. I found it was bringing me down and it was affecting every area of my life. I made the decision to quit for my own reasons not for someone else's.

The time came in year 10 for work experience. I couldn't be bothered looking for anyone to employ me, in fact I never wanted to do it in the first place. So I just asked my mate across the road if I could do my work experience with him and his mate doing bricklaying. So I did my work experience with Will (my mate) and Brendan (my boss). I really enjoyed it because I got a taste of what it feels like to be out of school, in the workforce and supporting myself and standing on my own two feet. I told Brendan if he ever wanted anyone to work with him he should give me a call, because I told him I was prepared to leave school and go to work.

Going back to school after work experience was hard because I knew where I really wanted to be. I was sitting in an English class and the teacher asked for comment on Romeo and Juliet and I gave her my comment after which one of the other guys in the class made an unnecessary smart arse comment, which outraged me. So I stood up and yelled at the little prick. The teacher stopped the confrontation and everything appeared to go back to normal. Lunchtime arrived and I was sitting on the oval with my friends when I saw a kid with about 50 guys walking towards us. I thought to myself, this can't be good!

The group was led by the same kid that made that comment in English. When they finally reached us, Geoff (the kid) told me he wanted to fight but by that time I had mellowed out and couldn't be bothered fighting. I told him I didn't want to fight but he and his mates didn't like that and told me I was a girl as they proceeded to throw dozens of eggs at me. I walked away from the group and continued to walk home, covered in egg. As I was walking home I thought, I can't take anymore of this, I have to leave school.

I rang Mum, told her the story and she backed me one hundred percent, which made me feel good. We then had a discussion about the possibility of me leaving school but there were conditions attached to this, one of them being that I had to have a full time job. I was already working at McDonald's part time and didn't really like the idea of going full time there. I needed to find another job. About one week later on a Monday night after losing my job at McDonald's because of my 'outrageous' hair cut, I got a call from Brendan the bricklayer who offered me a full time job as a labourer. I asked him when he wanted me to start and he replied, 'Tomorrow'. I said I'd see him the next day. My life changed that night all for the better. I am now a first, nearly second year apprentice bricklayer. I love my job and have learnt and am still learning about that grown up world I had so much wanted to be a part of.

Some of the things I have experienced have not been a bed of roses, particularly when my mate Johnny was killed in a car accident last September and that really knocked me around. But I would not go back to school for a million dollars. My understanding of the spiritual world helped me through Johnny's death because I knew exactly what was going on and he would be okay!

I feel particularly close to my mum and she has supported me through all the tough times and without that support things could've turned out very different. I had contemplated killing myself at the age of 13 and my dad talked me out of it. I still have a lot of learning and experimenting to do but now deal with things a bit easier by seeing from a different perspective and I am treated with respect.

My name is Adam and, for as long as I can remember, I have never been able to fit in.

During my primary school years I never had any friends. At recess and lunch I would walk around with the teachers because I never felt like talking to anyone. I think a lot of kids thought that I was strange. Everyone knew my name but no one really made the effort to let me join in. I suppose I never made the effort either. I never got overly depressed in my younger years because everyone always told me that I could do whatever I wanted to. As long as I worked for it, I could achieve it. I would never do any homework, as I believed it was unnecessary. Practise my spelling? Yeah right! My work at school suffered because of it. I could never learn my times tables.

When I was in year six, my teacher gave everyone the same work sheet apart from me. Without my knowledge I got a different one. She was trying to test me I suppose. Anyway, when I found that I couldn't copy the answers from anyone because they didn't have the same questions, I queried the teacher. She explained that I still had to complete the sheet. I never did because I was unable to. I was put into an extra class with another teacher where we would read the books by tape and work quite slow. Why was I moved into a class full of misfits that could not read or write when I could? I was taken to see a doctor who diagnosed me with a special disorder. He said that I could not remember more than eight digits at a time. I wasn't aware that this was a problem. I was never kept back in school. I found that I mainly enjoyed my music class and my art class where you were there to paint and play with clay. You get to see at the end what you have created, being made to make an object that was yours and would never go away. In music we all learnt recorder. I also took piano lessons, then guitar lessons and then saxophone lessons. I hated these once again because you had to do homework or practice. 'You must practise every night so you can achieve whatever'. This was another thing I believed that I didn't need to do. Starting high school at a private school was quite scary but it was a new beginning, a chance to make some friends. There was a camp the second week back. A sort of getting to know you camp. I was really looking forward to it. We all went down to Phillip Island on the bus and everybody was chatting away. I was fairly quiet, shy in fact.

Once we arrived, we all went up to the dorms. Now there wasn't enough room for everybody so I just went into another room with three other people. I guess misfits again. We would all participate in the activities but I never really connected with anybody. I still managed to enjoy myself though. We were outdoors, riding bikes, surfing and just doing loopy things. Every year we had a school camp. From the end of year seven and for the rest of my schooling there, I spent three lessons a week in 'special education' where I would get help with my work. I was the only kid in school that was allowed to have a laptop to take notes on.

Year eight was quite a good year where I started making some real friends. Ones that would last a lifetime … well maybe just one. I got this random phone call one day from my friend Jake, a lad in my class. He wanted me to date his sister. Well, yes of course I will. So after school one day we went up to his place in Belgrave and I met Sarah his sister. Now I was quite shy again but this was so good — I had a girlfriend. I never built up the courage to kiss her whilst we were seeing each other. This resulted in her dumping me. I was sort of heartbroken but I was inspired to stay friends with Jake. Jake and I were a good influence on each other. I was getting him out of the house more and experiencing new things and Jake was introducing me to new people who soon became my close friends. We would all go out on the weekend to someone's house and basically get pissed (the usual thing for a 15 year old). Over the next few years I dated a few girls from our circle of friends. Whenever there was a break up there was no loss in friendship for very long. We would just be up to our same old tricks getting drunk and 'picking up'. This was my life — simple. Not caring about school or anything. Things started to become serious. I was doing quite badly in maths. In fact I was kicked out of most maths classes for being noisy and disruptive. I was sent to the head of senior school office and put on a yellow card. It normally lasted for two weeks. I was on it for three months. This means every teacher must write if you have behaved yourself in that class and how productive you were in your work.

I hated the idea of this so I just didn't care what was written on it. The head of senior school wanted to suspend me. I wanted to drop out of school. In a desperate attempt to do this, we went through a whole thing of asking what I wanted to do. I decided on landscape gardening. Now this involved one day a week at TAFE studying horticulture. I had one day off school a week to attend this course. I went for a few weeks and found that everybody in this class was not only four or five years older than me but also three times as dumb. So I decided I didn't need to attend. I would have every Wednesday off of school. Nice bit of a mid-week break. I ended up not finishing the certificate, but still managing to pass year 10. The following year I started at public high school where I studied hospitality. The school was a very hands-on school — a lot of practical work. This school was a huge shock to the system as it was larger than anything I had ever seen. There were so many people. The first day I didn't meet anyone. Everyone acted as if they were better than me. I decided that I was there to work. So I did. Whilst being there I gained a lot of skills in this industry that would benefit me for quite a few years. I felt quite alone not knowing anyone and not really wanting to know anyone.

During my years at school I started working in the hospitality industry. I found that it was easier for me to talk to people if I knew I wasn't going to see them again, they were in my environment and my safety zone where I felt comfortable. I enjoy the idea of meeting new people every day. I worked in many different places over the years. Mainly I would stay at one place and then I would be unhappy after a while and look for something new and different. I eventually started working in a large hotel in the Yarra Valley. I enjoyed it for a while and I was working all the hours under the sun. I think mainly to keep busy so I didn't have to see anyone.

After a few months I started getting bored. It was the same thing over and over again every day every week. It was during this time when I started having visions. I could *always see spirits ever since I was about six years old. I can remember seeing lights and figures moving around me. When the visions started I never really paid any attention. I found that I was becoming more sensitive to energy. I would feel sad and depressed a lot of the time. I thought that this was just normal. I was living by myself in Warburton; I felt that this small town was full of energy. I could connect with living in the bush. Although I grew up in the suburbs I felt I always had a connection with the bush; living side by side with the land and everything around it.*

After being in my job for about ten months a group of friends and me decided to visit the United Kingdom on a working holiday. This sounded great. I would work in the industry I loved in another country. I guess the grass is always greener on the other side. I didn't look at it then but looking back it was sort of running away from any problems that I was having in Australia. Everything was going great. I made a great impression on my boss. I got myself a girlfriend that would soon become my fiancé after many months of on and off and on and off. This was great. I was promoted in my job. I became assistant manager of a hotel and pub. I loved it.

Like all things that happen in my life, they turn crappy all of a sudden and very fast. My fiancé and I were fighting, my boss had been suspended and we were constantly arguing with the holding manager. One day it got too much for me so we walked out. We went to live at Sam's parent's house till we found a new job. I thought it would be easy. Leaving did sort out a lot of things between Sam and I and we eventually found a job. I was unhappy as soon as we started. I didn't really gel with anyone there. Just went straight to my room and went to sleep. After a couple of months Sam decided to leave me, thus leaving me jobless and homeless. I had to resign from the job I hated which I didn't mind. I went back to the old company where I was manager again.

I was feeling depressed not only from Sam leaving me but just feeling everyone's problems. People sad about the debt they were in, work etc. I lived by myself above the pub but the room was a disgusting blue and the bathroom was a sickly green colour. Again, as in all of the places I go I didn't fit in, even though I was brilliant with the customers and did my job great. I always received praised from everyone but never really socialised. After leaving this job I slipped into a deep depression. I moved around thinking things would change but it only made it worse. Over the last ten weeks in the U.K I went from being sad to depressed, so much so I would cry on the phone to my mother. If it was homesickness it took 14 months to set in. On a whim I booked my ticket home then brought it forward because I needed something — I didn't know what and I still don't. But I came home anyway.

As soon as I got off the plane in Melbourne I wanted to go straight back to Heathrow. I couldn't though. I had just flown half way round the world on a whim because I was depressed. Now I had my family around me once again. I was happy but not thrilled. I spent the next few weeks travelling down to the beach to meet Jake. I was having fun. Then my money ran out and I had to go back to work. I tried for weeks to find a job. I mean I had so much experience why was it so hard to find work?

Was I supposed to? I went back to my old job in the Yarra valley. I started suffering from depression even more. I hate going to work. I hate having to be something that I am not; pretending to be this high-class waiter in a fancy hotel, for example. Every day was different in my moods. They changed from minute to minute. I would be happy and then I would want to hit someone over the head. I was glad to be home because the whole time I was in the U.K I never experienced any visions or premonitions or saw any spirits. When I moved back to Warburton it started almost instantly, and more powerfully. The dreams I had were quite strange. One dream that really sticks in my mind is that a group of friends and I murdered a friend of ours and to cover it up we chopped him into small pieces with a butter knife and buried him in the bush. I was quite upset about this because it was so real. But if you think about it, it was more of a sign that I was ready to move on and start again.

The next week I met Scott and I was inspired by his words. He told me that I was an Indigo Child and explained what it meant and what I could achieve. This made me feel really great about myself. I felt as though I was finally able to relax as I was finding out what I was all about. Learning about what makes me tick. It was like the world had been lifted off of my shoulders and I was able to now move forward and achieve anything that I wanted to. I have always known in my heart that I was able to do all of this stuff. I was always fascinated with the TV shows where there were witches and demons. Which I guess is a bit like real life. Good versus Evil. Although sometimes I hate that I can sense energy, I think that it is a real gift. A gift I wouldn't trade for anything in the world.

Crystal Children

Crystal Children are said to emanate multicoloured opalescent auras, similar to the prism effect caused when light is shone through a clear quartz crystal. Most Crystal Children have large eyes, a penetrating stare and charismatic, even-tempered, tender personalities. They are very affectionate and forgiving in nature. Many don't start talking until late in childhood, relying instead on 'telepathy' or self-styled sign language to get their message across to parents, siblings and friends. My sister, for example, did not learn to speak until late. As an infant, she would snort and point at what she wanted and when she did this, everyone would immediately respond. We laugh about it now, but her distinctive way of 'speaking' when she was an infant affectionately earned her the early nickname of 'Boo'.

Sadly, due to their propensity for silence or signed communication, many young Crystal Children are misdiagnosed and medicated for autism.

Crystal Children are highly sensitive and empathic, very much connected to nature and animals. They love the elderly and respond well to other children. They have no problems making friends. Many of these kids are fascinated with crystals and rocks and will openly discuss spirits and past-life memories. Most are musical and artistic, with all Crystal Children preferring a vegetarian or healthy diet over processed or junk foods (although some will have a very healthy sweet tooth – so be prepared). Being that they are very sensitive to the modern world, though, Crystal Children are generally more chemically sensitive than other kids and are naturally wary of strangers.

Rainbow Children

According to an extract from an article by Doreen Virtue from her Angel Therapy website, Rainbow Children 'are the embodiment of our divinity and the example of our potential'.

They are apparently few and far between. When they do appear, however, they are said to typically 'choose' Crystal Children to be their parents, carry no karma and usually only ever appear in proficient, supportive families.

2

Uniting As A People

This book was written in the hope that we might, some day, unite as a people and walk as one, with each of us being mindful of, but not fixated on, the differences, strengths and weaknesses demonstrated by *all* the children of the world – no matter what age they are or whether they be Indigos or not.

We all have a purpose. We all count. We are all here for a sacred reason, and it is our duty to find our purpose and to live it to the best of our ability.

Whether Indigo Children truly exist, whether they are here to save the planet or bring justice back to the system, none of it really matters if we (as their parents, teachers, siblings, mentors and guardians) don't perceive their existence as an aperture to heal ourselves and take responsibility for our own lives. We really do not need worry about our kids. They know what they are doing. It is *us* who must reassess life and how we live it. We are the ones who need to learn to fit in and comply with the (new) system.

Like everyone, I have my list of strengths and weaknesses, and my wife has hers. You have your strengths and weakness, as does your crossing lady, the girl managing the pet store and the guy who runs the local pub. We all have things we are proud of, good at or gifted in. We also have things we are lousy at, things we are ashamed of and things we do religiously even when we know we shouldn't.

Be they beneficial or not, these things are what make us unique. They are the things that, when viewed in context, make us sacred and special. Armed with these strengths and weaknesses, we are like individual jigsaw pieces that, when placed together, fuse to create the bigger picture. And as one of these jigsaw pieces, I have come to realise that I am not *apart from* the universe, but rather that I am *a part of* the universe.

It is my hope that this book will help bring people together; that it might facilitate mass realisation and celebration of the strengths and weaknesses found in others so that we might augment our own. And I hope this book makes people stop and look at Indigo Children as being more than just hyperactive trouble makers or real-life 'X-men' freaks armed with supernatural gifts of power by pointing out the strengths and weaknesses found in ALL children.

My strengths support my wife's weaknesses, for example, and visa versa. Without me and my eccentricities, her foibles might never have been acknowledged or shown the light of day, and without hers, my life would only ever have been half accomplished.

Just being an Indigo Warrior doesn't make me more aware than my wife or more spiritual, enlightened, frustrated or inherently angry for that matter. But acknowledging that I am one helps her become who and what she was intended to be. Her being a Peacekeeper, similarly, helps balance and ground me. Her strengths (of which there are many) enhance mine. They make me feel stronger, prouder and more alive. They lift my burdens and make my life worth living. Her weaknesses shore me up by giving my strengths purpose. They remind me that no one is infallible and that everyone needs rescuing at some time or another and that it is okay to ask for help or retreat into a place of silence when all other options dry up.

And that is the way life was meant to be: one life form supporting and nourishing the next; one life learning from and offering purpose and integrity to *all* lives. Being an Indigo Warrior does not mean that I am better or worse than someone who is not an Indigo. It just means that I am lucky in that, for some reason, people like me have had a spotlight shown on their strengths and weaknesses so that others may see us as a template on which to grow and heal. We have become the 'ideal' – a warrior archetype – a model on which to relearn and rebuild.

As an Indigo Warrior I know that we each hold a sacred position in the greater scheme of things; we all represent a vital thread in the Tapestry of Life and we are all equal. We are all unique and separate on one level, yet reliant and unified on another. I also know that putting Indigo Warriors up on a pedestal as the 'saviours of humanity' is not only a mistake; it is also a waste of time. For a start, the average Indigo Warrior (most of who love being the centre of attention, no matter what the rationale) would initially relish the fascination being showered upon them but soon forget why it was happening, with the truth being that Indigo Warriors make excellent rebel rousers and point makers, but, quite often, lousy leaders. They get bored easily and typically don't want or need such burdensome responsibilities. If you were to ask a true Indigo Warrior what they think of the current hype, few would respond enthusiastically. Indigo Warriors know, for example, that individually we all retain qualities needed to 'save humanity'. No one person or group of people carry the sole honour of fulfilling that responsibility. As 'a people', however, when everyone's qualities are considered and united as one, we collectively form the vital ingredients needed to brew the ultimate healing elixir. The role of the Indigo Warrior, therefore, is to empower *everyone else* to become leaders in their own right.

The Opposites That Are Equal

From my observation it is clear that humankind has always bounced spiritual power back and forth between the sexes. There seems to be an age-old bone of contention between the two as to who holds the greatest power, the strongest abilities and the deepest relationship with the Creator Spirit, but if we are to raise our children right and reach our potential as 'a people', we, as their elders and mentors need to set an example and address this power struggle, drop our self-importance and embrace both the masculine and feminine principles in a unified and respectful way.

For the ancients, spirituality was a shared responsibility, with both sexes acknowledged for their individual strengths and weaknesses on an equal standing. Spirituality was not something to be labelled. It was a way of life. It was what one did to live a healthy, abundant life. It was realised that for the Earth Mother and the Creator Spirit to continually supply the people with what was required for them to survive, they had to honour the source, live in harmony with nature and treat each other with love and respect. They also realised that what was given had to be acknowledged and offered back to the Earth in a sacred way.

And then darkness came, and for the longest of whiles it seemed that men ruled and all that was feminine was quashed, masculinised and pigeonholed as insignificant and weak. As with all things that are out of balance, the feminine power eventually reawakened and returned as a force to be reckoned with. After many years of female dominated spiritual development groups, goddess honouring, women's circles, womb-healing and moon lodges, however, the men are now, once again, beginning to look within for answers and are asking, "What about us?"

Personally, I am sick of comments like, 'women are more intuitive', 'men are muggles' and 'men need to get in touch with their feminine sides if we are to heal our planet'. The fact of the matter is, most men wouldn't be able to distinguish their 'feminine side' from a vanity basin, and secretly, neither would a lot of women. Not consciously, anyway. It is my belief that men are equally as aware as women, but since time was new, women have taken to the intuitive arts quicker and on a much easier, more natural level, and men have been allowed to forget. Sure, we hear the correspondences made between the phases of the moon and the three phases of women as maiden, mother and crone. Sure, we are encouraged to witness the presence of the goddess in all aspects of Creation, evident in the ebbs and flows of Grandmother Ocean and the changing of the seasons, but what of the youth, father and sage? What of the god aspect: the male consort to the goddess? We, as men, have forgotten what it means to be a real male, as apposed to a 'real man', while many women are striving to remember what it means to be a woman. In ancient times it was the women who dreamed the future and determined the path of the people. It was the women who visioned where the best hunting was to be found and the safest ground to set up camp. It was the women who governed the people, and they did so by trusting their intuition and their connection to Spirit. It was the men, though, who took these dreams and visions to the Creator Spirit and asked for signs as to how they should be brought to fruition. The men trusted Spirit because they trusted their women. They knew that neither would let them down, because they trusted their own Spirit and knew their purpose and who they were in the bigger scheme of things. The men honoured the menstrual blood as the driving force of life, and saw the bleeding of the women as a sacred time of immense power. In the days of our ancestors, the men and the women worked hand in hand. Their lives were interwoven on all levels. There was balance. They complimented each other physically, spiritually and emotionally and they supported and compensated one another's weaknesses.

Women were once seen as emissaries of the metaphysical realms, fulfilling the role of the romantic, prophet, healer, educator and philosopher. Men have always been the active ones: the developers, hunters and collectors, the foot soldiers and defenders. Despite these clearly defined roles, both men and women once gathered in sacred counsel. They may have gathered separately or at individual power times, but when they did, they stood opposite while honouring the other as a balancing force and equal in their own right. The women dreamed and shared their visions with the men, who sat collectively at peace within their role as the ones expected to consciously bring them to fruition. Although the women were the ones who visioned the future, the men were the ones who harnessed the energy and manifested the outcome. Vibrationally, masculine energy is intangible and cannot be held within the palm of one's hand. Masculine energy is generally witnessed or experienced rather than being physically contained. The warmth of the sun, the passion created by an intimate encounter, the violence of war; all these occurrences are energetically experienced and are therefore masculine in form. Feminine energy, however, is tangible and real to the touch. The experiences had within the womb, the birthing of children; the ever-changing cycles of nature and the growing and eventual harvesting of the crops are all energetically feminine in their form. They are physical experiences that can be bodily explored and recorded by the senses. The ancients knew this, and celebrated the fact on a daily basis in both ritual and ceremony as well as in their day-to-day lives. It was real, practical and afforded them great power. It was the way life was meant to be lived.

In Chinese philosophy, the Yin-Yang is the symbol of balance and harmony between all that is masculine and all that is feminine. The Yang aspect, the lighter coloured area, represents the light of the sun. The dark area, the Yin, signifies the night and the diminished light of the moon. The Yang symbolises 'man' while the Yin embodies 'woman'. It is a fundamental observation that affirms the Yang cannot grow and prosper without the Yin and the Yin cannot give birth without the Yang. The two halves that are opposite in form and equal in Spirit come together to create a perfect whole, a circle with representations of each honoured at the fullest, most potent times of the other as little 'fish-eye' dots. The power found within the feminine is neither different to nor the same as the power found within the masculine for, although they are opposite to all intent and purpose, they are equal at every degree. I believe that it is now time to understand our role as masculine and feminine energy forms, to come together as one and to live in harmony and balance with each other instead of arguing over who, what, when and why.

As men, it is time for us to remember the sacredness and power of the opposite sex while taking responsibility for improving public image of our own, and women need to do the same. Women get annoyed because their men 'do not understand' what it is like to suffer physically and emotionally during their bleeding time. They complain because their men do not help with the kids, offer to cook dinner or clean up around the house. They get frustrated because their intuitional realisations are labelled as 'fancies' and the wisdom of their elders are laughed off as old wives' tales. Why do women today get annoyed with their men? The answer, I believe, is that they unwittingly encourage them to remain ignorant. They keep them blind. They gently rubbish them in front of female friends and family, and get angry with them when they are alone. They expect their men to know what they want but remain silent as to how they should go about finding out.

Without making excuses, men cannot be expected to know what it means to have a period and how it messes with the daily aspects of life. They cannot know what childbirth is like. They cannot know how emotional and tired their women get after a day at home with the kids. They cannot know how to live their life trusting their intuition implicitly while still being expected to maintain a regular job that brings home x-amount of dollars at the end of each week to cover the mortgage and car repayments. They cannot know unless their women tell them and, by this, I do not mean sitting them down and instructing them with diagrams and training videos. I would love to see men inviting their women into the inner sanctums of what it means for them to be men, and visa versa. Just as men today need to let their guards down with their women, to heal their past and talk, cry and share from the heart, the women need to support the process by welcoming the men they love into their worlds. They need to trust that their men will not use and abuse them like the men who came before them. They need to invite their men into their sharing circles, healing lodges, temples and wombs. They need to educate their men by explaining the sacredness of being a woman and by teaching their men to trust their intuition and to share the burden of daily routine. They need to teach them how to show their love and appreciation by buying their men flowers or helium balloons and opening the occasional bottle of champagne with no other reason but to celebrate their love for one another. Otherwise, how will he know to do the same? A lot of men today want to know about periods, childbirth and 'women's intuition'. They want to be included in the shopping, the home decoration and the choosing of their kids' birthday presents. They yearn to trust their dreams and to vision their futures like their women do. They are learning to love their wives unconditionally and to participate in the lives of their children, because they are learning to love themselves, to forgive their parents and to openly celebrate their emotions. Today's men are tired of being 'blokes' who play footy, watch porn and drink beer. They want to do more, but their women need to show them how by encouraging them and providing space to explore, ask 'silly' questions without fear of ridicule and to make mistakes. Women must drop expectation and realise that their men are largely innocent (not ignorant) to the ways of Spirit and that they need time and patience if they are to catch up.

I believe we have come full circle. We are once again looking to one another as brothers and sisters, equals and as vital strands in the Web of Life. The spiritual reawakening and healing that women have collectively done over the years has been incredibly important, not just for themselves, but also for their men and for the Earth Mother as a whole. They have not only rebirthed themselves as beings of immense spiritual and sexual power, but they have also paved the way for their men to follow suit.

Although there are still some men today (and surprisingly, even some women) who view the male sex as the stronger and more potent, it is an outdated view that says women must remain passive to their men, be content to raise the children alone and keep house. We need to start taking responsibility for what happens in our own backyards: our lives and our families, our actions and our beliefs. We need to honour what it means to be men and women and what it means to walk hand-in-hand as a people. We need to drop stereotypes, peer group pressure, blame, guilt and fear. We need to celebrate our existence here on Earth as spiritual beings having physical experiences. Our mothers, wives, sisters and daughters must continue to learn physical skills, play sport, advance academically and consider themselves capable, if not more so, of achieving everything their brothers can, while maintaining their ability to vision, honour their bleeding time and commune directly with Spirit through song, prayer and chant. But, above all, it is also time for us to encourage our fathers, husbands, brothers and sons to cry, love, dream, trust their intuition and sing from their hearts, while still becoming the solid, grounded providers and protectors Spirit intended them to be.

Personal Power

Personal power describes the intrinsic gifts and sacred philosophies that drive each of us onward and upward. Personal power brings to light what it means to be unique and sacred. It is first realised the moment we are conceived, with the hope that we will embrace it and share it with others and teach them how to awaken their own during the course of our life.

Personal power must never be wasted or kept to ourselves, but rather developed and shared for the benefit of humanity. Personal power is knowledge; acumen gathered over lifetimes of experience that lifts us from the mundane and delivers us into the realisation of unlimited potential. When knowledge is gathered and is used for the betterment of the self (and others), it gathers in energy. This energy becomes passion, the motivation to move forward, grow and expand on all levels. Personal power is awareness that comes from being connected to Spirit and all things of nature.

Personal power is the quintessence of remembering who we truly are. It is represented by unique ancestral knowledge, particular abilities and the specialised strengths we have honed in order to 'separate' us from everyone else in a medicine way. Personal power is a gift to the people from Creation. To share our power and to teach others how to discover their own concept of power is the correct way to ensure that our path is kept clear, our journey made faster and our lives kept forever fruitful. Personal power must never be squandered or kept to ourselves.

Personal power represents our gift to the world and the inevitable mark we will make on it. It represents our purpose and the reason for which we were born. It offers us the chance to make a difference in the world and to make life richer for others. It is what future generations will remember us for when we finally shed our robes and return to Spirit. Personal power must be embraced, nurtured, developed and shared.

The Web of Life

The Spider weaves and reweaves her web on a daily basis, an act that embodies the cyclical nature of life. Each strand within the web is representational of each and every creature that exists on the Earth Mother. Each strand, although separate and independent, supports and nurtures the next. When one strand is broken or damaged, it threatens the integrity of the entire web.

According to Native American folklore, it was Grandmother Spider who sang the universe into being by weaving the web of all life. She wove the very first dreamcatcher, a beautiful and protective spiral web spun from a single thread within a loop of willow. At the heart of the netting she placed a single turquoise stone, a symbol of connection to the creative force, to clarity, peace, communication and protection.

It is said that with the aid of a dreamcatcher, our dreams can be harnessed and brought to fruition. Like a labyrinth, the dreamcatcher guides us to our centre; a journey taken by those determined to realise their true potential. Spider is the weaver of reality. Its medicine helps us to remember that we are the creators of our own lives, solely responsible for the directions we choose and the paths we follow. As the weaver of dreams, Spider assures us that if we do not like where life is taking us, we can return to our centre and metaphorically begin again.

Just as the Spider reweaves her damaged web each morning, we too can redirect our chosen life-path. As long as the web is strong enough to harness our dreams, we have the power to change direction how and when we want. This is because we each represent a vital strand in the Web of Life. Without our productive input, the web's integrity is breached, weakened and deemed incomplete, thus causing confusion and dis-ease in the world around us. We each embody a vital strand in the Web of Life; each offering individual strengths and sacred wisdom that promise to enhance the ways of our world.

We are encouraged by Spider's guidance to explore life and to investigate all the strands that lead from its centre and make the most of them. Some strands will offer reward and others will not. That's life. As we journey the positive strands, life is good and rewarding. We are nourished and our path seems abundant. A wrong turn, however, may lead us along a strand that offers little or nothing. Life becomes difficult with all attempts to free ourselves proving fruitless. The Web of Life is riddled with pitfalls, but it also promises greatness to those prepared to stay focused, take risks and work hard.

As the weaver of dreams, Spider helps us explore life and to reweave our web when our path becomes barren. She helps us reclaim our personal power and to bring our dreams to fruition. She warns, however, that in order to open new doors we must first find the strength to close old ones.

When we stand in our personal power and move forward with confidence and trust, we honour our sacred place within the Web of Life – particularly when we are determined to discover and embrace our purpose. However, if we slack off, deny responsibility or play the victim, we ultimately weaken the Web of Life, which dishonours the agreement we forged with Spirit at the beginning of time. It also robs our brothers and sisters of their chance to live better lives.

This is about recognising and honouring the place each and every one of us has in this interconnected universe. However, it is not about instilling guilt for things that are outside our capacity to influence or deal with. Rather, it is about appreciating and living the sacred connectedness we all share, and about playing our part in it.

We should view our life as a pebble about to be dropped into a pond, with every action, belief, spoken word or thought made creating a knee-jerk ripple effect fanning out the moment the pebble hits the water. It is our intent that guides the ripples and determines their productivity. Everything happens for a reason and all things have their place.

Instead of living independently, separate from everyone and everything else, it is time to pull together and work as a team instead of trying to force the 'square pegs' among us to fit into the antiquated 'round holes' stipulated by an equally passé society.

Labels

The first step toward living interconnected lives involves dropping negative labels that support racism, sexism, terrorism and all the other 'isms' that divide, persecute and oppress.

Labels, per se, are fine — as long as they aren't used to pigeonhole or reject those among us who dare to march to the beat of their own drum. Labels are fine when they are used to commemorate, encourage and congratulate, for example. We 'label' everything. We have to — it's in our inherent nature to do so. The trouble is, even when we say the word 'label', we automatically associate it with negative classification. We tend not to recognise words like 'academic', 'graduate' or 'champion' as labels. We tend to hear them, smile approvingly and say something sensible like, 'You must be so proud'. They are more like metaphors — they aren't 'labels'. When we describe our children as being achievers, for example, the response is always positive. It is assumed they will do well in life because they obviously work hard, are conventional and act respectfully. But when we describe our children as disruptive, challenging or angry, it is quickly (and erroneously) deduced that there must be something wrong with them and that something should probably be done to fix them and make them fit the form so they stand a better chance of becoming achievers. The system looks for reason. It points the finger and blames. It demands that we classify, separate and clarify what, why and how. Then, over time, we start to feel responsible, neglectful and ashamed of our children (and ourselves), until we eventually begin to believe the hype and point the finger ourselves. And that is what is starting to happen with labels like ADD, ADHD, and in some cases, the term 'Indigo'.

We need to look for ways to praise, encourage and inspire our kids without relying on labels to classify them or explain their ways. Saying things like, 'My child has ADD', is no less or no more potentially damaging as saying 'You will have to excuse my child for their behaviour. They act that way because they're a free-spirited Indigo'. Both statements equally focus on their weaknesses and vulnerabilities and deny their strengths and their right to be treated with equality and respect. Both effectively label our kids as disappointments. The first denigrates them in a way now sadly indicative of the whispered future of today's youth. The second, while attempting to polish up their reputation by making them sound knowing or enlightened in some way, only succeeds, in most cases, to do so on a superficial and fleeting level. If we don't watch ourselves, it won't be long before the term 'Indigo' comes to be just another label used to describe kids with ADD, ADHD and other fictitious, abbreviated conditions.

And that would be a shame. That would be heartbreaking for the kids and a backward step for humanity as a whole, and that is why I have decided to refer to each of the five types of children listed in this book from now on as 'Warrior Children', 'Nature Children', 'Peacekeeper Children', 'Winter Children' and 'Golden Children', for the simple reason that these names identify immediately both their strengths and their weaknesses with little or no need for further explanation.

3

Pathways To Power

The Four Humours

Based on the theory of four primary elements, Greek physician, Hippocrates (400BC), espoused that good health depended largely on the balance of four fluids, or humours, in the human body. In considering the four elements, he concluded that fire corresponded to blood; air to yellow bile; water to phlegm, and earth to black bile.

To this day we describe people as having a 'good sense of humour' or 'being in a bad humour', with the Greek or Latin names still used by some to describe the four primary personalities. From the (hot) blood, or sanguis, comes 'sanguine', meaning 'happy, hopeful and positive', for example; from the (hot) yellow bile comes 'choleric' (among others) meaning 'angry, irate and bitter'; from the (cold) phlegm, or phlegma, comes 'phlegmatic', meaning 'slow, cool and impassive' and from the (cold) black bile, or melancholia, comes 'melancholic', meaning 'depressed, irritable and sad' – hence the phrase 'suffering from melancholia'.

Some people, especially those of the older generation, seem to bridge the gap between two or more of the temperaments. The vast majority of people, though, continue to demonstrate one primary temperament type.

Although the correspondences no longer hold medical value as far as determining whether or not an individual is of good health or not, the temperaments remain relevant, despite being renamed and described as:

- The Guardian, who is fact-oriented
- The Rationalist, who is theory-oriented
- The Idealist, who is ideals-oriented
- The Artisan, who is action-oriented

A Fifth Temperament?

While only four temperaments are recognised, my observation of people (mainly through my work with children as a schoolteacher and mentor), suggests there may be five types. If I am right, the fifth — the Dreamer, who appears to be feelings-oriented — is still experiencing spiritual evolution.

Archetypes

Taking the concept of the Four Humours one step further, archetypes are personifications of universal energy; patterns, traits and behaviours that we all recognise, explains Brian Dale; a primary school teacher, librarian, storyteller, drama teacher and archetype consultant trained by the Caroline Myss Institute of Australia (as well as being my 'adopted' father). "We immediately understand the 'mother' archetype, for example," he says. "We automatically process a picture of a mother and recognise the energy that nurtures, cares, protects, teaches and models behaviours. However, all archetypes have both positive and negative aspects. So we also have the 'smother mother' or the neglectful mother.

Major or dominant archetypes are easy to detect and observe in adults. We all know someone who consistently operates on the negative 'victim' archetype. Which of our friends are 'damsels', continually in and out of relationships and still waiting to be rescued by their 'knight in shining armour'? Who in our life is the 'bully', the 'rescuer', the 'servant' or the 'martyr'? Adults consistently use archetypes in the different aspects of their lives. Remember, however, that there is both negative and positive energy with each archetype and adults may operate on either side. 'Balance' is another important issue. The negative 'addict' archetype may be so dominant that an individual will suppress their other personal archetypes in order to feed the addiction. The 'damsel' may become so involved with a love relationship that nothing else in their lives matters. Adults seeking awareness and personal growth will determine their archetypes, recognise and move from the negative energy to the positive energy of each archetype and strive for balance, that is, a positive contribution from all their chosen archetypes.

By their very nature, children are inexperienced in matters that surround them but are rapidly processing material about themselves and the world. Their individual archetypes are not fully realised and they tend to operate on two or three archetypes that best suit their needs and surroundings. Parents and teachers especially have an obligation to recognise those archetypes that individual children use. Because archetypes are universal energies, many adults do this naturally and subconsciously. How many fathers call their daughters Princess? There is a guaranteed special bond between that father and daughter.

Teachers, especially primary school teachers, can automatically tell you which children are the 'bullies', the 'victims', or the 'clowns'. How they react to these children will depend upon the openness of the teacher. Are they interested in encouraging the positive side of these archetypes or just suppressing the negative side? Which archetype of the teacher responds or reacts to the negativity of these child archetypes? We all have the 'child' archetype. Adults are often aware of their inner child energy that makes demands, plays, imagines, and creates. However, children, because they are children, rely upon their 'child' archetype to constantly learn about their position in the world. There are different types of 'child' archetypal energy.

As parents and teachers how aware are we of our children? Have we created the 'wounded child' and continue to feed and reward negative behaviours that damage self-esteem and limit expression and development? Or as teachers (in the parent or teacher role) do we recognise the 'wounded child' archetype? Do we adopt an empathetic (not sympathetic) attitude and encourage the determination and resilience of such children? For the 'spoilt brat', do we fuel the self-indulgence and placate the tantrums or do we model and teach the discipline of boundaries and limits, the joy and rewards (not bribery) of sharing? How do we encourage the positive energy of the 'Peter Pan child'? Certainly encourage the spirit of adventure and spontaneity but also teach responsibility, due process and consequences. Give credence to the 'magical or divine child'. These are highly spiritual, special children that need adults as a link between their giftedness and the grounding process of this physical earth.

As parents and teachers we fill a special role in the education and development of our children. They, like us, are individuals that use the universal energy of archetypes to learn and operate. We first must recognise this archetypical energy and then encourage behaviours that use the positive side rather than the negative side.

Consider those highly active, energetic kids. Many possess the 'warrior' archetype. Let us harness that power and direct it into a positive outlet. The development of modern technology and urban living imposes restrictions on these children. They are no longer free to roam the wide, open land in safety or with a sense of adventure. They need their sport, their martial arts, their bikes and skateboards. Most of all they need time away from the television and computer to be outdoors with adults and with active participation. These 'warriors' need positive modelling, nurturing and teaching. There is a code of conduct and chivalry. Others, whether they are in a position of strength or weakness, deserve respect, dignity and protection.

Recognise that the 'damsel' and 'princess' archetypes need times of indulgence, for example. However, they also need to be shown and encouraged to be independent. As a teacher, a good strategy when handling the 'damsel' child is as follows:

1. I'll do this for you.
2. I'll do this with you.
3. I'll watch you do this.
4. You can do this alone and by yourself.

Remember that there will be occasions when these children need the security to check their progress and re-visit previous steps. Take notice of the children who have chosen uncommon archetypes. The 'artist' who may not fit into the academic or sporty category has limited areas and opportunities for excellence and recognition in our modern education system. 'Artist' archetypes are continually planning projects and need to be given the time and opportunity to test their ideas and the encouragement to bring them to completion. The 'philosopher' archetype will question the pattern and worth of society, the 'judge' and 'detective' will question each individual, each rule and each decision while the 'rebel' will challenge society, the system and the administrators of that system. Parents and teachers! Be prepared! Where is your awareness? Will you react in a positive or negative manner?

As adults, we are responsible for the wellbeing of our children. Understand yourself and act upon that understanding. Understand your children and assist them to act upon their self-understanding. The key is balance and to use the positive energy of chosen archetypes."

Animal Spirits and Totemic Blueprints

I have seen animal spirits with people since I was a small child. When I saw the animals, I instinctively knew 'stuff' about them and their lives. I saw the animals as projections of their soul: archetypes, blueprints or externalised symbolic expressions of their personality and character. How? I have no idea.

As I grew and developed spiritually, I began to see these archetypes or totemic blueprints as 'totems', or power allies that offered explanation into where a person was at: what drove them, inspired them, supported them or frightened them. I was able to use this knowledge to 'read' them and to determine whether or not I trusted them or how I might help them or learn from them.

As an adult, it is now my understanding that each of us is born with a unique set of totemic blueprints that effectively showcase our particular strengths and weaknesses. These totems embody our fundamental character and personality; our principles and ethics; our ability to express our beliefs, our wants, needs and desires; our sense of home and security, creativity, sexuality and potential; our vocation, calling, hobbies and health, relationships, legal issues, death, spirituality, religion, education, wisdom and travel; our purpose and our gifts of personal power. Essentially, these aspects form the blueprints of individual expression, factors that dominate our lives and how we live them. And, to me, these totemic blueprints are archetypically personified within the spirit or essence that resonates from the world's animals, readily witnessed in the way they interact with each other and the particular environment they rely on for survival.

Although our set of totemic blueprints is unique to each and every one of us, it is interesting to note that most people can be quickly and accurately described as displaying one of four (recognised) primary temperament types. It is as though the combination of totems we innately carry magically shapes us to snugly fit into one of these categories, while offering us the chance to demonstrate ours in a specialised way — a way different to the millions of others who apparently match our 'type'. For this reason, we are all inherently similar, while simultaneously being profoundly worlds apart.

Identifying the Five Little Monkeys

I don't know why or how I am able to see animal spirits, or why I am able to interpret them the way I do. There seems little point, therefore, in trying to explain why or how the primary temperament types are, for me, embodied within the essence of the Five Little Monkeys I now see sitting on the left shoulder of the people I interact with each and every day: the Black and White Colobus, Ring-tailed Lemur, Capuchin, Squirrel and Golden Tamarin Monkeys.

After my awakening to the Indigo phenomenon at Doreen Virtue's Angel

Intuitive course, when I realised I had been unwittingly working with Indigo and Crystal Children my entire teaching career (I described them as being 'Warrior' and 'Nature' children back then), I was having a coffee with a friend who occasionally helped out at our shop, Circle of Stones. After a brief moment of silence, she put her coffee down and asked, "Do you see a Capuchin Monkey with me? Am I a Warrior or Nature Child?"

I accepted this as a challenge, because the answer was a resounding 'no' — I couldn't see a Capuchin Monkey. I could see other animals, but there was no Capuchin.

She then proceeded to verbally list mutual friends and associates, family members and favourite customers that frequented our shop. She even offered the name of the guy who owned the café we were drinking coffee in, asking me each time, "What do you see with them? Are they Warriors?"

It soon became evident that although not everyone had a Capuchin Monkey, and although many other animals were revealed, five Monkeys in total were repeatedly identified. I soon had a healthy list of people of all ages and walks of life; their names neatly grouped under five primate-oriented headings. The Capuchin Monkey people were automatically subtitled as Warriors, because they were the ones I knew to be angry, defiant, and restless and, at times, impatient — like me and the kids I taught. The list headed with the capitalised words 'Squirrel Monkey People' (the list containing the names of both my children), was just as quickly sub-tagged as 'Nature Children', because of their quiet nature, loving disposition, overwhelming love of nature and large innocent (but knowing) eyes. I likened the Golden Tamarin people to those celebrated by Doreen Virtue as the still-emerging 'Rainbow Children' and the ones I acknowledge as the Golden Children; the ones best described as pioneering, alternative, alluring and sometimes a bit unnerving in their ways.

But what of the two remaining groups: the Black and White Colobus Monkeys and the Ring-tailed Lemurs?

I sat and listed the most obvious characteristics of each of those on the two lists, including their traits, qualities, beliefs, likes and dislikes. I even considered their choice of career, their physical attributes, strengths and weaknesses among other things, and realised that, like the others, a sense of semblance bound the people on each list together that, in a similar way, cast them apart from those on the other. I realised that those labelled as 'Black and White Colobus Monkeys' seemed to display the propensity for moodiness, self-sabotage and, at times, bouts of depression. I was surprised to find, too, that everyone on that particular list could be fastidious, productive and inspirational when encouraged and supported in a productive way. I decided to subtitle these people as 'Winter Children' because of the way winter rouses me and how it influences the land, the animals and life in general. Winter is, in many ways, emblematic of their nature. The 'Ring-tailed Lemur' people, however, all seemed to be the sorts who were great at bringing people together in one way or another, sharing knowledge and taking in lost causes with the hope of rescuing or healing them. They also seemed to be the most athletic of the five, with a health-conscious, focused, no-nonsense attitude to life. I subtitled these people the 'Peacekeepers' because they rarely engage in arguments and have unlimited energy and patience to burn.

And so I had my Five Little Monkeys, neatly packaged and explained; each bearing the most obvious traits of the temperaments or 'humours' they represent. But that didn't help to explain why the Capuchin Monkey people — the Warriors — are so prolific right now. It didn't help to explain why we are seeing a swell in occurrence and a rise in interest targeted at these people in particular. And it didn't help to explain what could be done to support them and learn from them.

Keynotes of the Five Little Monkeys:

Monkey:	Child:	Keynotes:
Capuchin	Indigo Child Warrior Child	Militant Achiever Warrior Action-oriented Artisan
Colobus	Winter Child	Guardian Fact-oriented Martyr Logician Problem Solver
Ring-tailed Lemur	Peacekeeper Child	Rationalist Theory-oriented Loner Witness Pacifier
Squirrel Monkey	Nature Child	Idealist Ideals-oriented Activist Speaker Romantic
Golden Lion Tamarin	Golden Child Rainbow Child	Dreamer Feelings-oriented Prophet Intuitive

4

Power Time

'... *The sky is round, and I have heard the Earth is round like a ball, and so are all the stars. The wind in its greatest power whirls. Birds make their nests in circles, for theirs is the same religion as ours. The sun comes forth and goes down again in a circle. The moon does the same, and both are round. Even the seasons form a great circle in their changing, and always come back again to where they were. The life of a man is a circle from childhood, and so it is in everything where power moves ...*'

- Black Elk -
Elder of the Oglala Sioux People, 1863 - 1950

While pondering the Wheel of Fortune tarot card recently, it occurred to me that the 'Indigo phenomenon' currently sweeping the world may not necessarily represent the dawn of an evolutionary phase of humanity, as has been hypothesised by some, but rather a habitual return to a global 'power time' of truth, clarity and sincerity marked by an army of militant warriors recruited by inevitability itself.

The Wheel of Fortune describes the humbling roller-coaster ride that is life. It is all about the cyclical genesis of 'big things': luck, change and good fortune, abundance, happiness and elevation. It heralds a change that happens unexpectedly, but brings with it great joy. It reminds us to consider both the positive and negative aspects of life and the possibilities they afford, because when honoured for the lessons it presents, our journey through life may be plagued by difficulty and loss. The Wheel of Fortune espouses that even when things seem really hard, nothing is ever unachievable; things always work out in the end. So, even though we may be scratching our heads right now asking 'What have we done to deserve these kids?' it may be possible that they have always been here, lying dormant waiting for their power time to come around. Perhaps now these kids are at the pinnacle of the Wheel of Fortune and we are simply experiencing an episode of change embodied within a cohort of braver, more outspoken children that genuinely portends the card's interpretation.

There have always been generations that have been louder and more outspoken than those previous — prepared to protest and argue a point. There have always been individuals who have bravely stood in defence of their principles, daring to question the system and express their alternative beliefs and opinions while remaining steadfast in their convictions and resolvedly facing the consequences no matter how harsh. Warrior Children have always walked the planet, defying the system and breaking the code: Joan of Arc, for example; Ned Kelly, Lawrence of Arabia, Nancy Wake, Mick Jagger, Madonna and Robbie Williams, Jackson Pollock and Andy Warhol, Martin Luther King, Rosa Parks, Nelson Mandela and the 'unknown rebel', the nameless man who brought a line of looming tanks to a standstill during the 1989 Tiananmen Square protests in the People's Republic of China, to name just a few. To individuals such as these, freedom of speech is sacred, to be heard and acknowledged as a basic human right worth fighting and (in some extreme cases) dying for.

Instead of an evolutionary phenomenon, then, perhaps the kids celebrated today as Warrior Children are just regular people, once again, heralding the return to a time of peace and united global power? Suppose, like the countless times this opportunity has undoubtedly presented itself to us before, we are about to end a cycle of self-importance and manipulation, and suppose we are on the verge of beginning a new one? And suppose, too, as they have probably done many times before, our children are offering us a choice to continue to live life as we have always done or, alternatively, unite as a people, learn from our mistakes and rebuild the world from the ground up? Like the figures clutching tightly to the Wheel of Fortune as it advances through its phases suggest, we may be witnessing the return to power of those charged with the courage and inner strength to scream from their gut with an ear-piercing 'No more' to the lies and hypocrisies, the wrongs and devastations being inflicted on the people, the animals and our magnificent planet as a whole.

Whatever is happening, humanity is definitely being given a wake-up call. We are being forced to comprehend the abundance we have in our children and the planet as a whole. We are in a time of flux, of growing awareness and clarity. We are being summoned together to show responsibility for our lives. We are being forced to stand accountable for our past while being quizzed about our commitment to welcome the necessary change that will guarantee a fertile future. We are having our somewhat arrogant, 'throw away' attitudes and our controlling ways hung out for the word to see and our fears and weaknesses rubbed in our faces, and we are being mercilessly questioned and shown up by the last people we ever expected to point an accusing finger at our antiquated ways – our children.

Unafraid to fight for truth and justice when truth and justice in realistic terms are worth defending, Warriors have *always* been the ones to resist war, to denounce authority and question baseless orders and empty explanations. They have no respect for those who do not walk their talk, and they don't give a damn what people think of them. Although they embrace rules and boundaries (especially when they have played a part in their negotiation), they will blatantly defy any law until it is fully explained or proven. The degree to which our children are resisting 'tradition' while unashamedly disregarding the way things have always been suggests to me that now is the time to re-evaluate how we (as their parents, teachers and mentors) have always done things. Our children are giving us a golden opportunity to rethink tradition, redraft our plans and rebuild the system. It is pretty obvious, you might agree, that the customs of 'the good old days' are no longer applicable in our modern world and that they are in great need of revamping. We are being taunted and pushed to the limit by those who love us the most, to put our fears to rest, abandon our quest for control and surrender arrogance and jealousy. For the first time ever, we have the full support of our children. In fact, they are the ones initiating the change. Instead of us asking for their support, they are demanding ours. They are readying us for 'battle', standing beside us set to fight for a magnificent and selfless cause — a cause that promises to deliver us all into a time of abundance, acceptance and unconditional love.

So, just suppose, we are currently reliving the power time of the Warrior Child; the power time of those inherently armed with the courage and inner strength to scream from their gut with an ear-piercing 'No more' to the denigration and duplicity, the corruption and the oppression being inflicted on the people, the animals and our magnificent planet as a whole by those who should know better than them. But instead of experiencing a lone voice in a crowd, or a small band of rebel rousers we are witnessing a global call to power. It seems that now is the time for the masses and those best equipped to stand up and be heard with the purpose of bringing peace and truth back to the governments and the 'system'. If my thoughts are correct, then, it must be that humanity, like clockwork, has come full circle and we are again experiencing the reign of the Indigo Warrior; the militants, visionaries and idealists destined to return the Holy Grail to the people like Galahad / Percival once did.

They Have Always Been Here

According to the literature offered by the experts thus far, Indigo Children are proposed as those born any time after 1978 (with some exceptions). Crystal Children are apparently those born in 1995 or later, while the Rainbow Children are only now beginning to emerge, as the Crystal Children become adults . Although this theory makes a lot of sense on one hand, history seems to disagree. When you stop and assess the major events in history, and then consider the prominent types of people living at the time, a definite pattern starts to appear — a pattern that proposes the simultaneous existence of these children long before 1978.

The Indigo Warriors — the 'Capuchin Monkey' People

In Arthurian legend, surely the crusading knights questing for the Holy Grail were Warrior Children? In similar fashion to the youth of today, Lancelot, for example, (a well-known rules breaker), was supposedly driven by an altruistic desire to uphold a set of values and beliefs more enlightened than anything considered before. Along with his fellow knights, Lancelot gathered at an idealistically headless table where everyone was equal; they lived by their own rules and were unified by a simple and noble decree: to enhance the world by fighting for truth and honour whatever the cost.

Indeed Britain's debonair World War II Spitfire pilots and Navy Commandos were Warriors, as must have been the US Marines and the members of the French Resistance, like Nancy Wake, notoriously nicknamed the 'White Mouse'. They were heroic and action- based, as were, in a shadow sense, the Nazi Storm-troopers. Nancy Wake and her kin locked horns with in a blatantly opposite fight for perceived truth. They broke the rules and risked all, preferring to go out in a blaze of glory than fail or surrender.

And what of the outspoken, loud rebel rousers of the '60s? Without a doubt they *must* have been Warriors. The 'in your face' civil rights activists and black liberationists; the conscientious objectors, 'drop outs', hippies, members of the rampant drug culture and extroverted artists of the time whose main goal was to shock and agitate? They *must* have been Warriors.

The Crystal / Nature Children – the 'Squirrel Monkey' People

Just as the Knights of the Round Table were obviously Warriors, Guinevere, Vivien, Isolt and the Lady of the Lake (among others) were, in my mind, Nature Children. They personified the abundance of nature, the Other Worlds, the elements and the fertility of the Earth; the silence of The Void, the darkness of the womb and the sacred wisdom that is the feminine creative force. Merlin (glorified as a wizard and elder advisor to Arthur in some versions of the legend; defamed as a madman of the woods who ran with wild beasts in others) could be described as the masculine equivalent to the feminine creative force surging from the land during this time, and so was, therefore, probably a Nature Child too. The women of Camelot made flesh the true essence of the land, the inherent flow of nature, the goddess and the Earth Mother herself — qualities identified in the 'Nature Children' we see today.

During World War II, the Nature Children rose to the challenge of tending to the crops and the stock animals, keeping the farms functioning for when the men returned. Naturally gifted in the garden and ultra-sensitive to the animal kingdom, it became the Nature Child's responsibility to grow and provide adequate produce to nurture the people. It was their role to keep things as 'normal' as possible. As difficult as it was, they could not buy into war because they had to maintain a neutral state of innocence so as to ensure that hope and promise prevailed. They did this by taking on the role of teachers, nannies and governesses of children, many of who were secreted away to the country at the beginning of the war for their own protection.

During the '60s, it was the Nature Children who cemented the whole 'hippie / flower power' movement by endorsing organic produce and permaculture as an Earth-friendly and viable way of life. They saw it as their role to bring the people back into harmony with nature. Many Nature Children of the time unashamedly supported the Warriors as they blatantly did what needed to be done to disrupt the system. Many dropped out prematurely from school and university to join communes in the bush, to become introspective artists and musicians who produced material intended to make people think differently about life.

Today, Nature Children step into their power time whenever the forests are being ruthlessly logged, when the oceans are stricken by oil or when pods of Whales inexplicably beach themselves. They are the conservationists, liberationists, spokesmen and emissaries of Mother Earth. Nature Children believe in faeries, unicorns and dragons and openly acknowledge the trees and plants as sentient beings imbued with spirits that can be seen and conversed with. They are the animal communicators, diplomats and healers, fighting for their freedom and the right to be acknowledged as man's equal. They are the humanitarians, too, speaking up on behalf of the oppressed and disadvantaged among us, fighting publicly against racism, sexism, poverty and abuse. They are the romantics and the artisans. Recognised examples of Nature Children are Jane Goodall, Bob Geldof, Steve Irwin, Bob Dylan, John Lennon, Cat Stevens, Olivia Newton-John and animal communicators Billie Dean and Dawn Brunke.

The Rainbow / Golden Children – the 'Golden Lion Tamarin' People

In Scandinavian mythology, Ratatosk, whose name means 'drill tooth', was a Squirrel that scurried up and down the trunk of the Tree of Life, passing messages between the Eagle that lived at the top of the tree and the Serpent that dwelt deep among its roots. In this context, the Squirrel was a messenger: a bridge or 'walker between the worlds' that maintains balance between the positive and negative aspects of Creation. Ratatosk was an emissary of man and his quest for higher knowledge regarding the subtler aspects of life; a symbol of the journey we might take in our mission to better understand the connection that unites the realms of Spirit with the Underworld and the mundane world in which we live.

In many ways, King Arthur of Arthurian legend was Ratatosk personified. He was loved by the people, described as an 'enlightened ruler' and revered as a sacred meeting point between nature and man. He loved the land as much as he loved the people, and he loved the people as much as he loved the Creator Spirit or God. He was a bridge between the tangible, mundane world and that of Spirit; the material and the invisible; the masculine and the feminine. He was a balancer of the opposites and a link between the Pagan belief and the Christian faith. He was the bullseye on the 'dartboard of life', if you like: the hub on the Wheel of Fortune, with everything and everyone fanning out from its centre. His yearning for a perfect world, where it only ever rained at night, with the days as fine as any spring morning, matched the true essence of what the golden city of Camelot was said to represent.

If ever there lived a perfect example of a Golden Child, King Arthur was it.

During the Second World War, the golden baton of what it means to be a Golden Child seemed to pass to the painfully shy King George VI (who neither wanted nor ever thought he could become King) and his then Prime Minister, Winston Churchill, a visionary leader who vehemently shunned oppression and succeeded in renewing the world's faith in the pre-eminence that is democracy. Both these individuals were said to carry a 'golden energy'; a ray of hope that heralded powerful new beginnings that quickly spread through the land like a well-received wildfire.

The '60s, however, was riddled with people who resonated instinctively to the Golden energy and the higher awareness it offered. It was a psychedelic era that saw esoteric knowledge come out of the closet to be presented to the people as a way of life. The '60s made public UFO sightings and alien abductions, meditation, Indian philosophy, tarot and gurus, who were being introduced to the west at this time. The '60s were a point of 'conception' for the Golden Children, who are yet to unite as an assembly of any significant number. It provided a fertile foundation, though, for self-realised awareness while heralding a time of maturity and deeper understanding of the universe, spirituality and personal development as a whole. It was a springboard that saw people from all walks of life begin to question their purpose and the true meaning of life.

I don't know if the Golden Children have truly experienced their unified moment of glory as yet, although many are starting to have their presence felt through the remarkable work they are doing: people like Dr. Eric Pearl, for example, and others displaying gifts or knowledge they cannot explain — gifts that are raising eyebrows in the scientific and medical circles as well as in the spiritual arenas. I believe their power time will come when (and if) we ever see society forced to tap into aspects of human consciousness thus far labelled by the majority as 'new age mumbo jumbo' in order to survive. Golden Children are born with an incredible sense of self-knowing. They carry inherent knowledge best described as 'before their time', and although few and far between, Golden Children are here to awaken latent gifts of power within those they encounter. They are the dreamers and the prophets. Galileo, Albert Einstein, Isaac Newton, Shakespeare, Edison and Dr. Christian Barnard (a pioneer of organ transplants) were, with no doubt in my mind, examples of Golden Children.

The Peacekeeper Children — the 'Ring-tailed Lemur' People

Under the direction of King Arthur, it was left to the Peacekeeper Children to maintain a state of tranquillity throughout the land. When he was away, they spoke on the King's behalf and reported back to him on a regular basis, asserting his principles and policies with force and passion. The pages, messengers, sheriffs, bailiffs, judges and general law keepers of the time were most likely Peacekeeper Children, envoys that crossed the bridge between the worlds, maintaining concord, connection and kinship between the sovereign and its people.

The naval officers, sailors and members of the US and Royal Marines during World War II; the mobile infantry and foot soldiers, bomber pilots and the medical corps (the doctors, nurses, medics/ambulance drivers), were in no doubt Peacekeeper Children; those on the ground whose role it was to watch over and defend the freedom of those left at home and the security of the land; those best equipped to shepherd the public to safety and do what needed to be done to return them to a state of wellness.

Peacekeepers were evident during the '60s, too, and some of them enjoyed high profile positions. JFK, for example, surely had a Lemur on his left shoulder, as did historian Geoffrey Blainey and the senior minister of the then Australian Prime Minister Gough Whitlam, Jim Cairns, who both adopted a socialist, intellectual approach to the world's issues. During the '60s an alternative psychology started to emerge, as did a new way of thinking. We learnt to enhance our view of the world while staying within the familiar, established boundaries of society; an idealistic approach regarding morals and philosophy that, today, is indicative of the approach adopted by those celebrated as Peacekeeper Children. We saw white sympathisers, for example, and young university intellectuals, who, as a matter of principal and philosophy, were supportive of the black liberation movement while endorsing a non-violent approach and peaceful resolution.

During periods of devastation and upheaval is when we see the Peacekeeper Children step into their true power: when we need to regroup, pull together and work as a team. Examples include September 11, 2001 and the Asian Tsunami of Boxing Day, 2004, among others. The Armed Forces, Search and Rescue teams, and the Police, Ambulance and Fire Brigade are riddled with Peacekeepers who see it as their duty to serve and protect their broader community. We see them in their glory during times of unrest and disturbance, during war and times of natural disaster. They inspire hope as they rally people together, bringing the best out in those they encounter by offering a broader perspective, espousing a clear and precise understanding

KIDS! Indigo Children and Cheeky Monkeys

of the 'bigger picture'. Even when we are not experiencing major confusion en masse, however, we still see Peacekeepers uniting people for a good cause, raising awareness for some charity or quietly networking, matchmaking or counselling others so they may reach a place of personal greatness. They make great managers, teachers, carers, healers and leaders.

Peacekeeper Children touch the lives of many. They seem to be universally loved, bringing a little joy into our lives. Guy Sebastian and Stevie Wonder are Peacekeeper Children, as was Princess Diana and Wolfgang Amadeus Mozart. In general, they are the rationalists and the pacifiers, here to unite the people *today* in the hope of creating a more productive *tomorrow*.

The Winter Children – the 'Black and White Colobus Monkey' People

They say that a team is only as good as its players, and in the case of King Arthur, Camelot was no exception. The serfs, peasants, labourers and farmers, the villagers and the 'stay at home' knights: all these would have been Winter Children — the ones who kept and maintained the boundaries and who were capable of fighting or defending the kingdom when necessary, but happy to 'keep the home fires burning' while the king was away. The local landlords and squires; the 'country gentry'; the 'yeoman'; the country gent of good stock; those of good breeding but of little inspiration; the second class or slightly inferior noblemen — all of these would have been Winter Children, too: the ones who represented the backbone of the British Empire and the ones who did the hard work and kept things functioning effectively and productively until the king returned.

During World War II, the Winter Children made up the bulk of society. It was largely a traditionalist Anglo Saxon society, made up of 'good Christian' people, who relied on their faith and dogged determination to maintain a sense of pride and survival, particularly when it came time to rebuild society after the war. They were typically conservative types; average mums and dads and people of no great expectation. They formed the 'Home Guard', made up of wives, daughters and sisters and the families of those fighting the war who stayed behind and selflessly kept things going. They became the factory workers and manual labourers — roles normally filled by the men. The Trade Union reps and the British Government 'back home' — the people who worked for Churchill and effected his administration — these people would have been Winter Children, too.

It was with the onset of the Great Depression that we saw the Winter Children step into their supreme time of power, however. The Great Depression was the longest and severest time of economic crash ever experienced by the industrialised regions of the western world. It began in 1929 and lasted until approximately 1939. Such periods in history have called for us, as a whole, to make do, go without and think creatively. And these are those moments when we see the strength and resolve of the Winter Child shine through. Winter Children hate wasting things. They are hoarders and misers. They begrudge those who spend unnecessarily, but at the same time, they resent having to skimp and save, so they develop clever yet honest ways to live well, even when kept on the tightest of budgets. Winter Children know when to lay low. They know when to gather their resources together, not complain and make do with what they have. Winter Children step into their true power during times of hardship and adversity. They inspire others to keep their chin up, adapt and soldier on. The Dalai Lama and Mother Theresa are two inspirational people I would classify as Winter Children, people who live to remind us that at the end of every period of darkness there has to be a light; that in every negative there is always a positive, that after every night there is a dawn and that with patience and integrity, light will always be found at the end of the tunnel. They are the guardians and the martyrs.

Jesus – the original Indigo Child?
'The Kingdom of God Is Within You'

Daring to suppose, could not Jesus (as the earthly sage and teacher) have been a Warrior? Weren't his ways both rebellious and provocative? Wasn't he both loved and hated for what he espoused as a sacred truth? Didn't he dare others to think outside the box and do what needed to be done to reach their fullest potential? Jesus was a powerful harbinger of change. He was a loner, a prophet and, in his own way, a troublemaker who defied the system and dared to follow a higher calling. He was, in my mind, a Warrior before his time. But, as the divine redeemer, Jesus was also very much the Golden Child — a holy emissary of God and spiritual saviour of the people. The Bible, after all, portrays him as having a dual nature — an earthly revolutionary warrior and, simultaneously, a spiritual visionary and perpetrator of miracles.

Jesus was born during the time of Augustus Caesar (4BC). Augustus (a positive-phase guardian type Winter Child) was the nephew of Julius Caesar (an obvious Warrior, who took it upon himself to expand the Roman Empire to its fullest possible potential and, in true Frank Sinatra style, chose to 'do it my way'). Augustus put things right after Julius Caesar's assassination, by pursuing and killing all the murderers, thus putting an end to the civil wars. Augustus restored proper authority to Rome and established peace: the 'Pax Romana'. Augustus re-instituted the Roman Empire, with 'Caesar' as Emperor. Jesus was crucified at the age of 33 during the reign of Tiberius Caesar — the successor to Augustus and a well-known degenerate. Tiberius was a womaniser and something of a sadist who died of late-stage syphilis in 37AD.

The apparent dual nature of Jesus has long troubled the Church, with no one solution to the matter ever having been accepted. Recently, though, author Tony Bushby divulged the body of his extensive research into the historical records of this time in his book, *The Bible Fraud*. He proposes that there may have originally been two brothers; two brothers merged by the Church at the Council of Constantinople into the one legendary figure we recognise today as 'Jesus'. His research shows that this first Council of the Church, convened by the Emperor Constantine in 325AD, was probably set up to force the fragmented early Christian Churches into formulating one accepted overall doctrine. Apparently the plan allowed for Constantine to institute one official religion for the whole Roman Empire; a political ploy ultimately intended to bring about reunification, pacification and control of the splintering Roman Empire — and to place himself at the head of the Church.

As Jesus' favoured disciple, companion (and wife?), Mary Magdalene was probably a Nature Child, as presumably was Mother Mary (Jesus' mother). Both women embodied love, nurturing and unconditional trust; representatives of the Earth Mother herself. The apostles Peter (as the 'Father of the Church'), and Paul, as its emissary, may have been early examples of Peacekeeper Children, who together founded the Church and spread its message abroad, with all twelve male disciples (sent out to preach the 'Word of God'), similarly embodying the Peacekeeper principle. Pontius Pilate, as the official representative of Rome and 'the law', and Judas, the 'upholder of conventional values' seem to loosely fit the description of Winter Children. Judas betrayed Jesus to the Jewish council of priests (the Sanhedrin) in the hope that Jesus would be given the chance to present his case to the council and so gain endorsement from the Jewish establishment. But, like so many well-intended plans, his scheme backfired. The rest, as they say, is history.

So, when you stop and think about it, it really makes little difference in what year you were born, because even at the ripe old age of 102 you can be an Indigo, Crystal or even a Rainbow Child. They have always been here … and always will be. Perhaps the terms Indigo, Crystal and Rainbow are nothing more than new age, alternative words used to describe personality types that have been recognised for centuries? I believe they are.

5

Supporting Our Kids

General Advice

First of all, it must be emphasised that there is nothing 'wrong' with our children. Instead of focusing on their more negative qualities, we should acknowledge them as being equally as advanced and evolved as the next person, but realise that they (like most of us at one time or another) may simply have trouble functioning effectively in our seemingly indifferent, complicated world. Therefore, instead of 'treatment' per se, many just require consequential 'support'. Rather than 'treatment' in the traditional sense, I have found that most kids respond better when they are offered meaningful 'assistance' to help them cope with and understand better the rigours of this world, especially when coupled with conscious parenting and an initial 'cleanse' (with regular follow-up care) to help them recover from a possible (for a want of a better phrase) 'bumpy landing' at the time of their birth.

Healthy Beginnings

While in their mother's womb, babies are aware and able to hear every sound from the outside world. Theirs is a safe, secure world in which they, as far as they know, are all that exists. However, the slightest hint of external stress quickly sees the mother's heart rate rise. The epitome of innocence, the unborn child has no comprehension of what is taking place outside the womb, but as a matter of course, begins to feel its heart rate rise in unison with its mother's. Imagine then, that while in the womb, life for its parents remained stressful and difficult, with the only external sounds heard being those of raised voices and tears? What is the child to think of the outside world? Would their impression be a positive one? I don't think so.

Although they may learn to adapt to the tension and nervous energy shaping their view of the world, when a child is born, they often retain the anxiety they grew to know and trust whilst in the womb, carrying it through life with little understanding as to why. A child that has developed under a veil of nervousness and distress needs to have that energy explained not only after its birth, but while it grows in the womb. They need to be reassured they are not the cause of the sorrow and that their birth is something looked forward to with great anticipation. After their birth, too, they must be comforted and reminded constantly of their sacredness, told they are loved and safe and reassured of the incomparable place they hold in the family and in the hearts of their parents. A child that has grown in a womb under constant emotional attack instead of one nurtured by love, trust and peace, will grow to become a child who involuntarily feels responsible for their parents and somehow to blame for things they cannot explain. It is all unconscious. They do not wilfully make a decision or intentionally assume they are to blame for their parents anguish, but what else can they believe? To them, they are the only other factors in their parent's life. They have no knowledge of money, bills or mortgages. They know nothing of jobs, cars or bosses. They have not even been born themselves, so how can they comprehend the death of a loved one or unexpected illness? A child forming in an unhappy womb will automatically take the pain on board, and carry the guilt long after their birth. As small children, they will be clingy, needy and fearful, continually trying to prove their worth and seek acceptance and attention from their parents. They will innocently believe themselves at fault, unwanted or separate from the rest of the family. They will feel alone, nervous and apologetic. As they mature, however, and if their uncertainty is left unaddressed or unexplained, the child will grow to become an angry, resentful teenager and disrespectful adult.

The birth process itself can also imprint potently on the child. So often the events of labour and birth can create patterns that may replay themselves over and over during a person's life. Take for example when labour begins but gets obstructed, requiring a forceps extraction. This procedure can prompt recurring patterns throughout life that might see the child begin projects, only to find themselves getting into difficulty and being stuck, until some other person comes along, pulls them out and sets things right. Another upsetting circumstance is where the birth process is too rapid, resulting in damage to the mother. This situation can easily produce a pattern for the child of always doing things in a rush or feeling pressured with little control over proceedings. There may also be the frequent feeling of being unsafe and that both they and those around them are at risk or in danger. Any number of birth experiences can imprint themselves on a child's mind and body — and depending on how things pan out, can either be a real support or a major hindrance to their life. In recognition of this, a range of therapies have been developed to help reverse negative birth patterning, while reinstating functional patterns of behaviour. A good example is the process of 'rebirthing'.

There is no such thing as a perfect set of life experiences, so don't go blaming yourself for having had emotional upsets or difficult circumstances during your pregnancy. Instead, be honest with yourself about what happened and why, so that you can understand the events that occurred back then and those that have happened as a result since. Only then can you have real compassion for those occurrences, leading to genuine self-forgiveness and that of others involved at the time, after which you will be fully prepared and ready to talk candidly with your child about what life was like while they were in your womb.

Recalling what life was like during pregnancy and how the birth process went, helps explain why our children act and react the way they do. It explains, too, why they feel the way they do toward their family, why they hold their breath in times of stress and why their view of the world has evolved the way it has. Our sense of security, our confidence, our relationships, and even the type of employment we seek, are all determined by the quality of time spent in our mother's womb and the strength of the first breath we took. In order for us to reach our potential, therefore, we must revisit our sacred breath in order to fuel the fire of Creation that burns at our centre each time we conceive and 'birth' new ideas, create new things or embark on new relationships. We must reconsider our time in the womb and what life may have been like for our mother during that time, and consider the possibility that there may be some aspects of our life that may be blocked by an invalid or negative memory of our time spent in the womb. And we must consider the fact that our kids may be experiencing something similar. Their life may be tarnished by the anxiety or stress experienced by their mother during pregnancy, their birth, and their subconscious desire to make sense of it all.

So, talk to your kids about their time in the womb and what their birth was like. Consider the details that stand out and see them as a chance to re-map their journey, to check their life's blueprint and to review the sacred contracts you signed with them (and vice versa) before they entered this world. Share with your child affirmations of love as often as you can. They affirm your child's sense of self-worth and they open a channel for trust and love to flow between the two of you. My wife and I constantly tell our children "I love you"; "You are so special to me", and the most important one; the one all children are waiting to hear: "Being pregnant with you was the best thing that has ever happened to me". See this as an opportunity for you to reclaim your power and for them to review theirs, to rebirth as a family and for you both to finally honour (and heal) the first breath your child took as he or she entered this world. We must all do what we can to heal this first-breath moment so that even if it wasn't the most healthy or the strongest, we can be sure that the last one we take is a sigh that confirms contentment with our efforts and achievements during life; a sigh that ensures the first breaths taken by generations to come are those of abundance, interconnectedness and good health, and not a gasp that echoes centuries of regret.

Sound Parenting

I recently got an email about two cups of coffee and an empty mayonnaise jar. It was so applicable to this section of the book that I thought I would share it with you. It certainly made a lot of sense to me.

A professor stood before his philosophy class and laid some items out on his desk. When the class began, he silently picked up a very large and empty mayonnaise jar and proceeded to fill it with golf balls. He then asked the students if the jar was full. They agreed that it was. He then picked up a box of pebbles and poured them into the jar. He shook the jar lightly. The pebbles rolled into the open areas between the golf balls. He then asked the students again if the jar was full. They agreed it was. The professor next picked up a box of sand and poured it into the jar. Of course, the sand filled up everything else. He asked once more if the jar was full. The students responded with a unanimous 'Yes'.

The professor then produced two cups of coffee from under the table and poured the entire contents into the jar, effectively filling the empty space between the sand.

"Now," said the professor as the laughter subsided, "I want you to recognise that this jar represents your life. The golf balls are the important things: your family, children, health, friends and your favourite passions, and if everything else was lost and only they remained, your life would still be full. The pebbles are the other things that matter, like your job, house and car. The sand is everything else, the small, unimportant things. If you put the sand into the jar first, there would be no room for the pebbles or the golf balls. The same goes for life. If you spend all your time and energy on the small things you will never have room for the things that are important to you. Pay attention to the things that are critical to your happiness. Play with your children. Take time to get medical checkups. Take your spouse out to dinner. Play another 18 holes. There will always be time to clean the house and fix the disposal. Take care of the golf balls first; the things that really matter. Set your priorities. The rest is just sand."

One of the students raised her hand and asked what the coffee represented. The professor smiled. "I'm glad you asked. It just goes to show you that no matter how full your life may seem, there is always room for a couple of cups of coffee with a friend."

All children have friends who are more than happy to tell them what they want to hear. So instead of falling into the trap of trying to be a friend to your child (which is something they certainly do not want), be the authority figure they need. And as their parent, lay firm boundaries and always demonstrate impeccable, acceptable behaviour. Negotiate solid boundaries with older children, sure, but remain firm when it comes to defending them. Children respond well when they are given a say in how their future is to pan out, but they shut down when they fall victim to random leadership or disorganised parenting.

How can we ever expect our kids to become the best they can be if we do little or nothing to become better role models? As parents, therefore, we need to show accountability for all the decisions we make in life. The choices we make are our responsibility and no one else's. Our choices influence the relationships we have with our children and how they perceive us as helpful role models. Being able to identify bad habits or behaviour that gives mixed messages to our children means we are one step closer to becoming better parents. Knowing when we have spent more money than we can afford or when we are living beyond our means, for example; realising when our behaviour has resulted in the mistreatment or neglect of our children or acknowledging when we have placed work, habits and compulsions or new relationships in higher priority to that of our children, are some of the choices we need to show accountability for when we endeavour to become better parents.

Children respond best when they come to trust and rely on a set routine. Even those who are not accustomed to routine miss having it in their life. For those who are used to having a set routine, removing it or altering it (even slightly) can be both confusing and unsettling. An effective routine is one that operates at a mutually agreed pace with specific times allocated to meal times, bath time and bed time, taking into consideration any chores that must be done or homework that needs to be completed.

Support your child in their quest to succeed, but remain mindful the whole time of resisting the temptation to push them beyond their means or of feeding false hope. We all want our kids to achieve their goals, but some will always be out of reach and that is okay. It isn't a bad thing to acknowledge our limitations — it is only when we allow them to become 'what ifs' and shackle our hopes entirely do they become a problem. Support your child in their quest to pursue their own dreams. Do not expect them to follow your dreams. Allow them to choose the activities they would like to partake in, and resist the urge to channel them into things that you would have liked to do at their age. Allow your children to experiment. Encourage them to try as many activities as they want until they find something they're good at and enjoy doing. Let them be the judge of what is right for them, while you choose the activities that are right for you. There's a difference between expecting your kids to do what you love and loving what your kids do. Find the balance and, in doing so, avoid years of resentment and frustration between you and your children.

And when your child finally does tap into the one thing they can excel at, don't boast about their talent to your friends or theirs. No one likes a show-off. This sort of behaviour (no matter how honourable your intentions) will only alienate him or her from their peers. They need to know they are allowed to make mistakes and have off days like everyone else. By making them out to be gifted or better than their peers, you are putting unrealistic pressure on them to succeed. They need to excel at their own pace, without external pressure or expectation to do more.

Allowing your child to socialise properly is crucial. You cannot shelter your child from the real world forever. They need to be able to make their own mistakes and pick themselves up after they fall. They will never learn to socialise fully if you spend all your time wrapping them up in cotton wool. You need to make sure your child has had the firmest foundation from which to step out into the world. Do they know how to make friends, for example? Do they know how to share and negotiate? Can they demonstrate their strengths without being show offs? Can they take no for an answer? How do they handle criticism or advice? Are they able to successfully adapt to new or unfamiliar situations when they arise? These are questions that must be asked, with serious consideration given to the answers. As parents, too, it is essential that you take care and responsibility for the relationship you have with your husband or wife. It is good to be fully focused on seeing your child do well in the world, but not at the cost of the relationship you have with your partner. If your child is to develop fully, they must be given the chance to see you nourish your other relationships and understand that they require different kinds of attention to the one you have with them.

One such way is to allow our children plenty of opportunity to interact with children just like them, or children who compliment or balance them on all levels. During these play sessions, they soon realise they are not alone: that they may be 'different' in many ways (as is often unconstructively accentuated in the mainstream system), but that they are healthy and okay (this is also vitally important for the parents of these children, who also need to know that they are not alone — that there are other parents out there experiencing similar things to them). In fact, instead of reaffirming negative belief in themselves, 'medicine play days' help our children learn more about themselves — that, perhaps, they are the ones best equipped to decide what is right for them, while creating a support network that encourages them to unfold their wings in safety and get started on living their true life-purpose.

When we make an effort to get closer to our kids, we encourage our kids to get closer to us. Talk to your kids about normal, everyday, almost unimportant things. Ask them about school, their friends, their hopes and fears — and try to remain free of judgment, criticism and blame (no matter how hard that may be). Make an effort to become part of your child's world. Do not assume anything about the world your child is living in, by the way — it is totally alien to the one you or I grew up in. It is faster and more brutal on all levels to anything you could ever imagine. So make a point of asking your child regularly if they are happy, clear in their understanding and, most importantly, safe. And do not limit your child by expecting them to make safe or correct choices in life based solely on the ones you made as you grew up. Chances are the decisions you made as you grew up are about as relevant to your children as outside toilets, water wells and black and white television. But when you do offer advice, make sure the language you use is age specific and it goes well to explain why you're saying what you are saying. Sometimes it is best to say too much than regret not saying enough.

But, in case you do make the mistake of not saying enough to guide and protect your child, set a plan of action in place now so as to avoid or lessen the blow should a predicament arise down the track. If your relationship with your child is not ideal or conducive to open, honest discussion, for example, support them in their quest to find an 'elder'; a wise person, mentor, teacher, coach, police officer, counsellor or priest — someone to act as a guide and mentor; someone they can trust and open up to. But, if this does not apply to you and you are fortunate enough to have a good, working relationship with your child, do not hesitate to act yourself and immediately eliminate the threat should one ever arise. If your child reveals to you that they are at risk, make it clear that you will do what needs to be done (within reason) to remove that risk. This may involve having to call the police, sequestering hazardous items, isolating your child from certain people or moving them to a safer place. Never blame your child for something they have done before finding out why they did it and if they did it at all. Never raise your voice without good reason and never attack a child verbally just because you are upset with them. All this does is make you look like a bag of hot air, affording your children good reason to never open up to you again. Focus your worries and frustration into helping your child solve the problem instead and leave all morality based communication until after the case has been closed. And finally, never lie to your children. Not ever. Not even a little bit. Be open, honest and candid at all times, and they will reward you by being open, honest and candid at all times with you.

Remembering the 'Old Ways'

Traditional Chinese Medicine

Traditional Chinese Medicine, which dates back more than 3,000 years, derives much of its practice from Taoist philosophy and embraces the belief that everything in the universe, including our health, is created from the invisible life-force called Qi and develops through the interplay of positive and negative forces or polarities in all areas of life — called yin and yang. The physical world is governed by five natural elements: wood, fire, earth, metal and water. We also are made up of these five elements — both in terms of our physical organs and senses, and also our mind and emotions. Traditional Chinese Medicine supports the belief that people, both physically and mentally, are interrelated with and dependent upon nature. It also espouses that we are each ruled by the influence of one of the five main organs in the human body.

Treatment is aimed at restoring balanced energy flow and proper function to the whole person — body, mind and spirit. This is primarily achieved through the approaches of dietary therapy, herbs, massage, acupuncture and Qigong (focused breathing, movement and meditation).

Acupuncture has become a popular treatment in the western world and has been backed up by many scientific studies that demonstrate how it works via stimulating the nervous system, endorphins and natural chemical neuro-peptides in the human body. The classical Chinese view is that acupuncture points are like transformers in an electrical system — points at which energy flow can be regulated and rebalanced.

Ayurveda

Ayurveda is revered as the 'Science of Life'. It espouses prevention and longevity and is one of the oldest and most holistic forms of medicine available today. First documented over 5,000 years ago in India, it is described as a 'world medicine' dealing with both the body and the spirit; a form of healing that formed an integral element of the spiritual tradition of the universal or Vedic religion.

As a component of the ancient wisdom called the Vedas, the main purpose of Ayurveda is to restore proper health to the vehicles of mind, body and soul to assist the individual on the path of attaining true union with the divine — the goal of Yoga and the meditative path.

Ayurvedic medicine sees the human being as being made up of three principles that are found throughout the natural world. These are Vata (air in motion: wind), Pitta (fire) and Kapha (earth + water combined = oil).

In illness it is believed that one of these three principles is in excess, so treatment is aimed to sedate or pacify this excess. Approaches used include dietary therapy, exercise therapies such as specific yoga movements, herbs, cleansing treatments and lifestyle adjustments. The practice of meditation is seen as essential.

Homeopathy

Dr. Samuel Hahnemann (1755-1843) was the founder of homeopathy and, from his observations, derived the 'Law of Similars' which suggests that by giving a patient very small amounts of a substance that produces the symptoms of the very disease they're suffering from, the body will then be able to fight the illness properly and so be able to cure itself. It's a little like receiving a vaccination against a disease. According to classical homeopathy (which, as an 'alternative' form of medicine, is only about 200 years old), all ailments stem from an interruption in our 'vital force'. The vital force is the life-force energy that sustains life. Because homeopathy assumes that the source of all illness begins on the energetic level, the prescribed remedy must also be developed along similar lines.

In essence it is understood that this illness force has entered and disturbed the body's own vital force — this results in the mental and physical symptoms of the disease. In fact these symptoms are the human system's response to the illness, not the disease itself. So by giving a remedy that magnifies the specific symptoms, this actually strengthens the body's fight against the illness. So hopefully the disease force can now be expelled and the illness cured.

Homeopathic remedies are made from a range of substances—mineral, plant or animal products. Whatever substance is found by clinical experiments to mimic the symptoms of a specific illness can be used to prepare remedies. In addition as these remedies primarily act on the invisible vital force, they also need to be subtle. Hence the remedies are often prepared and diluted in a specific process to produce 'vibrational medicines' which act not on the physical level, but on the subtle body energies.

Naturopathy

Naturopaths have developed their treatment systems from centuries of experience in Europe as herbalists, 'wise women' and nature healers. Their aim is to cleanse accumulated toxins from the organ systems, to nourish the organs, and to restore proper function to the whole human being. The liver and gut are seen as common sources of disease in our society, along with disturbed emotions and stress.

Methods employed cover a range of approaches such as dietary therapy, minerals, vitamins, herbs, homeopathic remedies, flower essences, medicated baths, steam saunas, enemas, fresh air, exercise and lifestyle change.

Osteopathy

Osteopathy has developed in tandem with chiropractic as a means to treat disturbances in the structure and function of the muscles, tendons, joints and bones of the human body. It is understood that disturbances in this musculo-skeletal system can stimulate, aggravate or even in some cases cause a whole range of illnesses in the body. In addition osteopaths often focus on the flow of certain important fluids in the human body such as venous and arterial blood flow, the cerebro-spinal fluid (CSF) in the brain, and the lymph system.

Treatment techniques range from vigorous manipulations (cracking the joints) through to very subtle techniques which can feel like gentle massage but can yield major benefits as to how the joints and muscles function.

A further school of osteopathy has developed called 'cranial osteopathy'. This approach uses very gentle massage-like methods to correct disturbances in the bone structure of the skull, to improve blood and CSF flow to the brain and to even enhance brain function itself. These disturbances in the skull bones, often with resulting irritation to the underlying brain, can occur from a range of causes including head injury, too rapid or delayed birth, and forceps delivery, and are surprisingly common. Cranial osteopathy can bring relief for a range of conditions including chronic headaches, recurring colds or tonsillitis or ear infections in children, and behaviour disorders due to irritation of the brain.

Integrative Medicine

In recent years some medical doctors have become interested in the practice of 'mind-body medicine'. This is the specific use of counselling, meditation, hypnosis and other forms of 'altered state of consciousness' treatment, to allow the mind to induce positive changes in the body. In addition, complementary therapies are often utilised. This involves the use of a range of dietary therapies, nutritional supplements, herbs, homeopathic remedies and acupuncture in an ethical scientifically validated way according to the best traditions of the Hippocratic oath. In many ways this is a return to classical medicine as it was practised for many centuries until early last century when the use of drugs and technology started to take over. These doctors are finding new ways to treat illness, which they claim are much more effective and much safer to use, especially for the chronic illnesses plaguing our society such as cancer, heart disease, diabetes and arthritis. This is also bringing doctors closer to natural therapists, as well as to priests, theologians and meditators, in a truly integrative approach to medicine.

The Five 'Esoteric' Elements

The ancients referred to a set of archetypal elements in their effort to explain the cycles and models they witnessed in nature. The Greeks identified four primary elements: fire, earth, air and water that espoused the simple rule that all things of nature carry life-force, with all things being compatible and equal. A similar theory was adopted throughout Asia: a theory that formed the esoteric foundation of both Buddhism and Hinduism. The 'five great elements' of Hinduism are earth, water, fire, air and Aether. Japanese tradition refers to a set of elements called the 'five great': earth, water, fire, wind and void, while in Taoism there is a similar system that includes both metal and wood, but eliminates air. Chinese spirituality acknowledges four primary elements, each ruled by beasts known as celestial animals. These animals must be honoured in order to harness the power and potential of the four elements — energies welcomed into the home to provide protection, strength and prosperity to those that live and work within according to the Chinese art of Feng Shui. The Black Turtle, which governs the north and the energies of winter, for example, represents longevity, strength and endurance. The Green Dragon (as the guardian of the east and ambassador of spring), offers protection, vigilance and goodness. The Red Phoenix, ruler of the south and messenger of summer, wards off negativity while representing the five human traits: virtue, responsibility, conduct, compassion and dependability. The White Tiger, as the consort of the Green Dragon, embodies the west and the energies of autumn. The White Tiger not only emits submissive, feminine power, she is also extremely protective and strong.

Neo-paganism describes four elements (earth, air, fire and water) with some traditions adding a fifth: Spirit. The use of the pentagram, or five-pointed star, is associated with the practice of summoning the elemental spirits of the four directions at the beginning of a ritual. When describing the qualities of the four elements, fire is said to be both hot and dry, earth is considered both cold and dry, air is described as being both hot and wet, while water is obviously both cold and wet. Some describe the fifth element as the 'quintessence': an alchemical word that literally translates to 'fifth element' and which also means Aether or Spirit. It is interesting to note that five of the major planets in our solar system are named after the elements: Venus after metal, Jupiter after wood, Mercury after water, Mars after fire and Saturn after earth.

Many traditions look to the dragon as a protector of the four elements, with a specific dragon bearing certain qualities that correspond exactly to the elemental nature of earth, air, fire and water. The Earth Dragon, for example, is said to guard the treasures of the Earth as her 'legacy' to those of us who honour and respect the Earth as our mother. Earth Dragons, the large wormlike creatures that inhabit holes and caverns, speak of abundance and the wisdom obtained as we reach the maturity of old age. Water Dragons guide us as we meditate and contemplate. Water Dragon teaches the art of introspection by encouraging us to calm the inner chatter so that we may find the silence within. The winged dragons of the air bring clarity of mind while sharing the gifts of intuition and heightened intellect, while the Flame-breathing Dragon reminds us to honour the fire in our belly, the passion that drives our creative force, while teaching the lessons of enthusiasm and innocence. Fire Dragons are most potent at puberty when we seem to know everything, but in fact know nothing, when we are zealous about everything and hold the world as an oyster in the palm of our hand.

Subtle Energetic Therapies

Today's children do not react well to the heavy handed western medical treatments prescribed to make them fit in or act 'normally' like their peers. Sedating our kids with Ritalin, for instance, does nothing to help them adjust to living effectively in society. Instead it dulls their minds, making them docile and more compliant and not such a hindrance to the system. Sedating our children simply band-aids the bigger issue, while unashamedly violating their integrity, blocking creativity and self-expression, thus thwarting their chance of ever realising their true potential.

But of course there is always the exception to the rule. There is always the occasional case, for example, where conventional medicine *does* seem to make a difference (even if superficially), by helping the individual integrate, learn and grow and, in this case, proving beneficial to the child, their family and school. There are also those circumstances where, exhausted, stressed and, in some cases bullied by the system, we feel we have no choice *but* to medicate our kids for fear of making mistakes or doing them harm. If for no other reason, medicating our kids affords the opportunity to reassess, regain stamina and seek user-friendly surrogate treatments. Sometimes a break in constant negative patterning (offered by western medicine) creates a window of clarity, allowing us (and our children) to see clearly the alternatives being presented, which was one rationale for us writing this book.

Nevertheless, it should be remembered that, in general, all children (and not just those typically prescribed drugs such as Ritalin), often respond soundly to most subtle energetic therapies and specific gentle natural therapies, especially when combined with good parenting, a balanced diet, a harmonious home and plenty of outdoor activity and exercise.

If treatment is required, it is advised that the advice of an integrative holistic doctor, naturopath, cranial osteopath or spiritually aware counsellor be sought before heading down the traditional medical path. Requesting a live-blood analysis (a simple test that requires only a single drop of blood), ordered through your integrative holistic doctor or naturopath, is a powerful yet simple way of obtaining information about your child's metabolism, for example, while asking for a hair analysis to be done (a test that demands only a small amount of hair taken from your child's head, organised by your integrative holistic doctor or naturopath), will quickly and easily check for heavy metal toxicity and the health and wellbeing of your child's mineral levels.

Ask your integrative holistic doctor or naturopath to check to see if your child's liver and digestive system are functioning properly, and if they aren't, find out what needs to be done to restore them to their fullest potential. Have them check for and treat any chronic infections, including otitis media, sinusitis, bronchitis, enteritis, parasites, worms, and candidiasis. If left untreated (which they often are), all will markedly hinder your child's progress. If your child suffers from allergies resulting in asthma, eczema or hay fever, it may be useful to mention them, too, when you next visit your integrative holistic doctor or naturopath. He or she will be quick to suggest remedies that will effectively alleviate the symptoms, while treating the underlying causes and removing the stress they cause for your child.

Your integrative holistic doctor or naturopath may suggest cranial osteopathy, chelation (for heavy metal toxicity), laser acupuncture (a safe and painless form of acupuncture that does not require the use of needles) or prescribe homeopathic remedies, which are largely vibrational in nature. He or she may also suggest you incorporate the use of flower essences into your child's overall treatment plan.

Extensive research into vibrational remedies such as flower essences (homeopathic dilutions derived from flowers) has proven positive effects on the emotional state of adults and children alike. Only after an extensive initial examination is the individual recommended a formula, though, so visit a qualified therapist before self-medicating. For example, with flower essences, those who constantly repeat the same mistakes, the essence of chestnut bud is suggested; for daydreaming try clematis; for those who give up easily, gentian is recommended, while those who lack confidence, larch essence is the best remedy. For persistent unwanted thoughts, take white chestnut, and for those lacking motivation, prescribe wild rose. For stress in general, take a few drops of *Rescue Remedy* (a combination formula) directly under the tongue.

Considering the more 'alternative' healing modalities such as transpersonal counselling, kinesiology, colour therapy (such as Spirale or Aura Soma), intuitive healing, Reiki, crystal therapy, music, art therapy or even fire walking may seem a bit out there or bizarre for some, but many children benefit greatly from what they have to offer. Something as simple as strolling in nature or petting a companion animal (such as a cat or dog,) does wonders to lift the spirits and improve the general wellbeing of adults and children alike, while checking, cleansing and balancing your child's chakras is both an ancient and recognised therapeutic custom. Chakras (pronounced shack-ras) are energy centres found within all living bodies and are located in front of the spinal column. They are usually described as rotating vortexes where universal life energy enters and exits. The term chakra comes from the Sanskrit word for 'wheel' or 'disk', and originates from ancient yoga philosophies and Indian tantric texts. Many eastern religions and esoteric traditions have grown to incorporate chakras into their belief systems (over thousands of years) often depicting them as perfectly formed, appropriately coloured lotus flowers. The chakras are anchors, filtering energy from the environment and drawing it into the body. They ensure that there is an even, harmonious flow of energy within the body at all times, on all levels. It is vital that the chakras are in balance with each other so that the energy flows smoothly from one to another. When a chakra is in complete harmony, it is fully open, like a perfectly formed lotus in full bloom, spinning freely and in perfect balance.

The aura (pronounced or-rah) is the energy field that surrounds all living bodies and the force that radiates the subtle life energies within the body. Our environment, the people with whom we associate and our life style choices strongly influence the auric energies that form a record of who and what we are. The aura is an easily observed and interpreted account of our immediate condition: our health, mental activity and emotional state, often long before the onset of externally obvious symptoms. Closely outlining the body, and usually no more than half an inch wide, is the pale etheric aura. Looking like a thin layer of smoke tightly hugging the body, it is the easiest part of the aura to see. As we sleep, the etheric aura swells and reaches out far from the physical body in order to interact with, and store, the outer auric energies of the cosmos.

Often called the vitality sheath, the etheric aura levels contract and form a dense, protective field around the body as we wake from slumber. Emanating from the chakras, the main aura is banded around the body in protective layers of colour. Life-force energy is fed from Mother Earth through the feet and into our chakras, in much the same way as plants draw water through their roots. Each of the chakras generates different energy represented by a particular colour symbolic to that chakra centre. How each chakra operates, the rate at which it rotates, its balance with the other chakra centres — strength, vibrancy and so on — depend entirely on our present physical state and frame of mind. Working as one, the chakra centres generate the dominant hue of the aura, triggering change with each rotation. To simply 'rake, fluff and pat' the aura is a recognised and effective method of reviving the aura while repairing any ill effects caused by our way of life.

Chakra balancing has been used and adapted by many healing modalities and spiritually oriented groups and, like smudging, is still a very basic and popular form of auric care. You may need some assistance, but if you are able, you can do it yourself. With your fingers spayed like a rake, begin making quick, short, combing strokes, progressing gradually from the feet to the top of the head. No physical contact is required, but each stroke should be kept to about 30 cm in length and about 10 to 20 cm away from the body. Rake the space above the head while picturing the body's aura in your mind's eye as a huge bowl of well-whipped egg whites (this is what it looks like after raking). Repeat and move from the crown down. Once completed, the aura is all stirred up, but now needs to be 'fluffed' so as to loosen any edges and to separate any stubborn negative energy that may have been previously overlooked. Start again from the feet and work up. Make circular motions with the palms of your hands, while simultaneously wiggling your fingers in a gentle manner. Again repeat the action, from the crown down. This has a calming effect on the aura, especially after the rigorous workout of the 'raking'. Now, imagine the aura as a bag of cotton wool that was previously neatly packed into its wrapping, but that has now been pulled out, ripped apart and turned into an unruly cloud of fluffy white chaos. Try to fit it back into its wrapping. You couldn't without major reorganising. Cup your hands and work from the feet toward the crown, move your hands rapidly in and out from the body, between 20 cm and 5 cm in distance. You are effectively 'patting' the aura, to realign your energy field. Do it all over. Repeat from the crown to the feet.

Smudging, on the other hand, draws in positive energy, while banishing negativity and cleansing or purifying the aura on a vibrational level. To smudge, dry some sweet-grass, white sage, cedar or tobacco thoroughly and place one or a combination of all in a heatproof bowl or dish. Take a match and light the crushed herbs until they start to smoulder, keeping in mind that it is the smoke that is ultimately required and not a healthy flame. Brush the smoke, using cupped hands or a feather, so that it surrounds and touches every part of the body, the whole, while asking the spirit of the herbs to remove all negative energy. Visualise this energy leaving the aura and returning to the universe via the smoke.

Remember, the aim here is to rebalance your child's subtle energy system and help them to lead a full, happy, well-rounded life, to develop their inherent abilities and to fulfil their potential so they can play their part in making the world a better place. So, investigating or seeking what you might view as 'unusual' forms of healing must be considered if you are truly serious about supporting your child, as should investigating the possibility of unconventional schooling or participating in whole family therapy. Decisions such as these may seem a bit extreme (and confronting), but when you stop and think about it, isn't your child's growth and development worth it?

Whole Foods

Before any action is taken, however, it is essential that you first take a close look at your child's diet. Dietary modification is a key ingredient in rebuilding and improving your child's physical and mental fitness. You will see a marked improvement in their overall wellbeing when you pay close attention to what your child eats, especially when nutritional supplements are incorporated. Today's children have an inherent wisdom that enables them to see truth in all things. Food is certainly one area in which we can readily support them in their quest to be inquiring, and responsible for their own choices. Growth is not just about physical development — it is about wholesome eating habits, and foods full of life force that will support your child in fostering growth creatively, spiritually, emotionally and mentally. If we can imagine that whole foods bring children closer to their truth, and empty foods are like putting a barrier between them and their inherent beauty, then we start to move closer to an understanding of why real food is so important.

Some basic dietary guidelines follow below, but when reviewing them, be sure to spend time reflecting on effective and simple ways to make some grass roots changes to pantry items, eating habits and your basic nutritional knowledge.

When it comes to your child's general diet (no matter what sort of child they are), try to avoid or minimise the consumption of 'empty' foods: foods containing excessive unnatural colourings and preservatives, chemicals, refined sugar (white sugar), hydrogenated oils, sweets and confectionaries, added salt / sodium, pastries, cakes and biscuits, fizzy drinks, processed and preserved foods and junk food in general. Conversely, endeavour to drink fresh, clean (tank, spring or filtered) water (as apposed to regular tap water) and eat more 'full' or whole, unprocessed foods, super foods and foods rich in nutrients. Seek out and stock your fridge and cupboards with fresh seasonal produce and organic goods. Most mainstream supermarkets now keep a healthy stock of organic foodstuffs, but if yours doesn't, ask at your local health food store, produce deli or harvest market as to where your closest retail vendor might be. Thus, make a point of only eating fresh fruit and vegetables, free-range chicken, fresh or canned fish (suspended in spring water or brine) and organic, lean red meat. When organic meat is unavailable, however, lamb is probably the best alternative as it generally contains fewer steroids, antibiotics and hormones than meat gleaned from other animals.

This is a good model for the whole family to follow. It makes things easier, especially at mealtimes, if the whole family is seen to support your child's change in diet, with them enjoying the same food as everyone else. Not making your child's growth a family concern is not only hypocritical (it is hardly fair to expect your child to do something you are not prepared to commit to yourself) — it is also a healthier lifestyle choice for the family as a whole. Although some children may benefit greatly from an intensive, tailored dietary regime, this is something best handled by an integrative holistic doctor, naturopath or qualified dietician who may suggest you avoid dairy foods (some children are allergic to casein protein in milk) and wheat products, because the gluten in wheat often causes allergic reactions or induces 'Leaky Gut Syndrome'.

As with any process of change, however, it is worth trialling your new diet for two months to ascertain its overall effectiveness. If there are no obvious benefits within that time, you can go back to your old diet and then try a new dietary change after that. Sometimes, though, symptoms may get worse before they improve. This is because the body needs time to adjust to the new routine before it can work with it.

Perhaps you intuitively already know some of these tips and pointers. Perhaps you regard them as basic common sense. If so — excellent! Isn't that exactly as it should be?

Wholesome Choices

To really inspire wholesome choices, demonstrate the correlation between the Earth Mother (the source of our foods) and the kitchen table. Create a small vegetable plot, herb garden or plan a basic orchard, for example, and encourage your children to tend to its growth and harvest their yield for the table. Build a secure chicken coop and recycle their manure as fertiliser for your food garden and use their eggs in your cooking. Be sure to feed your chickens grain, maize and table scraps instead of the commercially produced, hormone-laced layers' pellets available through most local produce stores. Take your children on family field trips to pick berries, gather wild apples or visit a dairy and milk a cow — anything that opens their hearts to the richness of nature and the abundance of the Earth Mot her.

Stimulate interest in food through your basic appreciation of colour and consider the spiritual and psychological impact colour is known to have on us. The more naturally colourful the food, the more the chance increases of nutrients being present. Red or dark foods, for example, have higher levels of flavonoids that improve concentration and memory, so choose red lettuce varieties instead of the more traditional iceberg, and Spanish onions instead of the common brown variety. Foster a healthy relationship with food and eating by adopting a creative and multi-layered approach. Sing, dance, sculpt, play, draw, paint or write about food and health. Turn recipes into songs or laugh as you create a story about what would happen if a pea met a persimmon at the park one day. Such activities not only help bring food to life while deepening your child's understanding of what they are putting in their mouth, they are also fun ways of spending quality time with your kids.

Cook with love by involving your child in the simpler preparation tasks when it comes to readying their evening meal. Sharing responsibility by inviting them to help with the chopping and stirring inspires a sense of family togetherness in the kitchen. Be sure to choose tasks that are meaningful for your children and that are suitable for their age and developmental stage. Don't ask a four year old, for example, to peel and cut up a pumpkin or expect an eight year old to know how to dismember a chicken. Let your passion and enthusiasm for cooking show through with every meal you make by instilling pride in 'making it yourself'. Such a positive attitude will see your child choose a home cooked meal over a frozen or processed dinner every time. And be sure to make the sharing of the evening meal an important whole family event rather than a rushed bite in front of the television (a common occurrence, I am sure, the world over).

Teach your child to sniff, smell and taste and feel their food. Introduce foods that encourage hands-on tasting and make a habit of introducing new and varied produce to your family whenever possible. Involve all the senses, including the intuitive functions. Ask your child to assist with the writing of your weekly grocery list, and then locate the listed items whilst browsing the supermarket (a meaningful task that challenges their reading skills and their ability to choose wisely the most economical and health conscious products). Or let your children intuitively guide you to what they feel they need. Most children instinctively know what foods contain the nutrients their bodies require.

Instil healthy, self-empowered eating habits by allowing your child to regulate how much of anything they are going to eat while serving up, or better still, let them serve themselves! Enforce prudent boundaries if you integrate this approach into your routine of course, but be mindful of the fact that encouraging responsible intake is a vital life skill that will help challenge the obesity crisis facing many of today's children. Never use food as ammunition. Resist the temptation to dishonour good food by making it a bargaining tool with children. Reinforcing positive or negative behaviour through the offering or withdrawal of food can have disastrous and lasting effects on your child's attitude toward food.

And, of course, always praise good manners and respectable dining practice. Make it a habit to always give thanks for the food on your table. Teach your child to honour and acknowledge the food they are about to eat, the hands that prepared it and the goodness it will afford them.

Detoxifying your Environment

Chemical overload in our homes will potentially influence vitality, creativity and the general happiness of our children. Children are far more sensitive to the toxins found in cigarette smoke, cleaning products, standard bathroom items, tap water, plastic drink bottles and pharmaceutical drugs, etc., than we are as adults.

To protect your children, therefore, if you *must* smoke, do so outdoors and not in the confines of the home, office or family car (if you are truly serious about protecting your children, however, not smoking *at all* is the only viable option — eliminating it from your life will effectively eliminate it from theirs), systematically eliminate or exchange chemical-based product options for chemical-free alternatives and explain your decisions to your children. Expand your awareness of the ingredients that are in foods and the unseen additives that enhance flavour and shelf life longevity. Read labels and spend time learning the way in which food is marketed. Many products labelled as 'healthy' are not good for us at all, with descriptions like 'natural' hardly ever meaning 'free of pesticides or preservatives' and fabricated words like 'lite' often misleading consumers by meaning far more than just a reduced fat content.

By following these simple guidelines, you will not only establish a solid foundation of wholesome practice for your family, you will also ensure their healthy future. Try it and watch as your children mimic your conscious selection of only the best while programming a lifetime of wholesome choice.

6

A Quiz

How to determine which of the Five Little Monkey types
most relates to your child:

Do you or your child display any of the following characteristics?

Although the questions are aimed primarily at 'your child', you can ask these questions of yourself and others, and trust the answers you choose to be indicative of your nature. Please understand, however, that these questions were formulated as a guide only, with no formal study having been taken to determine the accuracy of their probable outcome.

1. Whilst in class, does your child:

a) Remain focused, listen attentively and retain information easily?
b) Quickly become bored and agitated, get up and walk around, disrupting other students?
c) Sit quietly as if in a daydream, or sit chatting to a classmate, while looking out the window watching the birds eating lunch scraps?
d) Complain that they don't understand, or respond well to being made a peer tutor?
e) Ask advanced questions, or request deeper information that will enable them to grasp the concept being discussed more effectively?

2. While playing sport, does your child:

a) Do well in team situations, play fairly and receive positive criticism well?

b) Tend to quickly fire up, become overly competitive, reject positive criticism, become revengeful against the other team members and display poor sportsmanship?

c) Prefer non-competitive activities that allow for quiet time in nature?

d) Either avoid sports activities entirely, or prefer quiet, low impact outdoor activities like fishing?

e) Choose sports activities with a spiritual or rich cultural history, like wrestling or track and field?

3. When choosing a recreational activity, would your child most likely:

a) Read, join a club or organisation, or a team-oriented sport?

b) Hang out with mates at the mall or sit in their room, alone, and listen to music?

c) Go horse riding, learn to paint, or join a dance school?

d) Watch TV, surf the net or play with their Game-boy?

e) Meditate with their crystals, draw their angel or spirit guide or play with their tarot cards?

4. At mealtimes, does your child:

a) Enjoy trying foods of new and exciting flavour or of different cultural origin?

b) Prefer foods that are quick, fast and preferably processed, eaten in front of the TV or in their room?

c) Prefer raw or vegetarian meals, with the option to 'graze' from a platter of dips and healthy nibbles rather than sit down to a meal of meat and vegetables?

d) Eat whatever, and as much as possible, of what is served up to them, while preferring foods of good taste and quality?

e) Ask to lead the family prayer of thanks, preferring vegan recipes or very simple foods?

5. When it comes to social interaction, does your child:

a) Seem to prefer the company of adults despite the fact they make friends easily, quickly taking up the head role as team leader or decision maker?

b) Tend to be a loner, having difficulty fitting in or being accepted by their peers?

c) When not playing with the dog, they look after the 'underdogs'; allowing those less popular to join in their games and activities (often to the disapproval of their peers).

d) Come across as being needy by constantly trying to prove their worth, working hard to get others to accept them or to include them in their activities?

e) Have difficulty making friends, because they are considered 'out there', strange or weird, because of their looks, beliefs or their mannerisms? Do they instead talk to themselves or their 'imaginary' friends?

6. Is your child:

a) Driven, focused, intellectual and good with people?

b) Rebellious, resentful, defiant, disruptive and, at times, aggressive?

c) Wide-eyed, innocent, peaceful, inquisitive and knowing?

d) Needy, protective, self-indulgent, impractical, but when inspired, they can become motivated and meticulous?

e) Content, restful, highly aware, 'an old soul' and, at times, a bit weird or uncanny?

7. When your child grows up, could you imagine them becoming:

a) A soldier, police officer or university lecturer?

b) An equal-rights activist, a youth worker, political lobbyist or rock-

and-roll band member?

c) A doctor or nurse, an artist, forestry worker or vet?
d) A mechanic, plumber, factory worker, farm hand or chef?
e) A priest, nun, spiritual teacher or intuitive healer?

8. Does your child prefer the company of:

a) Motivated, practical people with a good, dry sense of humour?
b) No one, mostly, but when forced, individuals inspired to buck the system or rebel-rouse?
c) Animals, plants or people who are gentle, empathetic and caring?
d) People who need people and those who love to indulge the senses?
e) People who are spiritually inspired, aware or connected to the Other Realms?

9. Has your child ever been diagnosed with the symptoms of:

a) Denial, disassociation, depersonalisation, drug-induced psychosis or hebephrenic schizophrenia?
b) Attention Deficit Disorder (ADD) or Attention Deficit Hyperactivity Disorder (ADHD)?
c) Autism, poor concentration, low intellect, reduced memory and confusion?
d) Severe or recurrent depression?
e) Psychosis, delusion, paranoid schizophrenia or disorientation?

10. Does your child suffer from any of these physical ailments:

a) Anaemia, or chronic asthma and eczema?
b) Allergies, multiple food or chemical sensitivities, migraines or painful menstruation?
c) Weakness, dizziness, fainting, lots of vague pains or flabby muscles?
d) Obesity, endometriosis, heavy periods, candidiasis, diabetes, asthma or stress?

e) Listless, disturbed blood pressure — high or low, either manic or apathetic, chronically either red-faced or very pale faced?

11. When it comes to authority and discipline, does your child:

a) Crave regimentation, respond well to direction and follow instruction without question?

b) Initially become angry and defiant, but when calm, acknowledge the fact that they respect boundaries that are consistent and fair? Do they look to you as a role model and demand that you act as such, while appearing intolerant of those who display hypocrisy, ignorance and arrogance?

c) Become apologetic, remorseful and do what they can to immediately mend the error of their ways (usually coupled with a deluge of genuine tears)?

d) Become defensive, deny knowledge and immediately try to blame others?

e) Take it on the shoulder, acknowledge their involvement and vow never to do it again (strengthened by a history of honouring promises?)

12. Have you noticed that:

a) Despite being a poor listener at times who demands attention, your child is sociable and a good networker?

b) Despite being powerfully motivated to make the world a better place, your child appears angry most of the time, emotionally volatile, reckless and even violent?

c) Despite being gentle, affectionate and a good listener, your child seems apathetic, aloof and, at times, distant?

d) Despite being practical and hard-working, your child is prone to bouts of depression, self-sabotage, poor self-esteem and self-criticism?

e) Despite the fact that they display inherent spiritual knowledge and advanced psychic gifts (which can be off-putting and scary for some), your child easily inspires others and is a born leader?

13. *Would you say your child was:*

a) Somewhat narcissistic, sarcastic, mentally alert, social and physically well built?

b) Angry, insolent, suffering from a short attention span, down on themselves, frustrated and restless, but motivated by causes that inspire them?

c) Gentle, loving, considerate, sharing, giving and kind?

d) Practical, matter-of-fact, sensible, but jealous and cynical at times?

e) Content, attentive, accepting, perceptive, and at times, unnerving and a bit eerie?

14. *Does your child have:*

a) Wide, curious, intelligent eyes that reveal a deep sense of humour and a love of a good, long chat with a group of friends?

b) Dark, taunting, defiant eyes that seem to question your integrity and invoke confrontation?

c) Big, round, trusting, innocent eyes imbued with unconditional love and the ability to communicate without the need for words or audible expression?

d) Small, near-spaced, deep-set eyes that seem to dart about as if looking for something or as if checking to make sure things have been done right.

e) Cat-like, almond shaped eyes that seem to look through you; eyes filled with understanding, wisdom and knowing.

Answers:

Although there is no right or wrong answer to any of the above questions, it is highly likely that:

If you have indicated a 'YES' answer to mostly the 'A' questions, then your child is most likely a Peacekeeper Child.

If you have indicated a 'YES' answer to mostly the 'B' questions, then your child is most likely an Indigo or Warrior Child.

If you have indicated a 'YES' answer to mostly the 'C' questions, then your child is most likely a Crystal or Nature Child.

If you have indicated a 'YES' answer to mostly the 'D' questions, then your child is most likely a Winter Child.

If you have indicated a 'YES' answer to mostly the 'E' questions, then your child is most likely a Rainbow or Golden Child.

7

Introducing the 'Five Little Monkey' Types and Their Qualities

Summary Analysis of the Five Little Monkeys

Monkey	Child	Keynotes	Four Humours	Esoteric Five Elements	TCM	Ayureveda
Capuchin	Indigo Child Warrior Child	Militant Achiever Warrior Action-oriented Artisan	Choleric	Fire	Wood Liver	Pitta
Colobus	Winter Child	Guardian Fact-oriented Martyr Logician Problem solver	Melancholic	Earth	Earth Spleen	Kapha
Lemur	Peace-keeper Child	Rationalist Theory-oriented Loner Witness Pacifier	Sanguine	Air	Metal Lung	Vata

Monkey	Child	Keynotes	Four Humours	Esoteric Five Elements	TCM	Ayureveda
Squirrel Monkey	Nature Child	Idealist Ideals-oriented Activist Speaker Romantic	Phlegmatic	Water	Water Kidney	Kapha-Vata Mix
Golden Lion Tamarin	Golden Child	Dreamer Feelings-oriented Prophet Intuitive		Spirit	Fire Heart	Tri-doshic: Vatta-Pitta-Kapha Mix

PART TWO

1

The Capuchin Monkey

Totem of the Warrior (Indigo) Child
Keynotes: Militant / Achiever / Warrior

Capuchin Monkeys are active during the day, foraging for food amongst the forest canopies of Southern Central America. Made famous as the 'organ-grinder's monkey', Capuchins are incredibly intelligent animals. They are often kept as pets and trained as therapy animals. *Capuche* is French for 'skullcap'. The Capuchin Monkey got its name from the fact that its fur resembles the cowl or *capuche* worn by monks of the Franciscan order. Capuchin Monkeys have slender bodies, thin limbs and opposable thumbs. They inhabit low-lying rainforests ranging from Costa Rica to Paraguay and Trinidad and have adapted well to living in close proximity to humans.

Capuchin Monkey people are awe-inspiring. They are born leaders, are energetic, dynamic and optimistic. They display the 'pioneer' archetype, while being undemonstrative in their approach. Capuchin Monkey people represent the initiators, the rescuers and the explorers among us. They make effective 'fixers', mediators and entrepreneurs. They are determined, independent and self-reliant. Capuchin Monkey people are confident, capable and are goal-oriented. Motivational and wise, Capuchin Monkey people are usually worldly, street-wise and experienced in life. Their knowledge comes from both a higher level of awareness and a lifetime of (often negative or abusive) experience. Many have experienced abandonment, for example, or have been adopted after a period of foster care. Many have endured years of sexual, emotional or physical abuse, rape or general oppression. Most know only too well the grief caused by the death of a significant loved one, a parent, perhaps, or a sibling or close friend. And most have either experimented with or have fallen victim to substance abuse, be it drugs or alcohol, and as a result have experienced directly or witnessed through a significant other, a life of crime, trouble with the law, imprisonment, institutionalisation, homelessness, prostitution or poverty, to name just a few.

Capuchin Monkey people are profoundly aware, highly intuitive and sensitive to the subtleties of life. They are grounded and practical in their beliefs, love nature, have green thumbs, are attentive toward animals and children and make good listeners. Capuchin Monkey people can identify a liar or deceiver even before they are given reason to suspect; they abhor hypocrisy and shun judgement. They walk their talk, are realistic and learn from experience. Innate survivors, Capuchin Monkey people lead by example, while delegating effectively, inspiring and stimulating their crew with enthusiasm and praise. They are productive team members, are competitive by nature and strive to achieve. Although they prefer their own company to that of a crowd, Capuchin Monkey people can be social, polite and patient when required. They are good in a crisis, great under pressure and are generally always proven right in an argument.

However, due to an unbalanced society that moves too fast, expects too much and places blame on the first to raise an inquiring brow, Capuchin Monkey people are best known for their impatient, domineering and quick-tempered natures. When working in their shadow phase, they often display impatient, impetuous, disagreeable qualities, and openly admit to having a deep, almost irrational anger at everything and everyone. They cannot relax. They are argumentative, pushy and resentful. They hate losing and can be inflexible and stubborn. Capuchin Monkey people do not suffer fools lightly, offering derogatory remarks, emotional displays and unsympathetic observations of those who irritate them. They say things as they see them, and refuse to mince words. Capuchin Monkey people question everything and can be hostile and even violent when cornered. Capuchin Monkey people appear suspicious of everyone and are typically overly emotional and volatile. When questioned, Capuchin Monkey people will tell you they feel frustrated, restless and angry at the world. They have no logical reason for their defiance. They don't mean to be challenging or disrespectful — they just are. Capuchin Monkey people are easily confused and distracted, seemingly approaching the world in a half-hearted, reckless manner. They protect themselves emotionally by detaching from family, reacting, instead, in indiscreet and vulgar ways. Capuchin Monkey people are often medicated for being hyperactive, self-destructive and uncontrollable. They are often misdiagnosed as having ADD and ADHD, simply because they can be manipulative, demanding and controlling. They display addictive personality traits, are demanding of loyalty and are often accused of being 'users'. Capuchin Monkey people are loners, independent and bossy. They are often unpopular with their peers and possessive when they are able to make friends, but no matter what, remain forever unapologetic.

Individual advice for the Capuchin Monkey / Warrior Child

Correspondences:

Esoteric Element: Fire
Traditional Chinese Element: Wood
Elemental Instruments: Trumpets, horns, drums, cymbals and plucked stringed instruments like electric guitars
Elemental Spirits: Salamanders, Fire Dragons, Fauns, Satyrs, the Phoenix
Direction: North in Southern Hemisphere / South in Northern Hemisphere
Directional Colours: White, green
Season: Summer
Time of Power: Midday, noon
Symbolic Phase of Life on the Wheel of Life: The teenager, puberty
Power Places: Deserts, volcanos, hot springs and hearths / fire places
Zodiacs as per the Corresponding Esoteric Element: Aries, Leo and Sagittarius
Organs: Liver, gallbladder

Chakras: Base (first), Third Eye (sixth)
Chakra Colours: Indigo, red, black
Crystals: Ruby, garnet, tiger eye, hematite, red jasper, dark amethyst, coral, aquamarine, rose quartz, clear quartz, and howlite
Totems: Capuchin Monkeys, Lions, Chestnut Horses, Venomous Snakes, Bees, Scorpions, Coyotes, Dingos, Red Wolves and the Red Foxes
Herbs: Cinnamon, juniper and garlic

Fuelled by an exceptionally strong will, the overall journey for the Warrior Child is to transform anger into drive. As a Warrior Child myself, I remember only too well the feeling of rage that built inherently within and the hatred that threatened to spew out at who-so-ever dared to raise a condemnatory eyebrow. But as I grew, I learnt to regulate my rage. I learnt to channel it in a productive way. I focused it, like a laser beam, into my relationships, building my business and the genuine investigation of spirituality. When working with Warriors, one of the key things I share with them is that in order to combat their anger, they must first discover what drives them, and then to channel their anger into that passion, using their fiery rage as motivation to achieve great things rather than allowing it to destroy all potential. Only then can they hope to realise and manifest their purpose and vision for the world through the productive application of will.

Growing up, Warrior Children are loners. As teenagers and young adults, they would rather have many partners than show allegiance to just one. They have difficulty showing loyalty or fidelity because few of them actually know what it means to be loved unconditionally. They are usually the offspring of Peacekeeper Children and the siblings of Nature Children (although there are always exceptions), and they tend to clash or have issues with Winter Children.

Often diagnosed as ADD or ADHD, Warrior Children frequently demonstrate addictive personalities that, when allowed to manifest negatively, can result in the misuse of drugs or alcohol. Time and again they turn to substance abuse in an effort to block out pain from the past and the difficulties of life. Believing themselves to be untouchable or invincible, most Warrior Children are more likely to take up cigarettes than others and enjoy nothing better than being invited to riotous parties, frequenting hedonistic nightclubs, getting tattoos, piercing their skin and making their mark through graffiti. They love skateboards, dirt bikes and fast cars. They can become hyperactive, workaholics, speed freaks and, in some cases, obsessed with gambling, pornography and sex.

Warrior Children enjoy sports and physical activity, but many of the more 'hardcore' Warriors do better when encouraged to participate in less competitive, solo types; sports that inspire them to improve on their personal best, temper their emotions and harness their innate power rather than forcing them to carry the burden of team expectation or competing against others who may be better skilled or more physically fit. Such contest tends to bring out the frustration, anger and low self-esteem readily seen in Warrior Children. They respond better to the non-disciplined forms of physical activity; sports that focus on them as individuals while encouraging them to harness and channel their aggression and passion into personal growth. Martial arts (tae-kwon-do, karate, jujitsu), for example, Horse related sports, like dressage, etc., archery, firing guns and rifles on a shooting range and fire walking (which dares the Warrior Child to harness their anger by fighting 'fire with fire'), gymnastics, callisthenics, jazz ballet / creative dance, aerobics and circus-oriented activities are all ideally suited to the Warrior Child. Regular horse and trail riding, mountain biking, dirt biking, four-wheel driving, hiking, bushwalking, rock-climbing, cave exploration, base jumping, walking, running, jogging, wind surfing, regular surfing, body-boarding and swimming are also fine examples of Warrior Child-friendly sports.

In order to reach their potential and move into their positive phase, Warrior Children must learn to temper their more impulsive qualities with a sense of balance and moderation in all things. Chapter 59 of Lao Tzu's ancient book *Tao Te Ching*, for example, speaks of a need to balance our earthly character so that we might cultivate our heavenly spirit. It suggests we do this by treading the 'Middle Path'. It explains that by walking the Middle Path, we will eventually return to our true nature and that by adopting moderation in all that we do, we will learn to care for and appreciate others. By adopting moderation, too, we stand a better chance of reclaiming our inherent relationship with God. Moderation is all about putting our own wants aside so that we may be of better service to the world and God (and eventually ourselves). When we live a life that appreciates all life, all people and all beliefs, we accrue a degree of sound providence. When we live a life of goodness, displaying integrity, honesty and morality in all that we do, then over time, the Tao says, nothing is impossible. And when we believe nothing is impossible, we are never again hampered by obstacles or limitations. And when we are free of obstacles, we stand fully in charge of our own destiny; ready to step out into the world as whole, healthy individuals set to live abundant lives. When we realise this simple truth, we also realise endurance and stamina. According to Taoist philosophy, this is called 'setting deep roots' and 'creating a firm foundation', thus guaranteeing oneself a long life and eternal vision.

Generally speaking, Warrior Children must learn to value their uniqueness and honour their individual gifts and the specific contribution they can (and will) make to the world as adults. They need to develop skills that will see them temper the inner fire so that it doesn't burn out of control and raze everything it touches to the ground. They must be shown how to cool their passions and their body so as to regain clarity and equilibrium. They must be helped to reclaim their innate joy so that they may laugh, love and trust like everyone else. Cooling and quietening activities (which don't have to be silent in nature) may involve hiking and bushwalking, swimming or surfing, canoeing, white-water rafting, horse riding or tobogganing and rolling in the snow. Simply spending a day in the country, too, where they will be surrounded by the greenness of nature will benefit Warrior Children greatly. After all, green is the colour of the heart chakra, the hub of balance and harmony. While, according to Traditional Chinese Medicine, the liver (the organ that rules all Warrior Children) resonates to the colour green and, in some cases, blue — which is interesting, especially when you consider that deep, royal blue is also known as 'indigo'.

Activities that promote balancing, harmonising movement, like Iyengar yoga and, for those who are serious about stilling their mind and combating their anger, Tai Chi (a gentler form of martial arts), are perfect for the Warrior Child. Tai Chi is the ancient Chinese art of movement. It was first created as a form of martial art, a form that inspires self-defence by emphasising stillness, inner balance and self-discipline. Today the flowing movements are practised as a holistic form of exercise designed to increase flexibility, body posture and balance and to return us to our innate place of ancient knowing and power; a place of life and death, light and dark, and choice. It affords a potent resource for Warrior Children who yearn to manifest their will in the world, as does Iyengar yoga: a physical, methodical, regimented form of yoga that promotes the assimilation of body, mind and spirit. Iyengar yoga encourages self-exploration, deeper perspective, contemplation and greater self-awareness, while promoting greater physical health and a stronger mind by striving to alleviate angst, lack of concentration and insomnia: conditions known to be aggravated, even instigated, by physical imbalance and poor health. Iyengar yoga works to build a suppler, stronger, more receptive body. As is often said, the body is the temple of the soul and therefore worthy of respect. The focus of Iyengar yoga is not to revamp the body per se, but rather to still the mind and develop clarity and greater awareness (with physical fitness and perfection being an added bonus).

As teenagers and young adults, it is vital for Warrior Children to align their interests with humanitarian goals and to make the pain that often haunts their past mean something on a tangible level, in a way that serves the greater good. It is important for the Warrior Child to find meaning for their suffering. They see little or no point in being overwhelmed for no reason. Essentially, the Warrior Child finds him or herself embarking on a quest to find meaning and purpose for their suffering; to create some value to the pain that they experience in life. It is not unusual for Warrior Children to have experienced an injury, tragedy or some form of abuse in their earlier years, with the purpose of the quest to learn from such events. In doing so, they are able to protect others and prepare them with wisdom deeply rooted in experience. Taking social action to create meaning out of suffering offers peace and understanding for the Warrior Child. Thus encouraging the Warrior Child to work in a way that serves the community, the higher good and advanced ideals is a profound way of helping them transform their inherent selfishness into altruistic endeavour. Although many find themselves travelling the apprenticeship path typically followed by the Winter Children, most resent having to dedicate their lives to physical labour. To the hardcore Warrior Child, apprenticeships offer nothing more than dead-end jobs for those considered the low-life 'shit-kickers' of society; the ones everyone has given up on or expects nothing better of. They lack the self-worth and patience to turn apprenticeships into lucrative careers (which many promise to become). Instead, they view them as pigeon-holes that prompt others to say ... "Oh yes, I knew that was all they would amount to." Warrior Children do well working as public advocates, such as counsellors, child welfare officers and youth workers, political lobbyists and journalists. For those who make it through university, they also make powerful, professional 'arse-kickers' as radical schoolteachers and principals, lawyers, economists and politicians.

Have them visit their local aged-care facility for inspiration, for example, their local primary school or child care facility or local hospital or doctor's clinic, and encourage them to volunteer their services or suggest they approach them as possible choices for work experience. Or instigate an exploration of the performing arts: drama, dance and song. Visit a theatre, the Opera House or a museum of performing arts for inspiration.

As Brian Dale says, "Imagine the times when you felt really good about yourself and what you have accomplished. Your self-esteem is high. Your confidence is booming. You know that you are capable of achieving whatever you put your mind to. This is how young performers feel at the end of a play or musical production. The risk of placing yourself on stage for all to see, the focus of drama/dance/music sessions, the individual practice and the hard work of rehearsals have reaped their reward. All of us need compliments and success. We respond to the positive. Achievement and recognition enhances our sense of worth. Children are no exception. At school our success as an individual is often measured by our academic achievement or our sporting prowess. There exists a group of children who have limited opportunities and choices. The reason is that the performing arts occupy a minor position within school life and a small focus in the curriculum. Drama, dance, singing and music fill the role of electives, an annual school production or activities that are pursued after school. Increase their significance and you increase the self-esteem of a wide range of children. The group dynamic and the achievement of group goals is a powerful feeling. Children and young adults working together for one unifying group dynamic is such a reward. To watch young performers, both boys and girls, assist and encourage each other and then to celebrate their performance with hugs, pats on the back and complimentary words is a joy to behold.

Performance is also a group achievement. As a performer there is the need to not only know your role but also to be aware of the group performance. If a performer goes blank, misses their lines or an introduction, then those around must have the awareness and capability to 'pick up' where the glitch occurred. This process creates a wonderful bond of dependence and friendship. We all need to express ourselves. Drama is an incredible tool for self-expression. It allows the performer to explore a range of diverse characters and opinions. It especially allows young performers the opportunity to examine a range of subjects, personalities and verbal expressions, many of which would be considered taboo in normal daily life, such as, sex, drugs, swearing, etc. Self-expression is about being creative. However, in drama performance, there are also technicalities that enhance an individual's expression. Breathing, voice projection, facial expression, body language, emotional content, phrasing, emphasis on key words are all skills that performers need to learn to enhance their self-expression. Participating in the performing arts requires incredible focus. There are so many things in today's world that scatter and scramble children's direction and energy. As a participant in the performing arts the prime requirement is that of concentration and focus. No matter how talented a performer is at role playing or characterisation, if the focus is not there, then all is in vain. Performance, by its very nature, demands focus. Performance makes many demands yet offers many rewards. Drama groups give young performers the avenue for challenge and personal growth."

Alternatively, investigate the fine arts: painting, drawing, sculpture, textiles and fashion design. Visit a gallery, a reputable fashion house or investigate the library, Internet or magazines as motivation. If such resources are not convenient, do not give up. Call your local community house and enquire about the programs they offer. Photography, for example, lends itself beautifully to those bearing the 'warrior' archetype, because it calls for them to literally 'stalk' their prey, while using a camera instead of the more traditional bow and arrow. Encourage them to learn to play an instrument, or if they are already adept and have mastered one, inspire their creative side by suggesting they use it to compose music appropriate to its intended use. If they express an interest in dance, channel them into styles that carry cultural significance: belly dance, classical Indian, tribal, Irish, etc. Your Warrior Child will respond favourably, I assure you.

As Per The Four Humours: The Choleric

Cholerics are famous for being domineering, intolerant, volatile and stubborn. They don't know what it means to feel continuously calm, are impulsive, love debates and need to have their opinions heard. They rarely quit (even when approaching certain defeat) and remain persuasive in their argument until the very end. They are disparaging, shun emotion and are indifferent to the needs of others. Hence the need for them to be 'cooled and moistened', according to the philosophy championing the Four Humours.

Cholerics are also born leaders, self-motivated and energetic, iron-willed and influential. They can suffer from an irrational desire to bring about transformation and must correct perceived wrongs at all costs. Given that they are quite undemonstrative, they are not easily disheartened and are self-governing and independent. Most Cholerics emanate self-assurance and can manage pretty much anything. To remain on track, though, Cholerics need to maintain a balanced attitude to life, while steadily directing their passions into constructive activities like energetic dance and vigorous music, which, believe it or not, pacifies the inner fire and 'cools the blood'. Cholerics benefit greatly from fostering high ideals and serving a higher purpose, so encourage this at all costs, and allow them to decide for themselves or negotiate what is right for them and what is not, otherwise their stubbornness and bloody-mindedness will rise up and get in the way. Provide outlets for them to exercise their typically high level of intelligence — especially in intellectual pursuits, which serve them and their need to be of service to the higher good.

As Per The Five Esoteric Elements: Fire

At approximately 12.00 pm each day, the sun is directly overhead and the plans for the day's events are established. The afternoon holds untold mysteries and, with the strength and warmth of the sun streaming down, life seems limitless and we are confident that we can face everything with an almost guaranteed degree of success. When the sun sits annually at its fullest, we find ourselves experiencing the longest day and the shortest night; it is summer and we are symbolically standing in the north (in the southern hemisphere / south in the northern hemisphere) — the direction affording the greatest heat.

When the sun is at its fullest, it is representative of the element fire. Fire is the element of great change. It is the element that represents will and passion and it is the most primal of the all the elements. It governs the realms of sexuality and innocence, growing within all at a great pace. According to the teachings of the Wheel of Life, we find ourselves working with the element of fire when we are standing symbolically at the peak of our youth, when we think we know everything when in fact we know nothing, with the potential to learn ripe to be picked, when we are more than willing to try everything that life offers. Evident primarily in the esoteric qualities of those born under the zodiacal signs of Aries, Leo and Sagittarius, fire represents not only the 'sacred fire' of sex, but also the spark of divinity that shines within all living things. It is both the most physical and most spiritual of all the elements, as it represents growth and maturity, connection and wisdom.

Fire symbolically invokes the projective energies within each of us, the energies that promote the masculine powers of spirit in its physical forms: the heat of the naked flame and of blood and sap.

According to the Five Esoteric Elements, Warrior Children correspond vibrationally to the energies of fire, and in turn, summer. During summer, the goddess is in her pregnant phase and the world is thriving, happy and at peace. It is at this point that we begin to realise our connection to Mother Nature, and we take full advantage of her by camping in the bush and taking trips to the ocean. Summer is cleansing, energetic, sexual and forceful in nature and is embodied within fire spirits such as Salamanders and Fire Dragons.

It is a recreational activity, favoured by many, to build a campfire and sleep beneath the stars, especially in wooded areas or dry spots overlooking a gentle stream, ocean inlet or peaceful lake (to extend the enjoyment with fishing and trekking). When we sit and contemplate the movement of the flames leaping from the wood fuelling our campfires, especially when the wood is driftwood permeated with salt, it is not hard to fancy small lizard-like creatures dancing among the hot coals. The association between the preferred sites for camping (with fire) and the small amphibious creatures spied at night taking advantage of the water, led to the belief that Salamanders were able to exist in fire, controlling its habits and harnessing its force. Over time, the Salamander became known as the elemental spirit of fire and the embodiment of its energy.

From the moment man 'discovered' fire and first harnessed its potency, he learned that fire shows little mercy for those who abuse or neglect it. He learned quickly that if he was to integrate fire into his life, he had to restrict its movements within a circle of rocks or some other fire-retarding vessel. To assume otherwise would see everything surrounding it swallowed up and enveloped in its wrathful flames. He also learned that the only way to quash its advancement was with water, an element both quiet and contemplative.

Salamanders, it was decided, although living near water but seemingly 'active' within fire, embrace both elements equally, and like the Chinese yin yang symbol, create balance between all that is deemed creative and destructive; good and bad; dark and light; nurturing and revengeful. Salamander Dreaming can be invoked to breathe life into and dampen the ferocity of fire in its tangible form, in the wilderness or in the comfort of our own home. When we ignite a candle, light a wood stove, or build a campfire, we essentially invoke the Dreaming of the Salamander. Fire is a living entity. It breathes oxygen. It must feed or it will die. It grows and travels across the land, and it seems to take on a mind of its own when it gathers in magnitude. Abuse it and it will bite back. Starve it and it will die. And, like the remaining elements of water, air and earth, fire is personified with each breath we take. As the element that rules the north on the Wheel of Life, fire symbolically governs our attitudes and how we conduct our personal lives. It governs issues related to the heart, the small intestine and pericardium, the cardiovascular and nervous system, digestive function and circulation. Whenever we set personal boundaries, partake in sexual activity or commence a relationship of any sort, we acknowledge the fire element, represented by Salamander Dreaming. We do, too, when we demonstrate self-expression, affection, enthusiasm, passion, joy or happiness. Anything that raises a sweat, the heart rate or encourages our blood to pump faster through our veins comes under the banner of Salamander Dreaming.

Fire people are passionate about most things, but not always in a productive way. They are inherently forceful, obstinate, opinionated and boastful, and when these qualities are allowed to intensify unchecked, they tend to result in broken or dysfunctional relationships, a fear of intimacy, deep sadness, shyness, insomnia and distrust; conditions associated with the heart, circulatory system, bowel, neck and upper back and environmental sensitivity.

As with fire itself, fire people must be careful to maintain control and not let their fiery disposition and forceful nature get away from them, because when it does, the rewards gleaned from years of hard work and dedicated effort can quickly and, quite literally, go up in smoke. Issues of the heart quickly become issues affecting the heart, for example. Love and joy quickly turn to pain and despair. Listening to, composing or dancing to 'fiery', grounding, martial music, especially that incorporating trumpets, horns, drums, cymbals and plucked stringed instruments, or wild rock music with electrical guitars primarily featured, are ideal sounds best suited to tame and quell the inner fire of most fire people. Fire people need to be themselves (or otherwise they appear false and shallow), but they must (more so than others, it seems), endeavour to walk the fine line between being true to themselves and being respectful and tolerant of the opinions, beliefs and values of those around them — especially when they differ from their own.

A Guided Visualisation that explores the Fire Element:

Find yourself a comfy place where you know you will not be interrupted. If possible, find a place in nature. Sit with your back supported by the trunk of a tree, a smooth rock or a mossy log. Sit with the intention of strengthening your bond with Spirit and of remembering your inherent relationship with the Earth Mother. You may want to wrap yourself in a blanket, because it is not uncommon for one's body temperature to drop as you sink deeper and deeper into stillness. Quiet your conscious mind and endeavour to silence your inner chatter. Wait for the moment when you intuitively feel inclined to open your consciousness to the Other Realms. Ensure that your subconscious mind is receptive and alert by speaking to your conscious mind. Allow visions and symbolic images to float through your mind. Keep your focus within yourself. Let any thoughts just go by. When you catch yourself engaged in an external conscious thought, take a deep breath and bring yourself back to your centre.

You are now ready to begin.

Picture yourself on a great grassy plane, dotted with the most beautifully coloured wild flowers. From where you are standing you can see two very different sights. To your right is a path leading up to a steep mountain peak and to your left is a path leading down into a deep valley. The point at which you are standing is in fact the intersection of time and reality; a mingling point of reality and 'the Other Worlds', of the physical and the mystical. It is where the miraculous can be found.

Visualise yourself taking the right path as it leads to the top of the mountain. It is noon and the full sun is directly overhead. The path leads you to the north, the direction of the greatest heat, past hibiscus trees, mustard plants, thistles, chilli peppers and bougainvillea vines, cacti and red poppies, all with Crickets, Ladybirds and Bees crawling through their leaves. It is summer and the air is warm. You watch a ginger Rabbit nibbling the dry grass. Above you, as lightning shards slash the sky, a fire-breathing Dragon circles with a Phoenix — a sacred bird with flames for a tail. As you reach the top of the mountain, you realise that it is a volcano. From the cracked, baked earth swirls of smoke rise and dance on the warm breeze and, at this moment, you feel like a teenager again — innocent and vulnerable, yet strong and courageous. You hear the sound of a harp, its music rising from the fiery heart of the mountain.

Suddenly, a great cracking sound pierces the silence and, from an explosion of heat and billowing smoke, Pele, the volcanic goddess of purification and upheavals emerges and stands in front of you: her whole being combusting, writhing with energy and enveloped in flame-blue robes. Beside her stand three fiery figures. They are Salamanders, fundamentally humanoid in shape, but wild and untamed in form. One is holding burning incense; one holds a lamp and the other, a red candle. They are the elemental spirits of fire, sent by archangel Michael, the warrior of the sacred flames and Adonai, the elemental King of Fire.

Theirs is a world of faith and trust, renewal and relationships with others, with the self and with nature. They are elusive yet protective. They teach self-healing, love and passion. They repel stress and tension, attracting energy, spirit and sexuality. They personify Creation; life-force itself and our blood as it surges through our veins. They know the truths associated with evolution, self-knowledge and the body, and their existence is governed by our obsession with candle flames, bon fires, hearth fires and explosions. They are ruled by the sun, volcanic eruptions and sexual energy and, like us, rely on oxygen for their survival, for without it, fire cannot exist. Theirs is a world of destruction and transformation, of life, death and rebirth, of physical activity, vitality and change and they beckon you to join them, to explore their world and to become one with it.

The Salamanders race off aboard blazing golden chariots — one drawn by Lions, one drawn by Horses with sparking hooves and the other drawn by Snakes, as scarlet as fire. You notice there is a chariot for you, too, drawn by two red Foxes with eyes like green obsidian. The Salamanders have altered you and your perception of reality and in this world you are capable of travelling in their blistering terrain. They have gifted you with a cape crafted from red feathers — symbols of courage and spiritual strength. You step into the fire opal and red amber encrusted chariot and follow in a cloud of steam.

They lead you on a wild ride, the scorching wind burning your face and melting your hair. You know these sensations represent your greatest fear, so you close your eyes and focus, repelling feelings of panic and vulnerability. You open your eyes and to your relief, realise your skin and hair are fine. You have passed a test of inner strength that you once may have failed. You race past goldmines, blacksmiths and white-hot forges, through bubbling hot springs, sun-baked deserts and raging forest fires until you finally find yourself back at the mouth of the smoking volcano.

The Salamanders stand in front of you, pleased with your efforts. They take your hand and speak to you through your base chakra — the energy centre that governs passion and Creation within all living things. They speak to you of dance, drama and free-form movement. Of exercise, physical communication, sensuality and love, while sharing with you teachings influenced by their element — body awareness, philosophy and spirit vibration. They release your hand and return to Pele and their volcanic world.

Make a silent prayer to Spirit for a reason sacred to you and offer thanks, taking three breaths in through your nose and out through your mouth before returning to the physical place in which you are seated.

As per Traditional Chinese Medicine: the Wood / Liver Person

According to the teachings of Traditional Chinese Medicine, Warrior Children, as 'liver people', have their mind, body and energy systems focused on the wood element. Wood, as an element, corresponds with spring and the bounty of nature: new life, rebirth, abundance and opportunity. The dominant colour during spring is green, indicative of the new shoots and buds of flourishing plants. Autumn creates a sense of vulnerability in liver people, as does extremely hot weather and strong wind. The centre of attention for those governed by the wood element, therefore, lies in the desire to manifest their will through focused action that will, in turn, help to bring their dreams and visions to fruition. They are the militant types who go out and put things right in order to build what they perceive as being a more promising future.

Liver people, when working in harmony with their element, have a clear vision of their future with defined goals and objectives. Most importantly, though, they know exactly what they need to do in order to bring them to fruition. They are excellent planners and decision makers, are influential and forceful, with penetrating eyes that can both fascinate and attract while (more often than not) concealing a ruthless nature. On a bodily level, a greater level of wellbeing for the bodily tissues related to the liver is realised (according to the teachings of Traditional Chinese Medicine): healthier muscles and tendons for fast, active movement, for example; stronger eyes and clearer vision and enhanced health for the liver itself as a chemical factory and detoxifying plant (as per western medicine). When the wood person's Qi (essential life-force) has been allowed to wane, they may appear uncertain, directionless and befuddled, forced and repressed. When the liver Qi is blocked or sluggish, they may come across as arrogant, scheming and irritated. This is when they display the tendency to become workaholics, allow their inherent addictive personalities to show, or when the likelihood of drug or alcohol abuse will emerge. They may seem unbalanced (usually due to too much work, lack of sleep, keeping irregular hours, poor diet, lack of rest, little time in contact with nature and over-indulgence in rich, spicy food, alcohol, drugs and even sex). Symptoms such as bloating, gas, constipation and/or diarrhoea, fatigue, muscle aches and pains, headaches (especially on the sides of the head), ringing in the ears, a dry mouth and unquenchable thirst, dark, sparse urine, insomnia, constipation, a bitter taste in the mouth, muscle tightness in the neck and shoulders, blurred vision, red eyes, acne, itchy skin, irritability, anger and frustration begin to emerge. If this imbalance is prolonged, it can lead to more serious problems, such as migraines, allergies, asthma, eczema, hay fever, heartburn, painful or heavy periods, depression, sensitivity to alcohol and drugs and even to serious degenerative or auto-immune diseases such as rheumatoid arthritis, inflammatory bowel disease, multiple sclerosis, multiple food and chemical sensitivities and CFS (Chronic Fatigue Syndrome). When diagnosed, people suffering from these symptoms are described as being 'liverish' or as having 'S.O.L.: *Shit on the Liver*'.

In accordance with the teachings of Traditional Chinese Medicine, Warrior Children (as people prone to wood / liver excess) need to sedate their excess liver energy and cool their mind and body if they are to fully realise their potential. Eating plenty of leafy green vegetables, such as broccoli and cabbage, and salads, for example, will help immensely. Adding melons, apples, asparagus, barley, celery, cucumber, eggplant, gluten, mangos, mushrooms and pears to the diet will also help relax the liver, as will drinking plenty of lukewarm water (not chilled, as this is said to damage one's 'core feminine' or Yin energy) and fresh, green juices derived from foods such as apples, wheat grass and barley green (especially when enhanced with supplements such as spirulina, which provides a potent concoction of vitamins, minerals and phytonutrients —nutrients found in the skins of many vegetables and fruits and some grains and seeds — and chlorella, which helps the body to naturally break down persistent hydrocarbon and metallic toxins that may build up in the system). Beef and chicken liver, black sesame, celery, kelp (seaweed), mulberries, plums, spinach, chestnuts, rye, vinegar, asparagus and eggs are also believed to reduce liver excess. Warrior Children would do well to avoid (wherever possible) spices, alcohol and drugs, seafood, coffee, heavy red meats, sugar, sweets, food additives, preservatives and over-indulgence of any kind.

Other therapies endorsed by Traditional Chinese Medicine for the treatment of excess liver / wood energy in Warrior Children include the application of natural, alcohol-free cooling / soothing lotions to the skin, soaking in a mineral or lukewarm freshwater bath imbued with bergamot enhanced Earl Grey teabags or permeated with sea salt, acupuncture (for more severe blockages), taking dandelion-based herbal remedies (for the more severe disorders) and getting plenty of good quality sleep.

As Per Ayurveda: Fire Energy / Pitta

According to Ayurvedic philosophy, 'Pitta' is a force created by the dynamic interplay of the elements water and fire. Warrior Children must learn to appease their excess fire energy if they are to reach their fullest potential. The golden rule, once again, is balance and moderation. They must find a balance so that their fire does not dry out their water, and so that their water does not extinguish their fire.

From an early age, Pitta people must be encouraged to remain focused, organised and on task. They are capable of being so, but are easily distracted, especially when it comes to things of little interest to them. They must to be taught to be precise about following directions and keeping to plans. Pitta people can be obsessive, though, so when it comes to fulfilling tasks, they need to find a balance so as to not become preoccupied with reaching the goal. Moderation in all things is the key. They enjoy being in charge. When stressed, they quickly become snappy and heated. Pitta people are prone to rashes, redness of the skin, acne, boils, skin cancer, ulcers, heartburn, acid stomach, hot sensations in the stomach or intestines, insomnia, anaemia, jaundice, bloodshot or burning eyes and other vision problems. They (especially the single or young) love spending money, wear designer label clothes and accessories and have the best car with all the extras. They prefer to live in the best part of town and be seen with the 'beautiful' people.

Pitta people are intelligent and attentive, systematic and determined. Many would describe them as being confident, self-assured and entrepreneurial when displaying their more positive qualities, but violent, challenging and aggressive when not. They are generally highly spirited individuals who don't mind confrontations and love arguing their point. Romantically, they are both obsessive and passionate. Pitta people can be inflexible, aggressive and opinionated, although they do make effective public speakers when given the opportunity. They can be critical and sardonic and use hurtful words when annoyed or frustrated. When balanced, Pitta people display good organisational and managerial skills, but can become dictatorial when not. When they cannot get their own way, they are not above throwing tantrums, intolerance and moments of pure rage.

Physically, Pitta people have medium builds, tending toward being both strong and muscular, with fair to reddish skin and freckles. They tend to sunburn easily. They have fine, straight, blond or red hair that usually greys prematurely, with a predisposition to baldness or early thinning. Because they perspire a lot, most Pitta people dislike excessive hot weather and will avoid sitting in the direct sun. It makes them overheat and lose energy. They usually have a healthy digestive system, and display good appetites. They need to partake in activities that are cooling, restful and recreational — preferably in a way that incorporates nature. Camping, hiking, swimming and leisurely strolls are ideal. In order to mollify their fire energy, make a habit of watching what your child eats. For example, encourage them to eat plenty of salads, fruit and starchy foods like vegetables in general (except those listed at the end of this paragraph), barley, wheat, oats, white rice, tofu, soy, chickpeas, mung beans and olive oil, and 'cooling' herbs and spices, such as cardamom, coriander, cinnamon, dill, fennel, mint, saffron and turmeric. Flavours that are bitter, sweet or astringent are okay.

Poultry, black pepper, cumin, butter, ice cream and milk should be eaten in moderation, while red meat, chilli, fiery herbs and spices, fat, pickled food, salt, vinegar, yoghurt, sour cream, cheese, coffee, fermented items such as beer and vegemite, fried foods, carrots, eggplant, garlic, hot peppers, onions, radish, spinach, tomato, lentils, apricots, bananas, berries, cherries, peaches and grapefruit should be avoided completely.

Do not expect Pitta people to be as organised as you, but similarly, Pitta people must learn not to expect others to be as focused as them. It works both ways. To ease the frustration felt by Pitta people who cannot find a sense of balance, encourage them to sit outside on a warm night and ponder the moon or watch the tide come in or stroll with them beside a slow moving stream and contemplate the deliberate yet irregular movement of the water. Give them exercises that help still their mind while helping them further develop their great memory and intellectual mind; activities, for example, that help them remember important dates, such as birthdays and anniversaries. This will help them shift their focus beyond their immediate world so that they may begin to acknowledge and appreciate the wider world and the people who share it with them. Regular sessions of yoga, meditation or Panchakarma, an Ayurvedic deep tissue cleansing treatment that removes toxins and impurities from the system, will also help the Pitta person find the balance required to equalise their fire energy. Herbs known to support the process include aloe vera, comfrey root and saffron.

As Per Homeopathy

The homeopathic remedies listed below may be beneficial in helping to balance the Warrior Child's constitution:

- Arsenicum – album
- Ferrum met
- Lachesis
- Medorrhinum
- Nux vomica
- Sulphur

For a deeper explanation of these suggested homeopathic remedies, please refer to the section at the rear of this book dedicated entirely to homeopathy and its history, and the chart listing the keynotes of each remedy on page 281.

Other Advice

Herbal remedies known to generally assist the overall wellbeing of the Warrior Child include St. John's Wort (*Hypericum perforatum*), taken as an herbal tincture to treat mild to moderate depression, anxiety, restlessness, night terrors and insomnia; valerian root, a calming herb often taken to increase concentration; hops, which also helps to calm the nervous system; skullcap, a natural sedative; ginkgo, which eases forgetfulness while helping to increase concentration and focus. Ginkgo is believed to have positive effects on brain neurotransmitters, while chamomile is both soothing and calming, as is lemon balm and finally, hawthorn, which apparently supports blood circulation to the brain. 'liver herbs' such as dandelion, St. Mary's thistle, silybum or blessed milk thistle are advised, while Swedish Bitters, a 500-year-old remedy promoted by European herbalist, Maria Treben, is certainly worth a try. The bitter taste of Swedish Bitters is said to trigger the rejuvenation of the body's vital organs, improve regularity, aid digestion and cleanse the entire internal system, among other things. Of course, as with all herbal medicines, it is wise to seek advice from your integrative holistic doctor or naturopath before self-prescribing remedies of any sort.

Investigate the properties of aromatherapy, particularly the sweet, cooling scents of sandalwood, rose, mint, cinnamon and jasmine. By gently dispersing their aroma into your child's space via an electric oil burner or releasing three or four drops directly into your child's bath, you will undoubtedly discover a treasure trove of calming, healing potential, as you will if you make deeper exploration into the realm of crystals and their vibrational healing properties. Crystals are gifts offered directly to us by the Earth Mother, each imbued with powerful medicine. Carry crystals in your pocket, in a pouch around your neck or in your sock or bra. Many crystals are ideal as support for the Warrior Child. Hematite, for example, is a powerfully grounding stone that promotes a healthy flow of blood (and life-supporting energy) through the body, and as such, is profoundly balancing in nature. Rose quartz offers a gentle, soothing sense of calm and perfect trust. Amethyst connects its carrier to the spiritual realms and the higher self, while clear quartz offers clarity, awareness and spiritual insight. Aquamarine is both cooling and refreshing, while labradorite inspires us to follow our destiny, turns anger into action and helps to instil a sense of endurance. Tiger eye is great for the development of intuition and is believed to soften stubbornness, while howlite alleviates pain, stress and rage.

Warrior Children are powerfully intuitive. Encourage them to join and participate in a spiritual development group, visit a psychic fair and attend the workshops and seminars being offered, or buy them a deck of tarot cards and teach them how to use them properly by explaining the symbolic journey of growth they convey. Show your Warrior Child how to create a medicine pouch; a compact drawstring purse worn around the neck made from suede, light weight leather or cotton fabric. Inside place sacred items that connect them to Spirit, their guides or those in Spirit; items such as leaves, twigs, seeds, stones, crystals, shells, feathers, fur scraps, claws, bones, teeth or hair, and/or personal items which hold emotional or spiritual value to the wearer, such as jewellery, coins, photos, knick-knacks, etc. Medicine pouches are worn as a way of remembering someone in spirit, as a means of harnessing specific healing energies or as a way of identifying and radiating one's personal medicine, or spiritual strengths and gifts. Encourage them, too, to call upon archangel Michael for guidance and their patron saint, St. Francis of Assisi for help. The Capuchin Monkey was named after the Capuchin monks who were members of the Franciscan order. The Capuchin monk aspired to do only good in the world. Following the example of St. Francis of Assisi (who was an avid lover of animals and people), Capuchin Monks gave priority to two ministries: working with the poor and preaching the word of God.

And speaking of animals, the therapeutic advantages animals offer is a documented fact. Warrior Children love and respect animals, so allowing your child to have a pet of their own will offer purpose, immediate love and someone they can tell their secrets to. It will encourage them to take responsibility for something other than themselves, while helping them realise that unless they take the responsibility no one will be there to care for their pet. Allow your child to choose their own pet as the bond is often forged right there in the pet store, and is always a personal thing. Salamanders, Rats, Snakes, Dragon Lizards, medium to large Dogs, stray Cats, Rabbits and hand-tame Parrots make excellent pets (and companions) for Warrior Children. If you are not in the position to have a pet, regularly visit your local zoo, wildlife sanctuary, wildlife rescue centre, pet adoption agency, local pound or park. Many zoos and sanctuaries offer benefits to regular attendees: Friends of the Zoo, for example, allows limitless access to all affiliated parks for a minimal annual fee. Tap into this love of animals in a therapeutic way, too, by having them draw a picture of their favourite animal and a picture of the animal they fear the most. Explain that the 'medicine' or Dreaming of the favourite animal represents their strengths and aspirations while that of an animal they fear represents their vulnerabilities, fears and weaknesses. The animals we fear are equally as important and as valuable to our growth as the animals we love. They represent those aspects of our psyche that we choose to ignore — our fears, our secrets and dark thoughts. They characterise our personal boundaries, our self-imposed limitations and those parts of our selves that reject spontaneity, risk taking and the development of self-esteem. They also represent our dark side — the shadow aspect of our soul that we tend to ignore or suppress due to the connotations that they represent and the responsibilities that they force upon us. They make us to look at ourselves, to stand before our weaknesses and our frailties and to honour them as lessons and as stepping-stones to power.

Ancient wisdom clearly illustrates our relationship to all things. What may be initially seen as inert, the ancient teachings depict as living. It is said that all things of nature, ultimately being created from the one source, deserve equal honour and respect. As a result, the traditions of many indigenous people encompass nature as a whole, with the understanding that Spirit lives within all things of nature forming the core of their belief system. The teachings imply that the Earth is our mother — that from her we came and to her we shall return. She supplies us with everything we need. She cradles us when we are despaired, feeds us when we are hungry and shelters us when we are vulnerable. She loves unconditionally as mothers will. She scolds, too, when we disrespect her by lashing us mercilessly with storms and drought. She instructs us well in all of life's lessons — of giving and taking, of love and war, of birth, death and rebirth. She teaches symbolically, her lessons clearly marking our rites of passage with the changing of the seasons, the transition of day into night and night into day, the waxing and waning of the moon and the ebb and flow of Grandmother Ocean's tides. She gifts us with healing herbs, medicine stones and vibrational wisdom hidden deep within her heart and made available to us as needed. She employs the animals as our mentors, healers and guides, each symbolically gifted with a unique and sacred message intended to guide us to a place of wholeness both individually and as a united people. Her animals present themselves when we need them most. They share their knowledge unconditionally, even if we do not consciously heed their wisdom at the time. Her animals, our 'creature-teachers', can assist us in the manifesting of change; they can help us to bring about healing for ourselves and others; they can return a traveller safely home, or ensure a safe passage for someone about to embark on a journey. They can ease the pain a mother feels as she watches her children leave home, just as they can ensure health, peace and happiness when a new baby enters the world. There is an animal imbued with the wisdom to help us with every aspect of our physical lives, just as there are animals in Spirit that act as vibrational teachers, totems and spiritual guides, there are also animals here on Earth that are more than willing to help us whilst in their physical form.

Essentially, this philosophy embodies the ancient spiritual path known as 'Animism', a path very similar to that of Shamanism, but more generic and open to personal interpretation. Typically the sort to shun organised religion, Animism is a path ideally suited to the Warrior Child; a spiritual path that will serve them on all levels until the day they die. Animism espouses the belief that all objects and living things are imbued with a soul permeated with wisdom, insight and choice that preside over their reality. Put simply, Animism advocates that everything is alive, conscious and having a soul, and should be treated with the respect it deserves. It also says that the world is a community of living 'persons', only some of which are human. It portrays all things as equal: the humans, rocks, plants, animals, birds, ancestral spirits, and so on. Animism offers a 'belief in spirits', be they mystical, paranormal, unseen or illusory beings. Animism, as a spiritual path, celebrates beings for their own sake, whether they have or are souls, or because they are 'persons', or not.

Shamanism, however, refers to a range of traditional beliefs and practices that claim the ability to diagnose and cure human suffering by forming a special relationship with 'spirits'. Shamans are said to control the weather, practice the art of divination, interpret dreams, astral travel and drift between the upper and lower worlds. Shamanism, as a tradition, has existed since prehistoric times. Shamans are said to form a bridge between the natural and spiritual worlds and to travel between worlds in a trance state, where they call upon the spirits to help with healing and hunting. Shamanism champions the belief that the tangible world is infused with invisible forces or spirits that influence the lives of the living. Unlike Animism, Shamanism requires specialised training, initiation, knowledge and ability. Shamans, it could be said, are the 'experts' employed by Animists to instigate necessary and beneficial change on behalf of the wider community.

Two facets of Shamanism that could be explored by the Warrior Child, however, with almost guaranteed positive results are Sweat Lodge (when over the age of 16) and the drum. Only ever participate in a Sweat Lodge, however, when you are sure the 'pourer' (the central person running the lodge) is fully trained and qualified and not motivated by potential monetary or egotistical gain and, for girls, only ever participate when not experiencing a bleeding time. Sweat Lodge is a sacred custom embraced and modified by many shamanic communities the world over, with orientation most commonly witnessed in Native American tradition, and should be treated and celebrated as such. Its composition is a total re-enactment of Creation, documented in a plethora of varying forms. Sweat Lodge is a tangible way for us to return to Spirit and to reconcile our relationship with Creation so that we may reconnect to the place we have and the role we play within it. It is a cleansing ceremony for all aspects of being on the physical, mental, emotional and spiritual levels. Sweat Lodge is powerful. It is capable of bringing about profound change in the form of healing and personal growth and reconnecting us with the nurturing energies of Mother Earth. On a physical level we sweat, cleansing our pores of deeply imbedded dirt and grime. On an emotional level we shed tears, actively releasing in a sacred way, years of personal baggage, with the intent of bringing ourselves back to the centre point of balance and inner harmony. On a mental level, our perception is snapped back into clarity so that we may see, perhaps for the first time in many years, what is really important to us, what is sacred and what is burdening our load on an emotional, physical and spiritual level. As we exit the lodge, we fall exhausted upon the earth like newborn babies: crying with joy, limp, wet and covered in mud, the blood of our Earth Mother. We are reborn and so deeply humbled by the magnitude of the experience that life is never the same again. The Sweat Lodge reconnects us to Spirit – the Grandmothers, the Grandfathers, Creation, Great Mystery, our spirit and the Spirit in everything. Everything with a life-force is a reminder of Spirit. Everything with a life-force is Spirit. Sweat Lodge affords the powerful ability to bring about profound change in the form of healing and personal growth, reconnecting us to the sacredness of the Earth Mother and her wisdom.

The drum echoes the pulse of the Earth Mother's heart. Its rhythm guides us to other dimensions, new opportunities and heightened levels of awareness. The steady beat of the drum offers clarity and awareness and the avoidance of tunnel vision. We are often so consumed by mental and spiritual activity that we tend to neglect the tangible world, our health and other responsibilities. The drum reminds us to tap into our inherent rhythms and to intuitively listen to what our body may be trying to tell us about our physical wellbeing. The drum reinstates a sense of emotional balance, buoyancy and stability. It helps us regain a solid foothold on life and rekindle the fire in our belly so that we can make practical but long-overdue decisions potent enough to instigate powerful new beginnings. The drum returns us to our centre; it refocuses intent and affords symbolic rebirth and renewal. It reveals our potential gifts of power, while tempering arrogance and self-importance with the grounding influence of the Earth Mother's wisdom. The drum stabilises our emotional body and heals physical imbalance by tapping into our DNA, retrieving our sense of identity and personal truth. The drum's beat is reminiscent of the double heartbeat all children hear while in the womb. The power of this sound is realised audibly and vibrationally, thus realigning us on a united heart-felt level. The drum reawakens ancient knowledge stored in the memory of all people. It nurtures us as we seek the wisdom held in store, to be remembered when we re-embrace the heartbeat of our Earth Mother. It teaches us to interpret the sacred sound frequencies that nurture memories of ancient knowledge and how to reconnect with universal consciousness so that we may again, one day, walk as one.

To create a drum, you will need to purchase a Goat or Deer rawhide, which will be used for both the 'face' of the drum and the thonging, a drum frame (either round or octagonal) or traditional size (an adult-sized frame should be at approximately 42 cm across, while a child's frame is usually only around 30.5 cm across. You may need to seek the assistance of an experienced carpenter or someone who is comfortable working with timber), a cardboard template (required to determine the size and shape of the drum face and the location of the thonging or lacing holes. The template needs to be around 10 cm wider in diameter than the drum frame), a square of red cotton fabric (which will be used to create a prayer tie to be tied inside the drum), scissors, a bucket, two bath towels, a rock or heavy crystal (used to keep the drum face and thonging submerged during the soaking process), a pinch of tobacco and a pinch of sage (which will be used in the prayer tie), a pen and pad, a hammer and a leather hole punch.

To begin, place the template on the hide, making sure to position it as close to the edge and as near the end as possible to minimise waste. Use the pen to mark around the edge of the template and to indicate the location of the punch-hole marks. With the scissors, cut out the Drum face and use the hammer and the leather punch to cut the lacing holes. Using the scissors again, start at the edge of the hide and cut in coil fashion, a continual strip 1cm wide but as long as possible. Keep circling around the hide until there is nothing left and, in its place, there is a healthy pile of thonging. Place the drum face and dry thonging into the bucket and fill with water. Place the rock or heavy crystal into the bucket, so that the hide remains submerged. Allow the hide to soak for 24 hours. It is encouraged for the drum maker to place items of personal value into the bucket, such as jewellery or crystals as it is believed that their energy will be absorbed by the hide, facilitating a firmer bond between the crafter and the drum on a deeply spiritual level. Next, compose a prayer of thanks to the tree and animal that gave of their life so that this sacred drum may be birthed. Write from the heart and consider it a message intended for Spirit's eyes only. Should anyone see it and mock it later, however, understand the prayer itself was never the motivation for their scorn, but rather their own fear, ignorance and naivety. Once complete, rewrite the composition inside the frame of the drum. It can be written in any fashion and of any size.

Lay one towel on the floor, and then lay the (now wet) raw hide drum face (face down) in the centre of the towel. Place the drum frame in the centre of the drum face and lay the overlapping edges over the rim of the frame. Use the other towel to gently dab the thonging so that it is touch dry. If it is dripping wet it can get messy, but don't let it get too dry either. Take one end of the (wet/damp) thonging and thread it through any one of the lace holes and again through the hole directly opposite the first hole threaded. Thread the thonging through and then stand up. Holding the original end in one hand, allow the other end to run through your other hand until you can hold your arms above your head. Cut the other end of the thonging now, so that you have a length of thonging threaded through your drum face with an end in each hand above your head. Place the leftover length back on the floor (or in your empty bucket). Now, go back to the two holes just threaded up, and twist the lacing between the two holes so that it looks like cord and not just a flat piece of wet rawhide. Continue to twist the thonging beyond the holes and bring the lacing back into the centre between the two holes and tie it off with a loose knot. It does not have to be taut, just tight enough so that it does not sag. So, basically, you should now have thonging between two opposite facing holes laced together with twisted lacing that should be knotted in the middle. If the drum is laced up too tightly, it may snap the thonging as it dries and retracts. Imagine your first lacing went from east to west. Repeat the above points through the holes in the north through to the south. Ensure that the holes are directly opposite one another. Continue the lacing and twisting procedure through the north-east holes through to the south- west, and so on until all the holes are laced together. Should you run out of lacing, tie off and continue on as before. Even if the knots appear loose, once the hide has dried, they will never come undone. Rawhide dries rock hard! Bind the centre of the lacing together (where all the central knots are), keeping it tight and neat. It should look like a giant star or the centre of a Spider's web.

Now that you have completed the lacing of the drum, it is time to bind the lacing together to form the handle. Look at the back of the drum, and take special notice of the laces leading out from the centre of the drum to the edge of the hide. Imagine the top of the drum facing the north, the bottom facing the south, the right facing the east and the left facing the west. What you have to do next is evenly distribute the laces leading out between these four directions. This can be done by counting or using your eye as judgement. Once you have determined how many laces will be distributed to each direction, take the laces allocated to the north section, and tie a length of rawhide thonging to the base (the end closest to the central knots in the middle of the drum). Grasp these laces in your non-writing hand. With your other hand, begin binding them tightly with the thonging until you are three quarters of the way to the end. It should look like a thickly bound stem with several 'branches' sticking out of the top. Continue this procedure for the other three directions. Remember, it is traditional for all knotting to be done in groups of four. No single knots (except in times where any more is impossible due to lack of length, etc.) should be left, without finishing off with a further three. The number four is sacred, as it represents the four races of man, the four directions, the four elements, the four seasons, and so on. You must now massage all the wrinkles from the edge of the drum frame. The sides and all edges must be smooth and free of wrinkles, bumps and crimps. Turn the drum upside down, and using your thumbs, work the wrinkles out towards the lacing side of the drum with firm, even strokes. Your drum is now complete.

Cut off any loose ends, and allow the hide to dry for one to four weeks. Do not be tempted to use it until it is completely dry, as this may damage the drum forever. You may want to make a beater, and this can be done by binding a round piece of leather stuffed with wadding onto a stick taken from your favourite tree, some driftwood or a length of doweling. If you choose to paint your drum, it is advisable to use oil-based paint, as it bonds with the natural oils in the hide and will not crack off, as acrylic or water - based paint will tend to do. Keep in mind though, that oil paint takes several days to dry, so don't think its slow drying is because of something you have done wrong. A prayer tie is traditionally bound to one of the laces on the back of the drum as a way of keeping the drum safe and your intent and reasons for using the drum pure. A prayer tie is simply a red square of cotton fabric tied up to form a pouch in which tobacco, a sacred herb of prayer, and sage is placed. The prayer tie is usually tied to the drum using green thread (embroidery cotton will do). Some people make carry bags to keep their drum in. This way the drum and the beater can be carried together, lessening the chance of it being knocked and damaged. Some people place sage, lavender, sweet grass or even cedar in these bags to ensure the safety of their drum on a spiritual level.

The drum is an ancient tool powerful enough to reinstate a sense of direction, focus and healing within the Warrior Child. When held over the body during times of crisis and repeatedly struck with the padded beater, for example, the rhythmic, comforting sound produced will effectively deliver him or her into a relaxed, peaceful state, inspiring a productive release of emotion; a release that will initiate communication and surrender of all anger, resentment and frustration.

While all these suggestions will certainly bring about profound change within the Warrior Child, making a pact with the self (and sticking to it) is the most powerful step any Warrior Child can take, especially when they have not alerted anyone to the fact that such a decision has been made. The law of attraction brings to us the things that we resonate best with, while the law of reflection shows us the things we need to address in our life by putting it in our face via an external source. Attitude, therefore, can either make or break a Warrior Child's spirit. Unfortunately, this is a step your child must decide to take for themselves. All the encouragement or coercion on your part will make little or no difference to the Warrior Child; in fact, it will only encourage them to dig their heels in deeper, thus slowing the healing / growing process down even more.

2

The Black & White Colobus Monkey

Totem of the Winter Child
Keynotes: Martyr / Logician / Problem Solver

The beautiful glossy black coat of the Black and White Colobus Monkey, or Guereza, contrasts with the long white mantle that runs down the full length of each side of the its body. Black and White Colobus Monkeys also have luxuriously long tail-tufts. Forest dwellers, these Monkeys spend much of their time hidden high in the canopy, blending in with the dappled sunlight that forms both the light and shadows of the forest. The blatant dissimilarity between the black and white of the Monkey's fur against the green foliage of the forest creates a powerful form of camouflage known as disruptive colouration: the illusion that the animal is not there despite its obvious presence. There is also a plain black variety of Colobus Monkey (*Colobus Satanas*), which has grey skin and a naked face, and a form known as the Red Colobus, *Piliocolobus pennanti*, which has rusty brown fur, black head, white ruff and white underparts. Led by a dominant male in a clearly defined territory, Black and White Colobus Monkeys travel in troops made up of several family groups, but totalling anything up to 200 individuals.

All Black and White Colobus Monkey people are hardworking and loyal; meticulous in everything they do. Most are intelligent, methodical and determined in their approach. Intense and overly solemn at times, Black and White Colobus Monkey people are sympathetic toward others and are capable of achieving admirable levels of personal greatness (when they remain focused and driven) because they are complimentary, affable and helpful. Black and White Colobus Monkey people love working with their hands, being both artistic and musical. They have analytical minds and love to figure things out. They need to be needed and respond favourably to praise, and when acknowledged for their high level of skill, they are idealistic, sensitive and reliable. Black and White Colobus Monkey people are romantics at heart — helpful, encouraging and systematic. When encouraged and entrusted with responsibility, they are organised, economical and cautious with money. Black and White Colobus Monkey people are trustworthy, loyal and make good listeners, particularly when the favour is reciprocated. Their empathy makes them effective problem solvers and mediators, despite being overly emotional at times (bordering on being 'drama queens' when backed into a corner).

In the shadow times Black and White Colobus Monkey people can appear negative on first meeting. They suffer from moodiness and unpredictable bouts of depression. They will self-condemn for attention, may seem blatantly self-sabotaging and often have low self-esteem and poor self-image. Black and White Colobus Monkey people will self-punish when they feel they are failing, are threatened or overlooked. They intentionally do things they know they shouldn't (they seem to love being growled at, for example, almost espousing the erroneous belief that 'negative attention is better than no attention at all'). They readily skate on thin ice and tempt fate with an almost wilful abuse of their health, relationships and other responsibilities.

So, Black and White Colobus Monkey people will, on occasion, come across as being arrogant, vague and, at times, unapproachable. They suffer from selective hearing and can be morose, needy and selfish. They fluster easily and have quick tempers, drawing on petty argument to almost bully their way through confronting situations. They will also stretch the truth and make weak excuses to superficially cover up their shortcomings, when backed into a corner. They like to get their own way and will readily display childish behaviour to gain control or make a point, in which case tantrums are never out of the question. They externalise blame, deny responsibility and show signs of hypochondria.

Individual advice for the Black & White Colobus Monkey / Winter Child

Correspondences:

Esoteric Element: Earth

Elemental Instruments: Percussion instruments, such as the drum and hitting sticks

Elemental Spirits: Gnomes, Dwarfs and Trolls, Earth Dragons, Centaurs

Season: Winter

Time of Power: Midnight

Symbolic Phase of Life on the Wheel of Life: The Elder / Wise One / Crone / Sage / Teacher / Grandmother / Grandfather

Power Places: Mountains, open plains, fields, caves and mines

Zodiacs as per the Corresponding Esoteric Element: Taurus, Virgo and Capricorn

Direction: South in Southern Hemisphere / North in Northern Hemisphere

Directional Colours: White, green, brown

Organs: Spleen, stomach

Chakras: Sacral (second), Solar Plexus (third)

Chakra Colours: Yellow, orange, ochre

Crystals: Pyrite, malachite, carnelian, citrine, brown, ochre and red-coloured jasper, yellow calcite, rock salt, coal, diamonds, peridot, iron and lead

Totems: Black and White Colobus Monkeys, Wolverines, White Horses, Kangaroos, the Emu, Bulls, Bison, Stags, Dogs, Ants, Polar Bears and White Wolves

Herbs: Benzoin, comfrey, ivy, grains, oats, rice, rye, wheat, patchouli, vetiver, moss, lichen, nuts, roots, acorns and oak trees

The principle idea of the Winter Child's journey is to transform impracticality (stubbornness, obsession and arrogance) into realism and function (flexibility, consideration and protection).

Winter Children are the guardians, the facts-oriented logicians. They can come across as martyrs, but nonetheless, are expert problem solvers and proficient leaders when made to feel important. They are traditional in approach, yet encouraging and doting in nature. They tend to lack peripheral vision, trusting in what they know and believe to be true above the 'fancies' or ideas of others. Like the season itself, Winter Children are reflective and contemplative, reclusive and retiring. All Winter Children are extremely serious and matter-of-fact in attitude. When they believe themselves to be unappreciated, however, Winter Children appear 'heavy' and stuck. They become aloof, cynical and despondent, irritable and resentful. They seem to shut themselves off to everyone and everything around them, closing the door on the beauty that surrounds them, while silently punishing those who love them. They make sarcastic comments, while superficially hiding them under a veil of forced humour. They resort to a submissive, irresolute attitude, their movements become deliberate, self-conscious and attention-seeking. When working in their shadow, Winter Children are distrustful and prone to immaturity, melancholy, depression and revenge. Some will go as far as getting themselves into trouble by intentionally doing the wrong thing or sabotaging important responsibilities in a perverse attempt to regain attention. Being reprimanded makes them feel worthy, somehow; recognised again, as part of the team. Winter Children only ever see the negative in a situation, feel cut off from the divine and are openly incensed by what they perceive as injustice and deceit.

To move to the positive phase, Winter Children must get active by participating in physical activity, be it only low impact or recreational in nature, or some other interest that inspires them and draws attention away from their everyday lives. Winter Children do a lot of thinking, but not in a scholarly way. They watch and think on a gut-felt level. And this is where they come unstuck if they have nothing else to occupy their time or stimulate their gut feelings in a productive way. Often coming from nothing or born into families of low income and matching expectation, Winter Children are secretly envious and resentful of achievers and those seemingly 'born with silver spoons in their mouths'. Winter Children are quite materialistic, and so love nothing better than shopping. They love eBay and Internet stores, television shopping channels, garage sales, factory outlets and discount bins. They always have their eyes peeled for a bargain and will purchase things they don't need 'for later', 'just in case', because they are the hoarders, misers and squirrels who cache stuff for later. Winter Children will do what they can to make a dollar. As adults, they often have their fingers in many pies at once, doing as much as possible to create a good, residual income, but often choosing things that never pay out. Winter Children are dreamers and, in rare cases, gamblers. They see opportunity in most things, but generally hate taking risks that may fail. They hold great potential within their hearts, but honestly have no idea how to access it. Winter Children can be generous to a fault. They can't say no, and because of this, often find themselves in situations hard to back out of. They hate letting people down, especially those not closely related or of their immediate family. Unafraid of hard work, they are always on the lookout for an easier alternative, repeatedly investing in get rich quick schemes only to discover soon after they have been conned — again. They are the providers and the protectors, and so despise being 'have nots', especially when forced to serve the 'haves', and so, in their desperate bid to become one of the 'haves', they can become distressed and hard on themselves. During their darkest hours, Winter Children panic and become desperate, transforming into neglectful parents and rancorous friends and partners, often losing everything and winning it back time and again in a frantic attempt to achieve, expand and grow.

In order to access and celebrate their potential, Winter Children must first find meaning and purpose for their existence by connecting with the divine and by acting as a true benefactor for humanity. As children, they need to be given responsibilities that make them feel wanted, needed and special. Schoolteachers would see an incredible improvement in behaviour, for example, by simply giving the Winter Children in their class the trusted roles of responsibility. Taking the attendance roll to the office after it has been called each morning, for example, or collecting and dispensing the lunch orders prepared by the school canteen, or simply cleaning the blackboard at the end of the day are simple ways of bringing out the best in the Winter Child. They love spreading paper out on art room tables, checking books out for those borrowing from the library and being the one in charge of locking and unlocking the bike shed before and after school. So long as they feel appreciated, Winter Children remain as compliant as soft putty in the palm of your hand. It is handy to know, however, that Winter Children are no good at rebel rousing. They are not great at firing people up or inspiring them to reach a place of greatness. That is a role best left to the Warrior Child. Warrior Children are excellent at inspiring people to the point where they become excited, motivated and ready to do something great. But then they lose interest. Warrior Children are great inspirers but hopeless leaders. They don't care what people do with their newfound passion, so long as they find it. Winter Children, on the other hand, are excellent leaders. They are the ground workers and the providers — the ones on the same level as the 'ordinary folk'. They are fully equipped to step in (often with the help of a Peacekeeper Child) and bring the roused mob together and channel them into productive action, and they do so with dexterity and calm. Although they make proficient leaders and role models, they do best when they have someone to look to or an example to follow. Superb chiefs and principals, Winter Children need guidance and direction. When they know what is expected of them, they excel in their role. However, they are poor initiators, so do best when they are able to follow an instituted master plan. When they have a blueprint to follow, they proudly show others the way in a grounded, matter-of-fact way. Consequently, in order to channel their energy productively, Winter Children are best nominated as team-leader or captain, but never the coach.

As they grow, Winter Children must find the one thing they are passionate about and stick to it, so that when they become adults they can easily transform what was once a hobby into a profitable career.

Despite the fact that I am a Warrior Child, some aspects of my persona reflect distinct Winter Child traits. Nearly ten years ago, for example, my wife and I were at our friend Susan's house. I had recently resigned from teaching and was at a crossroad in life. I didn't know where I was supposed to be heading or what I was supposed to be doing — all I was certain of was that I had a wife and a child and no paying job to support them with. During dinner, Susan said, "When I ask you what you want to do with your life, what is the one vision you see in your mind's eye?" I sat and pondered whether I should tell her or not, and then said, "I see myself sitting in a small cottage making things, with people coming to me for help and advice." Now it so happened, tragically, that my friend's husband had died some time before and she had been wondering what to invest his life-insurance money into.

She wanted it to be used for something significant, something that would become a legacy for her children.

On hearing my vision, she announced that she had decided a cottage was something worthwhile, a good investment and something that would honour the memory of her husband and his life. So she bought that cottage and we decked it out to incorporate a meditation room, several consulting rooms and a little shop that stocked tarot cards, crystals, candles and incense — things typical of a spiritually oriented business. We worked the cottage as a healing centre and called it Circle of Stones. Eighteen months later, however, we had outgrown the cottage to the point where we were ready to take the plunge and move to a shopfront location in a major tourist town. I had run workshops, spiritual development circles and had offered personal readings through the cottage, and they lifted to a whole new level when we moved to our new location. The shop took off straight away. It was well received by the tourists who visited our town and the locals who had never had a shop like ours in their business district before. Being positioned in a traditional Seventh-day Adventist town, we figured a business like ours would raise a few eyebrows (and we were not wrong), but despite placing a figurative Cat among the Pigeons, our business boomed. Because of the animal medicine workshops I ran in the space 'out the back' and the popularity of my animal card readings, my reputation as an animal spirit oracle began to spread in a favourable way, especially when people realised that I was able to see animal spirits with the people I read for. The weird thing was, even though I could see the animal spirits and I knew why they appeared with my clients, I persisted with reading the cards and only mentioned the animals I saw near the end of the readings I gave. I don't know why I had been paying so little heed to them, except that I was perhaps so used to them being there I had understated their power, or perhaps I was subconsciously worried about how people would respond if I suddenly dumped the cards in their favour.

Then one day (and I cannot remember what triggered me to do it), I decided to put the cards aside and purely rely on the animals I saw and the messages I received in order to deliver the readings I had booked in. To my surprise, my readings were not only easier to give, the messages were far more accurate and to the point. I was also able to offer more than the normal three or four, and I was not left exhausted at the end of the day. I realised that because I was working with Spirit and not resisting my inherent ability to translate the symbols I was being shown, everything had become 'easier'. After that day, my reputation exploded and I was booked out weeks in advance because I was unique, accurate, and, more importantly, living my purpose.

Around this time another friend, Roz, had been pleading with me to compile a basic list of 'common' Australian animals that included their spiritual meanings. She thought a simple chart would be a good idea, something that people could refer to when they needed help interpreting the symbology of the animals they encountered. I took her advice, and started writing the chart. It was fun, but I had difficulty limiting the animals to what was considered 'common'. By the time I had finished, therefore, I had a healthy list of over 200 animals, and instead of a simple chart, I ended up with a self-published book. I called it *Animal Dreaming*. The book was taken up by a major distributor and was well received throughout Australia. It received favourable reviews by most of Australia's new age and spiritual magazines, as well as a few international ones. It saw me being interviewed on television and on radio and appear as a guest speaker at some of the biggest spiritual fairs in the country. Most fantastic of all, however, was when it afforded me the chance to be offered a publishing deal with New Holland when they asked if I could expand it to include animals from all over the world. That book I called *Animal Messenger*, which was followed closely by this one.

So you see, my practical, earthy, Colobus Monkey aspect had simply been waiting for someone peripheral to my everyday life to ask about me and invest energy into the answer I gave. Although my wife had nurtured me and provided the forum for me to heal and learn about myself, she couldn't lift me to that next level. I knew she loved me unconditionally, and that she always would. And that, I guess, was the problem. My wife was too close, so I couldn't hear what she was saying or see what she was showing me. I needed someone separate to quiz me and dare me to do more. The moment someone respected shows belief in their natural born abilities and throws a guiding light on their path, Winter Children usually honour the process and do what needs to be done to hone their skills and present them to the world in a productive way. They simply need to have their vision for the future confirmed or their belief in themselves established on a tangible level before they grant their visions any real worth.

Winter Children must learn to trust their ability to turn the ordinary, uninteresting, routine aspects of their life into veritable pots of gold. Most Winter Children unwittingly carry the 'alchemist' or 'Midas' archetype, a trait that promises to literally turn everything they touch to gold, so long as they believe in their self-worth and their place in the greater scheme of things. The only thing preventing them from realising their potential (in most cases) is the tedious, resentful, fearful streak that runs through their nature, and their inability to believe in things they cannot physically see or things wished for but not yet brought to reality. To move into their positive phase, therefore, Winter Children must work hard, stay focused and never be afraid to spend money to make money. They must see their role as making a difference to the world and constantly ask themselves, "What skills do I possess that may help to transform the planet?" and to see their potential as lying dormant under the snow-covered Earth's surface, waiting to burst through to benefit the people when the time is right.

As adults, Winter Children will often pair up with Peacekeeper Children or other Winter Children with whom they often produce Nature Children (although there are always exceptions). They do not get along with Warrior Children. They tend to lock horns on first meeting for no obvious reason. And many don't understand Golden Children at all, labelling them as weird and scary.

As per the Four Humours: the Melancholic

Melancholics can be pessimistic, seeing only the negative in a situation. They appear temperamental and disheartened, displaying the defeatist traits of the classic dark horse. They seem to enjoy being hurt, persistently putting themselves in the line of fire over and over again. Melancholics are said to display feigned modesty and to live in a fantasy world. They suffer from low self-esteem, selective hearing and feelings of guilt and shame.
They can be selfish and brooding and believe themselves to be constantly discriminated against. Many are hypochondriacs.

But when working in their positive phase, Melancholics can be profound and sympathetic. They make methodical leaders, although appearing solemn and overly determined. Being intellectually brilliant, many are classified as 'gifted' or bordering on genius. They are imaginative and creative, truth-seeking and prosaic, enjoying nothing better than surrounding themselves with things of rarity and beauty. Melancholics are insightful and sensitive, altruistic, diligent and, at times, a little naïve.

Activity and productive work are helpful, so long as they inspire the Melancholic to only ever look on the bright side of things, hence the need, according to the philosophy advocating the Four Humours, for the Melancholic to be given the chance to be 'warmed and moistened or lubricated' in order to reach their potential. Positive affirmations can be helpful especially when they are prepared to accept difficulty and pain, but refuse to surrender to it, and when they are prepared to make an effort. Melancholics need to know that one person can genuinely make a difference to the world no matter how modest they are. They do well to avoid media stories and news that focuses on the misfortunes of others or problems facing the world. Instead, Melancholics should seek out inspirational success stories, stories that convey motivational 'rags to riches' scenarios such as the life-narratives of celebrities like Mark Wahlberg, Oprah Winfrey, Madonna and others.

As per the Five Esoteric Elements: Earth

According to the teachings of Ancient Earth wisdom, we symbolically visit the south on the Wheel of Life as a Grandmother or a Grandfather; an elder with much knowledge to share and wisdom to pass down to the younger members of the family. The south speaks of the wisdom, abundance, prosperity and wealth offered by the earth element. It is stable, solid and dependable and is seen as the place of the greatest darkness, as is winter, the season energetically associated with the south. During winter, the veils between the worlds are at their thinnest. It is a time of great transformation. The seeds shed during the fertile months lay germinating under the seemingly dormant, frozen, barren ground, preparing to burst through the surface as the crops of the new season, thus completing the Great Cycle of Life, of birth, death and rebirth. The goddess is in her Crone stage, when she realises her purpose and is able to understand better the complexities of life with the attainment of wisdom and experience. The lessons had during winter leave us complete and whole, with nothing left to do but return to the east and the freshness of spring, to start life over. We 'shed our robes' as an elder in winter, to be reborn as an infant in the spring, ready to relearn life's lessons all over or to 'polish up' on those learned last time round.

Winter is both feminine and receptive in nature, as is the earth element, the force that rules the zodiacal signs of Taurus, Virgo and Capricorn. The earth element teaches those ready to listen the lessons of personal and physical growth and the surrendering of will, of sustenance, prosperity and abundance; of creativity, fertility, birth, and death, inner silence, compassion and stability, success, healing and strength, all of which are lessons of maturity and wisdom often learnt best through experience, hardship and, at times, loss. At winter's end, we emerge from quiescence to rejoice and start again. Winter Children, it becomes clear, seem to embody a lot of the same qualities as their namesake, being gentle, appealing, nurturing and contemplative on one hand and unforgiving, bitter, punishing and relentless on the other.

Earth people are grounded, practical and unpretentious. They are reliable and solid, steady and focused. They need to be organised, but they aren't always rational in their approach. Earth people are the motherly carers, the plodders and the ones happy to stay at home and tend to the domestic chores: cooking, cleaning, washing, ironing, gardening and acting as veritable taxis for sports-mad kids and pub-visiting partners. So long as they *feel* safe, loved and needed, they are able to operate effectively, but the moment they feel unsafe or unappreciated, they freeze up and emotionally fall apart. People of the earth element tend to make decisions based on gut feelings, following hunches and listening to their most basic instincts and by making educated guesses rather than thinking things through in a logical, rational manner. When things don't go to plan, earth people quickly collapse in a heap. They tend to be over-reactors, the drama queens and the ones often accused of living in denial.

Earth element people are often slaves to their physical senses. They seem to live for things best described as earthly pleasures: all things beautiful and delicious — good food, fine wine, enchanting music and intoxicating flavours. They are constantly seeking things that bring pleasure, from aesthetically agreeable works of art to sex and physical intimacy. 'Indulgence' is the key word for all earth element people, with most falling into one of two categories: the gourmets and the gourmands — the gourmets preferring to eat a little a lot of the time, dining only on the finest of produce in restaurants known to be the best of the best. The gourmands, however, would rather eat a lot of anything at any given opportunity. They are the gluttons (the ones working primarily from the shadow phase of their element) who prefer to make junk food bought from fast food outlets the staple aspect of their diet, the whole time deliberately ignoring the strain such a regime puts on their health. As a result, many earth people are overweight or suffer from weight related conditions, tending to gain weight quickly while taking ages to lose it.

Whenever I think of earth people who choose to operate principally (for whatever reason) from their shadow side, I am reminded of the Wolverine, or Skunk Bear; the rarest member of the Weasel family; an animal known for its tenacity and determination that aggressively defends its freedom. They are found in high elevation forests and alpine regions, enjoying a life of solitude and isolation. Wolverines are adept tree climbers and will eat just about anything, from fruit to carrion. Their Latin name is *Gulo gulo*, which means 'glutton'. All members of the Weasel family have large appetites. The Wolverine is no exception. They protect their cache by marking it with a musky odour immediately recognised by other carnivores. With a stocky build, the ferocious dog-like Wolverine powerfully protects its territory against intruders. Once a Wolverine identifies a regular source of food (even if it only yields once a year), it will visit that source again and again until exhausted of resources. A Wolverine that discovers a berry patch, Salmon spawning bed or Elk calving ground, for example, and returns each year, is likely to remain well fed. Names like 'devil bear', 'demon of the north' and 'evil one' have helped confirm the malevolent reputation of the Wolverine as an uncompromising scavenger. Wolverines are completely intolerant of humans ... and Wolves. They depend solely on the wilderness for their survival, and anything that threatens that way of life creates chaos in their world. Sensitive to the encroachment of roads, tracks, agricultural pursuits, deforestation, oil and gas exploration and basic recreational activities, the female Wolverine has been known to move her den five kilometres away after being disturbed by the one-time passing of a single skier.

To appeal to the sympathetic, productive qualities of the earth element, earth people should look to the energy that can be raised via ritualistic dance, rhythmic drumming and trance evoking chants and mantras. They should spend time alone in the wilderness and connect to the ancient energy that is the Earth Mother by going caving, hiking and camping in the bush. Many benefit personally by seeking the advice of a respected elder or by apprenticing themselves to a Wise One or Medicine Teacher. Earth people need to get their hands dirty by designing and planting a vegetable garden or herb plot. Many tend to take things further by studying naturopathy or medicinal or esoteric herbalism. The dominant colours associated with the earth element are those reminiscent of the Earth Mother herself and those inspired by the mountains, forests and valleys: ochre, ox-blood red, mustard yellow, rusted or burnt orange, chestnut brown and auburn, olive green and white (as in the colour of snow). Therefore, it can be therapeutic for the earth person to wear these colours due to their grounding, earthy, practical qualities and their nurturing, warming implications.

A Guided Visualisation that explores the Earth Element:

Find yourself a comfy place where you know you will not be interrupted. If possible, find a place in nature. Sit with your back supported by the trunk of a tree, a smooth rock or a mossy log. Sit with the intention of strengthening your bond with Spirit and of remembering your inherent relationship with the Earth Mother. You may want to wrap yourself in a blanket, because it is not uncommon for one's body temperature to drop as you sink deeper and deeper into stillness. Quiet your conscious mind and endeavour to silence your inner chatter. Wait for the moment when you intuitively feel inclined to open your consciousness to the Other Realms. Ensure that your subconscious mind is receptive and alert by speaking to your conscious mind. Allow visions and symbolic images to float through your mind. Keep your focus within yourself. Let any thoughts just go by. When you catch yourself engaged in an external conscious thought, take a deep breath and bring yourself back to your centre.

You are now ready to begin.

Visualise yourself standing in an open field. From where you are standing you can see two very different sights. To your right is a path leading up to a steep mountain peak and to your left is a path leading down into a deep valley. The point at which you are standing is in fact the intersection of time and reality. A mingling point of reality and 'the Other Worlds'; of the physical and the mystical, it is where the miraculous can be found in the silence.

Visualise yourself taking the left path as it leads down into the deep valley. The path leads you to the south, the place of the greatest darkness. When we journey to the south we must learn to weigh and measure our growth and progress in order to step out of our physical confines, and to evolve. It is in the south, the direction ruled by the earth element, that we apply the knowledge that we have gathered, as well as receive deeper wisdom. We combine sacred wisdom with practical wisdom to enhance our journey. We are walking the path of one who has reached advanced age — the wise elder — the wisdom keeper of the people.

It is midnight, and winter is upon you. The mountain towering above the valley is thick with snow, but in the valley the giant redwoods and oak trees are dripping with dew and the icy air is dense with fog. From where you are standing it is difficult to make out the market gardens and nurseries that fill the valley, let alone the surrounding forests, farms and fields planted out with grains, oats, rice, rye and wheat, due to the darkness, but the lights from the cottage windows glimmer through the mist like honey-coloured crystals.

Boreas, the wind that springs from the darkness of winter, whistles through the trees, chilling even the warmest heart to the core, heralding the death of outworn modes of thinking, old habits and things no longer needed in preparation for the new birth and re-growth of spring. You walk until you come to a great circle of ivy-covered standing stones. This is a sacred place; a place of hallowed knowledge, teaching and learning, ritual and truth. It is a place of the ancients.

As you walk into the centre of the moss-lined stone circle, you feel the ground trembling, and right in front of you, the earth cracks and opens up, revealing a deep crevice that leads down into a huge gold mine. The sound of hammering and voices shouting directions drift up through the ravine, riding on the back of billowing clouds of dust and warm air. You look down into the gaping hole, and consider what might be down there. You hear a sound behind you, and you turn to see a woman on a white Horse with eyes as green as peridot standing next to a queer looking creature, who appears to be half man and half Goat. He has the torso of a man, but the shaggy legs and cloven hooves of a Goat, with two little horns sticking out of his forehead and a shaggy beard on his chin. He notices your stare, and introduces himself as Pan, the god of the woodlands and domestic animals. He is a deity of the earth, representing all that is masculine. The lady on the Horse now speaks up and informs you that she is Rhiannon, the protector of animals, and, like Pan, a deity of the earth, but representing everything feminine. She dismounts and offers you her Horse. You accept, knowing that with the invitation is the expectation that you are to enter the ravine and explore its depths. You hesitantly look down the hole again, and return your gaze back to Rhiannon and Pan, but they are gone. The Horse speaks, reassuring you that their essence will travel with you, protecting you from harm.

You hear the sound of drums, the heartbeat of Mother Earth, as you begin your descent into the nadir. To your surprise, a path has been prepared, making your journey easier. You notice, too, that with the gift of the Horse came a new wardrobe. Your attire consists of a green velvet tunic with gold trim and brown leggings. On your head is a black skullcap with a violet Ostrich feather sticking out. You are dressed in colours that represent the earth element, and have been gifted with them so that you may be welcomed by the spirit creatures that reside within her. Three beings approach you, in greeting. They are dressed in olive green tunics with ochre-coloured leggings. On their heads they too are wearing black skullcaps, but with no feathers. Their faces are covered in grime, for they have been working the mines in search of gold, coal, iron and lead. They extend their hands, and you notice that one is carrying a gold pentagram, one is carrying a pouch of salt, and the other is holding a handful of precious gems — rubies, emeralds and diamonds. They are gnomes, elemental spirits of the earth, sent by Ariel (Uriel), archangel of the earth, keeper of sacred wisdom, Ghob, servant to Ariel and guide of all earth journeys, and Agla the elemental king of the earth. Their world is fertile, moist and nurturing, stabilising and grounding. Gravity is a manifestation of the earth element. It is feminine and receptive in nature, filled with the promise of prosperity if one is prepared to use one's energies for material growth. The gnomes invite you to enter their world, and to share in their secrets. They turn, and each mount a Pony that had until now been out of your range of vision. One Pony is black, one is chestnut and the third is golden in colour. With your white steed, you realise the four colours of the medicine wheel have been honoured, and that you have begun a sacred journey of learning. You all turn and trot off at a steady pace into the darkness of the Earth Mother's heart — the womb of all Creation.

The first thing you notice is that the drumming sound you heard earlier has eased into a steady, metrical rhythm, which has a very soothing, grounding effect on you. They lead you past great airy caves, water filled canyons, fiery chasms, lushly forested groves, leafy arboretums, wind swept parks, dank mines, and lava filled holes and subterranean mountains. You realise that all the elemental spirits find refuge here, the Earth is Mother to all, and that without her, the other elements would not exist; they would have no grounding, no purpose and no stability.

The scent of myrrh, sagebrush and patchouli fills your nostrils, and you notice that these herbs grow wild down here. They are herbs sacred to the earth, and carry with them the vibrational energies of abundance, materialism and prosperity.

The gnomes lead you into a great jade lined cave that is decked out for a banquet. A massive oak table, covered in red velvet and scatterings of onyx plates and clay bowls, filled with mushrooms, lichens, nuts and root vegetables stands in the centre of the room. Meat roasts on a spit over a huge fire, and Deer antlers and Bull horns decorate the walls. A Dog and a Badger crouch under the table, waiting for any titbit that may happen to fall from the forks of the feasting guests. The floor is covered in layers of comfrey and Bison skins and the air is thick with the smoke from the many sticks of burning benzoin incense.

The walls, decorated with works of art depicting images of various forms of shamanic studies, sweat lodge, people taking woodland walks, mountain hikes and cave explorations, seem to speak to you on a vibrational level. Their spiritual qualities seem to resonate with you, and as you watch, begin to writhe and throb, as if alive and pulsating with life-force. The feast stops, and the Dog begins to howl. Rhiannon and Pan enter the hall, and it is assumed that they wish to talk. They welcome you to their home, and begin to speak. They talk in a monotone voice, about many things: wisdom, practicality, symbols, ceremony, patience, responsibility, codes and authority.

The gnomes now face you, and, for the first time, speak. They speak in a tongue not unlike English, and it is pleasant to the ear. They speak of the need to respect one's body, of growth and the natural ways of things. They speak of material gain, of wealth, money and prosperity. They speak of structures, of bones, industry and business, of wisdom, fertility and employment, of stability, healing and possessions, and the need to combine them all with the forces of nature to harness its power and bounty — the gifts of Mother Earth intended for each of us equally. They show you, by example, as they sweep their arms in an arc, how simple hard work, determination, drive and passion can result in personal reward, material abundance, emotional security and spiritual strength. With this, the gnomes lead you back along the path that brought you to the hall, and back up to the surface. They leave you in the circle of standing stones, and return to their earthy world with the white Horse in tow. You feel empowered and symbolically richer for your experiences.

Make a silent prayer to Spirit for a reason sacred to you and to offer thanks, taking three breaths in through your nose and out through your mouth, and return to the physical place in which you are sitting.

As per Traditional Chinese Medicine: the Earth / Spleen Person

According to the teachings of Traditional Chinese Medicine, Winter Children, as 'spleen people', have their mind, body and energy systems focused on the earth element.

The spleen person has their dominant focus on digestion and nourishment, be it the digestion of experience and being nourished by this, bodily nourishment via the hormonal system, or the physical process of digestion, which feeds the body. At a bodily level, when this relationship is understood and the spleen person is working in harmony with his or her element, a greater level of wellbeing for the tissues related to the spleen is achieved, according to the teachings of Traditional Chinese Medicine: hearty digestive and hormonal systems, healthy blood, supple flesh, well-built arms and legs, a generous mouth and full, sensuous lips (the mouth being the point through which food is passed into the body). People with dynamic earth Qi are typically described as well grounded, caring and sympathetic. They love having friends over for dinner, taking pleasure in both the preparation of the food and its consumption.

When out of balance with their element, however, the spleen person develops obvious signs of fatigue, exhaustion and overall 'heaviness'. They may also endure diarrhoea, wind and bloating, obesity, oedema (fluid retention), growths, menacing sores, benign tumours and cysts, hormonal problems, chilliness, 'dampness', excess mucus production (especially in the lungs and sinuses), excessive sweating and moist skin, food allergies and sensitivities, eating disorders, heartburn and digestive problems. More serious problems may include heavy frequent periods (menorrhagia) and other menstrual complaints, ovarian cysts, endometriosis, candidiasis, infertility, diabetes, catarrhal disorders, 'wet' asthma, obsessive thinking, and stress. The spleen person typically slips out of balance due to dietary excess. Lovers of food and drink, an over indulgence in food containing high levels of sugar, salt, preservatives or food colourings, processed foods and cold foods will see the spleen person suffer. Prolonged periods of indolence or living in cold environments or damp houses may also aggravate the problem, as will living the life of a 'couch potato'.

When people have weak earth Qi, they can be fretful busybodies who often burn the midnight oil, especially when reading, doing research, cramming for an exam or other academic work. When they push their limits, they tend to become confused, weak, light-headed and incoherent. Minimising cold, raw foods and dairy products seems to benefit those suffering from weak earth Qi. Instead, they should include warming foods and grains in their diet — foods known to be both grounding and calming, while sweets containing processed sugars should be replaced with sweet tasting grains, vegetables and fruits. People with low earth Qi are prone to spleen deficiency, so boosting their spleen energy must be considered a priority. According to Traditional Chinese Medicine, the spleen is all about building and the process of digestion — both the digestion of food and the digestion of experience. To aid in the restoration of digestion and the proper circulation of fluids, the colours yellow and orange are healing. It is a simple rule of thumb, therefore, that prescribes the eating of yellow or orange foods: pumpkins, squash, oranges, lemons and ginger, for example.

Spleen people should avoid eating cold and damp-forming cuisine such as raw or cold foods, sweets and dairy foods. They should also avoid highly processed foods, choosing, instead warming foods that are easily digested, such as soups, stews and rice congee. Cooked squash, for example, carrots, sweet potato, turnips, leeks, onions, pumpkins, well-cooked soft rice and oats are all foods that should be consumed, as are butter, cooked peaches, cherries or strawberries, dried figs, custards, arrowroot, cardamom, ginger, cinnamon, nutmeg and black pepper. Sweeteners, such as honey, molasses, sugar, rice bran syrup, barley malt and maple syrup should only be eaten in moderate amounts, while small portions of chicken, turkey, mutton, beef and anchovies, are encouraged, especially when prepared as a broth or soup. Salads, citrus fruit and their juice, excess salt, tofu, undercooked grains, millet, buckwheat, milk, cheese, seaweed, agar, liquid foods and excessively sweet foods should be avoided, while warming spices are considered helpful: ginger, for example, and small amounts of pepper and chilli. Beetroot soup with a touch of pepper and chilli (better known as borscht) is excellent.

Like the Nature and Peacekeeper Children, Winter Children are also said to greatly increase their life-force by practising Qigong and Tai Chi and by embracing the benefits of both acupuncture and Hatha Yoga. Qigong refers to the combination of 'Qi' (air, breath, vital energy and life-force) and 'gong', the mastering of self-control and accomplishment. It incorporates meditation, relaxation, physical movement, mind/body integration and various breathing exercises. Acupuncture is deeply rooted in the belief that illness is caused when an imbalance is caused in the body's energy system. It is said to re-establish harmony by balancing the body's yin and yang. Acupuncture involves the painless insertion of fine needles into the body's meridians or energy channels (named after the organs they represent) to clear blocked Qi, releasing energy flow through the body. Hatha Yoga is all about uniting the mind and body by means of exercise, meditation, focused breathing, healthy attitude and meaningful posture, while Tai Chi offers us insight into an ancient Chinese art of movement. It is said to have been first created as a form of martial art, a form that inspires self-defence by emphasising stillness, inner balance and self-discipline. Today the flowing movements are practised as a holistic form of exercise designed to increase flexibility, body posture and balance and to return us to our innate place of ancient knowing and power. One Chinese herb known to boost spleen Qi is dong quai, a herb also used to treat gynaecological conditions and to strengthen the heart, liver and kidneys and as a tonic for the blood.

Regular steady physical exercise, like walking, swimming and cycling and low impact or recreational sports, like surf fishing, Horse trail-riding and hiking are all thought to strengthen the earth element, as is daily, disciplined (seated) meditation. Meditation is said to connect the mind and body with the spiritual aspect of self, as well as our creative side and the inherent healing abilities that exist within us all, and as such, is an effective way of boosting depleted earth Qi.

As per Ayurveda: Earth and Water Energy / Kapha

Kapha is the balancing force between water and earth. It represents composition and lubrication. It is the blending and binding element that helps keep water and earth from separating. When earth and water are mixed together and then left to their own devices, the earth will gradually sink to the bottom, thus extracting itself from the water. Kapha is the force that prevents this from happening. It binds the elements, thus providing for physical structure and endurance. Water is the main ingredient of Kapha; a vital component physiologically needed to ensure biological power and natural tissue vitality. 'Oily' in nature, Kapha is said to lubricate the joints, moisturise the skin, repair wounds, plug 'gaps' within the body, afford biological strength, vigour and solidity, enhance memory and provide extra energy to the heart and lungs, while helping to maintain good health and immunity.

Kapha people are generally more laid-back than other people, with a peaceful, unhurried attitude to most things. They are demonstrative and devoted toward their friends and family, and magnanimous, empathetic and permissive as parents. Overall, they are constant, dependable and loyal and approach life in a placid, calm, uncomplicated manner. They are docile, languid and charming. They speak with a drawn-out inflection, indicating a methodical, reflective mind. Energetic, balanced and lasting, Kapha people are usually physically powerful and with a brawny, thickset build. They have a healthy appetite, a sluggish digestive system and a predisposition to obesity. Kapha people have a propensity to suffer from grave, burdensome bouts of depression. They are patient and do not anger easily. Kapha people often fill the role of dependable 'rocks' for those around them. They appear more independent, needing less external motivation than the other types. It takes a long time for Kapha people to learn new skills, but once mastered, they never forget. They have an exceptional long-term memory, which can be annoying when they are owed money or when it comes time for them to call in favours. Kapha people can be possessive toward people, places and things — especially money. They have the potential to be wealthy. Once they find a way to earn good money, they are hesitant to let go of it. Typically, Kapha people display exceptional health and rarely become ill, however they don't like cold, damp weather because when they do get sick, they suffer from colds and congestion, sinus headaches, respiratory problems including asthma and wheezing, hay fever, allergies, and atherosclerosis (hardening of the arteries).

The golden rule with Kapha energy is to acknowledge the person's earthiness, stability, compassion and ability to nurture themselves and others. Vary their schedule every so often by changing their routine. Remember, variety is the spice of life. Never allow them to overeat and encourage them to partake in regular exercise (to help control weight, if nothing else) and associate with people, places and things that stimulate their mind. Hobbies are great, especially when they offer a variety of experiences that enhance recreation time. Kapha people need to preserve body warmth while remaining mindful of their level of 'dryness' and their intake of sweets. Elecampane and wild honey are known to pacify Kapha energy, while aromatherapy oils believed to soothe excessive Kapha energy include the warm spicy aromas of juniper, eucalyptus, camphor, clove and marjoram.

When addressing the diet, focus on bitter, pungent or astringent foods, warm light foods, dry foods and stimulating foods, while avoiding foods cooked in too much water, oily fatty or buttery foods and sugar. Eat plenty of apples, apricots, cranberries, mangoes, peaches, pears and pomegranates, vegetables in general, salads, light, dry foods and herbs and spices, such as black pepper, cardamom, cinnamon, clove, coriander, cumin, garlic, ginger, fennel and nutmeg; raw/natural honey, small amounts of chicken, rabbit, seafood, venison and eggs, goat's milk, ghee, and black tea and coffee. Minimise or avoid sweet, sour or salty foods, frozen or fried foods, fatty foods, dairy products, grains, potatoes, tomatoes, water chestnuts, excessively sweet, sour or juicy fruits, red meat, legumes, nuts and seeds, oils and fats, sugar, sweets and salt.

As per Homeopathy

The homeopathic remedies listed below may be beneficial in helping to balance the Winter Child's constitution:

- Arsenicum –album
- Baryta-carb
- Calc-carb
- Calc-phos
- Carcinosin

- Ferrum met
- Nat-mur
- Syphinilum
- Thuja

For a deeper explanation of these suggested homeopathic remedies, please refer to the section at the rear of this book dedicated entirely to homeopathy and its history, and the chart listing the keynotes of each remedy on page 281.

Other Advice

To inspire your Winter Child's belief in their potential and their creative instincts, organise a visit to a school of performing arts and explore the world of drama, dance and song. Visit a theatre, the Opera House, a museum of arts, or, alternatively, investigate the fine arts: painting, drawing, sculpture, textiles and fashion design. Visit a gallery, a reputable fashion house or the library, the Internet or the many artistic magazines that are currently on the market for inspiration. So long as they are given reason to believe in themselves, Winter Children are highly motivated and driven to make something of their lives. Hobbies that lead to careers are the best, because they are more likely to remain on task and focused on their goal. Earthy, practical, hands-on activities are ideal, activities that stimulate the mind and offer an immediate sense of accomplishment.

Winter Children represent the bulk of society; the ordinary folk; the 'salts of the earth'; the everyday men, women and children who excel in practical and manual jobs, working with their hands, in nature or on the land. They are the ones most likely to take up apprenticeships as mechanics, electricians, plumbers, carpenters, bricklayers and landscape gardeners (although, of course, the other types commonly do as well). They make excellent farmers, market gardeners, orchardists, nurserymen, flower growers and tree surgeons, because of the earthy component these jobs afford, as well as architects, graphic designers and any work that involves computers and computer programming— fields that make them feel needed while appealing to their practical mindset and their desire to accomplish, protect and provide for those they love. With this instinct in mind, Winter Children also make solid, reliable, practical and hard-working GPs or doctors who dedicate their time to the casualty department of major hospitals. They stand out because they remain cool and collected, thoughtful and effective in a crisis.

Not afraid of honest work, Winter Children love the thought of living on a farm or living off the land. The thought of returning to a self-sufficient lifestyle, for example, is both intriguing and stimulating. It appeals to their desire to provide for the people and to feel appreciated for what they do. It also affords them the opportunity to keep and raise animals (something they enjoy doing), but in a way that is both practical and productive. The thought of keeping animals appeals to the Winter Child, but due to their sensible approach to life, animals need to have a purpose and to earn their keep in some way. Winter Children are typically disinterested in keeping animals for the sake of it. Keeping Trout, Chickens, Ducks, Geese, Rabbits, Goats, Cattle, Pigs and Sheep, however, becomes a viable option when the possibility of making a few dollars by selling the produce they bestow is thrown into the equation. The concept of providing eggs, milk, cream, butter, yoghurt, meat, grain, fruit and vegetables for their own kitchen table (not to mention the fleece, down, and other produce a self-sufficient lifestyle yields) excites the earthy Winter Child greatly, with permaculture tempting further investigation because of its 'no dig' policy and its Earth-friendly doctrine. They also enjoy keeping Ferrets, especially when the animals are working stock and used for flushing wild Rabbits from their warrens. Winter Children enjoy breeding pedigree animals, too, and showing them at Royal Shows, collecting ribbons and improving the breeds of the animals they keep; animals like Dogs, Cats, Rabbits, Poultry, Sheep and Cattle are among the favourites. Volunteering their time at animal rescue centres, lost Dog and Cat homes and local pounds not only affords the Winter Child access to the animals they love in a useful way, but it also appeals to their ego by giving them a respected role of responsibility, thus boosting their self-esteem and sense of worth.

Winter Children love practising traditional, useful handcrafts, the techniques of which have long been forgotten by many of today's children.

Crafts such as basket and rug weaving, for example, knot work (macramé, among others), knitting, crocheting, spinning, sewing and quilting, were not only considered practical and essential for everyday life, they also afforded skills that formed valuable stepping stones to a plethora of employment opportunities. Winter Children respond well to being included in the cooking of the evening meal and the baking of the occasional cake or batch of biscuits. They particularly enjoy measuring the ingredients, relaying the recipe and licking the mixing spoon. Reading and watching a game of football or cricket on the television, playing cards and board games (both solitary and involving other players), building towers with Lego, designing the perfect robot with their Meccano set (www.meccano.com), playing 'farms' or 'zoos' with their Schleich plastic replica animals (www.modernbrands.com.au), dressing their dolls or touring in their Matchbox cars, model aeroplanes, ships, racing car sets and model trains, dressing up, or drinking 'tea' from their tea sets while playing in their tree or cubby house are all favourite pastimes of the no-frills Winter Child. For them, the simple things in life are often the best. As they get older, encourage them to join a band, particularly the more traditional pipe band, marching band or brass band. The time-honoured qualities of such companies will appeal greatly to the nostalgic Winter Child. Encouraging activities that take the Winter Child outdoors (away from the computer, video games and television) are essential, and more likely to appeal if they are largely recreational in nature and not too physically demanding: pond-dipping, bug-catching, bird-watching, gardening and Worm farming will attract a positive response.

The following is a list of crystals and minerals imbued with energy that will sustain the Winter Child in their practical, grounded, pragmatic endeavours. Have them carry their crystals in a pouch around their neck, in their pocket or, alternatively, in their sock or bra. Pyrite, for example, is a stone that protects against negativity. It is both powerfully protective and shielding. Pyrite promotes good health, focuses intellect and builds emotional wellbeing. Malachite is a stone of transformation. It aids with spiritual evolution by being both balancing and equalising in nature. Malachite represents fidelity, loyalty and friendship. It is good for business as it promotes practicality and responsibility. A stone of abundance, malachite is literally the colour of money. It often costs a lot of money to buy, so it espouses the 'spend money to make money' principle. Carnelian, an inspirational stone, kindles analytical aptitude and precision. It fosters discernment, dexterity and one's inherent gifts of power. Carnelian protects against envy, fear, rage and helps banish sorrow. It disperses laziness, indifference and submissiveness and combats neuralgia. Citrine dissipates and transmutes negativity. Otherwise known as 'the merchant's stone', citrine is said to produce greater income for the merchant when placed in the cash register. It is a stone of abundance, used in both the creation and maintenance of wealth. It also stimulates mental clarity, focus and endurance. Jasper (particularly the brown, ochre and red-coloured varieties) is revered as the 'supreme nurturer'. Jasper reminds us that we are not to live selfishly on this planet, but that we must consider others and do what we can to make their life better. Jasper provides for the realisation of responsibility and protection. It is a sustaining stone that offers strength and endurance, particularly when energy is low, while yellow calcite, a teacher stone for all of humanity, enhances awareness and appreciation of the creative forces of nature. It is an excellent stone when studying the arts and sciences. Rock salt is both protective and shielding. When sprinkled around the perimeter of one's property, for example, rock salt energetically creates a safe boundary that negative energy cannot penetrate. Coal is a primary symbol representing the earth element, whereas diamonds help to combat cowardice, rally strength and stimulate unity and unconditional love. Coal also helps to dispel anger, invoke love and harmony. It is a stone of innocence because it inspires purity, constancy and love. Peridot emits a warm and friendly energy. It inspires openness and acceptance, love and personal growth. Iron brings mental and emotional balance, while affording the strength to dismiss traditional issues and to implement new ones. It helps us learn from experience while augmenting the qualities of diplomacy. And finally, lead is a mineral that brings harmony to a group by raising awareness of the goals or intentions of the group. It helps bring out the best in the self and others.

Like the Warrior Children, Winter Children would do well to investigate the philosophies of 'Animism', an earthy, practical spiritual path that espouses the belief that all objects and living things are permeated with wisdom, insight and choice that preside over their reality. Animism is a path not unlike Shamanism that advocates the belief that everything is alive, conscious and comprising of a soul, and should be treated with the respect it deserves. It also says that the world is a community of living 'persons', only some of which are human. It portrays all things as equal: the humans, rocks, plants, animals, birds, ancestral spirits, and so on. Animism offers a 'belief in spirits', be they mystical, paranormal, unseen or illusory beings. Animism, as a spiritual path, celebrates beings for their own sake, whether they have or are souls or because they are 'persons', or not.

A sacred aspect of the Animist philosophy is the Medicine Walk, a meander of intent not viewed simply as a stroll in nature, but more as a journey undertaken with the purpose of communing with Spirit, Creation and Mother Earth. It encourages us to find and honour the silence within so that we may communicate with *all* of Creation — the crystals, stones, feathers, trees, flowers, animals, shells, birds, sticks, leaves, insects, weather, rivers, oceans, forests, deserts, parks, gardens and the clouds. It is hoped that the walker will find it possible to take their experiences and the significant things they see, hear, smell and touch, as gifts and messages from Spirit, purposefully integrating the wisdom into their life. Encourage your Winter Child to partake in regular Medicine Walks, especially when they feel alone, confused, misunderstood or frustrated. You may want to join them the first time they venture out. While walking, have them pick up objects that grab their eye or seem to call to them. The items found do not have to be natural objects. They may find that after walking for a while they have found only five or six things. Not all the items will want to go home with them, so it is important that they ask permission and wait for a reply. A 'yes' may be felt as a tingle in the stomach, while a 'no' may come to them as a pain, heaviness, or a definite 'negative' feeling. As you walk, look for the things that have unusual shape, length, appearance, colour or texture. Look for things that are a little different from the norm: twigs that have moss or lichen growing on them, a small log with fungus on it, a stone with a hole in it, a mussel shell with both halves intact, an Eagle feather or any feather of significance to you, or a skeleton leaf (a leaf with the flesh eaten off leaving only the delicate vein membrane). These are all sacred items as they all have special meaning and hold secret messages and healing potential. Animal signs or evidence that animals have passed through an area are symbols that may have spiritual, emotional or physical significance to you. Goanna marks on trees; Lyrebird scrapings on the edge of bush walking paths; Owl scats (evident due to the small bones and fur scraps found within); Wombat droppings on top of rocks and logs; and the distinctive stale smell of the Fox are perfect examples that should be acknowledged. Taking a small tape deck with you will also enable you to record any sounds that you feel are significant. It you cannot take a tape recorder with you, describe the sounds in a journal. Sounds to listen for may include the laugh of a Kookaburra, the whip of the Lyrebird or the sardonic call of a Raven. You should also record the immediate feelings or sensations you experienced when you come across them. When the walk is completed, and it comes to receiving the messages from the pieces found, have your child lie on their back and take three deep breaths — one for the body, one for the mind, and one for the spirit. Remind them to focus on their breathing and the silencing of their mind. Wait until they have cleared their mind to the point where you believe they have reached the point of inner harmony where nothing is important enough to disturb them from the task at hand. Take each of the items in turn and place them on their stomach. This area is the centre of their energy system and it is from here that they communicate with everything in existence. Mentally ask the items why they presented themselves to your child. They may not talk to you using words. A telepathic connection may occur. You may receive colours, shapes, a vision, or a dream-like image may even form in your mind, or your child may receive a response in a way sacred to them. Refer to the list below to help you interpret the symbols further, and print it out so that your Winter Child may receive personal clarity, too.

- **Stone**: Personal records and ancient knowledge will be revealed to you soon
- **Feather**: A sign of confirmation and acknowledgment from a higher source
- **Shell**: Mother Earth is nurturing your inner child and urging you toward greater things
- **Leaf**: Expect change
- **Fur**: You are being offered a sense of warmth and protection
- **Bark**: Your aura is in need of maintenance and your defences are down
- **Cloud**: Look to those in Spirit by considering what your ancestors would suggest you do
- **Scent**: Know your territory and set definite boundaries
- **Flower**: You are being offered the nectar of life, the inspiration to

manifest what you deserve

- **Grass**: Your field of options are lush and fertile
- **Puddle**: We are all teachers
- **Seed**: New beginnings are yours for the sowing
- **Gumnut**: Feelings of being forsaken
- **Snail Shell**: Dance the sacred spiral that leads to a deeper knowing of the true, innate self
- **Thorn**: A warning of a potential obstacle, gossip or false friend
- **Stick**: Support is being offered as you walk your path
- **Bird**: A recognised symbol of the soul, birds lift us out of the mundane by awakening potential
- **Mammal**: Acknowledge issues, abandon them completely or commit to dealing with them later
- **Insect**: Find the silence, trust and be at peace now
- **Fish**: Your intuition is ripe, your creative abilities are sound and your imagination is primed
- **Reptile**: Listen to your dreams: day and night
- **Fungi**: Suspicion that you are being kept in the dark is highly probable
- **Bone**: Death represents endings; conclusion
- **Moss**: Dormancy is only positive if you are resting. The negative is redundancy and avoidance
- **Bulb**: After every night there is a dawn. All will be revealed at the right time
- **Rain**: Your tears are productive and cleansing of your soul
- **Log**: Stop playing the victim
- **Scats** (animal droppings): Let go of guilt
- **Scrapes**: There is nothing as important as leaving your mark
- **Cocoon**: You are experiencing a time of sacred transition
- **Sand**: Trust that everything happens in its own time
- **Mud**: You are being reminded of your sacred inherent life-force
- **Water**: Meditate
- **Sun**: Now is a time for commitment
- **Moon**: Now is a time for re-evaluation
- **Sky**: You can reach any height
- **Thunder**: Don't waste your energy by huffing and puffing
- **Lightning**: Choose your words carefully
- **River**: Surrender your worries

- **Pine needle**: Stop giving your power away by surrounding yourself with 'vampires'
- **Acorn**: Trust your own knowledge
- **Cone**: You offer wisdom and insight
- **Soil**: Life is only as barren or as fertile as you believe it to be
- **Fern Frond**: Let life unfold with time
- **Shed Skin**: Make way for new beginnings by freeing up energy
- **Egg Shell**: Although fragile, you are ready now to birth a new idea
- **Egg**: You are 'pregnant' with possibility
- **Nest**: Regret nothing
- **Spider Web**: You will bring a dream to fruition
- **Ice**: You waste energy on resentment and doubt
- **Fire**: Do not let things get out of hand
- **Wind**: Barriers, obstacles and fears are diminishing
- **Smoke**: Your heart's yearnings have been received as messages by Spirit
- **Cave**: A time of birth and rebirth
- **Burrow**: You are not running away or dumping responsibility
- **Litter**: To pollute Mother Earth is to pollute your own life
- **Sound**: You are relying on learnt behaviour, indoctrinated belief and cyclic patterns at this time
- **Tree Roots**: What are you hiding?
- **Tree Trunk**: Set realistic goals
- **Tree Branches**: There is never one correct answer
- **Hive**: Your dedication will pay off, but you may have to start alone
- **Stump**: An opportunity cut short
- **Bud**: Reintroduce yourself to the world
- **Seedling**: You have instigated a new cycle, phase or aspect of life
- **Tree Hollow**: You provide shelter, help, insight and warmth freely
- **Mist**: Things are not always what they seem
- **Snow**: Emotional truths being held in stasis
- **Charcoal**: Rekindle the sacred fire
- **Ash**: End of a cycle
- **Tracks**: Finding ones spiritual life path or purpose

3

The Squirrel Monkey

Totem of the Nature (Crystal) Child
Keynotes: Activist / Speaker / Romantic

Squirrel Monkeys are very peaceful, arboreal creatures. The future of the Squirrel Monkey is threatened due to habitat destruction from logging and agricultural encroachment. The Squirrel Monkeys eat insects, small birds, seeds and fruit. They have thick, orangey tan-coloured fur but are almost hairless around the muzzle, which is black. The fur on its head is dark and so is the tip of its tail. They are, indeed, beautiful Monkeys. The males are typically larger than females. Squirrel Monkeys inhabit the rainforests of South America. They are also found in cultivated areas, particularly near water. Squirrel Monkeys travel in mixed species groups, often associating with Capuchin Monkeys. The Squirrel Monkeys initiate communication by following the Capuchins, who help them find food more efficiently.

Squirrel Monkey people are easygoing and peaceful. They are composed, tolerant and objective in their approach to life. They make reliable friends and are gentle in their ways. As a rule, Squirrel Monkey people are funny, compassionate and nurturing. Reticent in nature, though, many are submissive, attentive and universal to a fault. They have large, innocent eyes that captivate and lure. They are emotional and passionate, usually presenting themselves as communicative, animated and entertaining, or reserved, silent and watchful. They choose to be one or the other, rarely alternating between the two. Often misdiagnosed as autistic as small children, the more reticent types will stare at strangers. They don't mean to be rude, but prefer to communicate telepathically. Laidback and accepting, and due to the fact that they are outwardly composed and stable, the majority are grounded enough to lead effectively when required to do so. Squirrel Monkey people negotiate well, are reliable in foundation and are pacifists at heart. They make dependable, sociable partners, pleasant, cooperative workmates and inoffensive neighbours.

Like all people, Squirrel Monkey people have a shadow side. They can appear apathetic on first meeting, for example, due to their habit of separating themselves from emotional issues to disguise fear, apprehension and lack of self-worth. They may present as being introverted and nonchalant. Because they oftentimes emanate an air of aloofness, they can be described (even by those close to them) as being detached, inattentive, or stubborn and reserved. When they allow their shadow side to rule, Squirrel Monkey people can be poor listeners who crave attention. When working from their shadow side, Squirrel Monkey people are only ever onlookers who despise change, often demonstrating a cynical, judgmental, discouraging air. Although they yearn to know unconditional trust and acceptance, Squirrel Monkey people often have difficulty maintaining relationships, but keep many friends and even more associates.

Individual advice for the Squirrel Monkey / Nature Child

Correspondences:

Esoteric Element: Water
Elemental Instruments: Reed instruments, harps and bowed string instruments (violins etc)
Elemental Spirits: Undines, Nymphs, Water Dragons, Sea Serpents, Merpeople
Direction: West
Directional Colours: Dark blue, purple, black

Season: Autumn

Time of Power: Early evening, dusk

Symbolic Phase of Life on the Wheel of Life: The mother / father / parent / guardian / carer

Power Places: Streams, rivers, lakes, oceans, beaches, waterfalls, wells and springs

Zodiacs as per the Corresponding Esoteric Element: Cancer, Scorpio and Pisces

Organs: Kidneys, bladder

Chakras: Heart (fourth)

Chakra Colours: Green, pink

Crystals: Iolite (water sapphire), emerald, turquoise, aquamarine, obsidian, apache tears, onyx, jet, sodalite, jasper, carnelian, rose quartz, tourmaline, pearls, blue topaz and lapis lazuli, aventurine, jade

Totems: Squirrel Monkeys, Serpents, Dolphins, Koalas, Fish, Seals, Sea Birds, Frogs, Turtles, Otters, Platypus, Swans, Crabs, Bears and Black Horses

Herbs: Myrrh, willow, the boab and eucalyptus trees, chamomile, seaweed and water lilies

I remember when my son (a Nature Child) came home from kindergarten one afternoon in tears, unable to speak without choking on his grief. His eyes were red and puffy and his hair was stuck to his head with sweat. When we had settled him down sufficiently, my wife asked him what was wrong. Through a fresh wave of tears, Kaleb attempted to explain how he had tried to stop his friend from breaking the branches off one of the trees that stood in the kindergarten's grounds. "I tried to stop him," he said. "I tried to tell him he was hurting the spirit person that lives in the tree, but he wouldn't listen. He just didn't care."

The challenge for the Nature Child as they journey through life, you see, is to transform weakness, fear and separation into connectedness, expectation and vitality in a meaningful way; to become one who nurtures; one who understands and fosters the 'mother' archetype; one who sponsors new life and honours the sacredness of all life and one who finds meaning through birthing, raising and nourishing other life forms. Theirs is a path that encourages all people to move graciously and in harmony with the ebb and flow of life — wherever it may lead, to face the difficulties and opportunities of life with equal respect and to flow with or around them, just as water would. By being so 'at one' with nature, Nature Children quickly find the peace, security and structure they crave, and by following their lead, others can realise an equal degree of connectedness as well.

Just as a Squirrel Monkey troop will instinctively follow a family group of Capuchin Monkeys in the wild, Nature Children inherently know they are here to follow, watch over and pacify the Warrior Children. Nature Children are sometimes born into families containing one or more Warrior Children, and will almost immediately step into the role of mediator, counsellor, and spokesman. They are the ones best equipped to say 'relax' and 'calm down' with little fear of retort, hastily returning the fiery Warrior Child to a place of clarity and cooperation. In turn, Warrior Children offer Nature Children courage, strength and self-esteem by creating a forum for them to speak up and be heard.

As adults and teenagers, Nature Children often find themselves in relationships with Warrior Children. Apart from finding 'bad boys' or 'naughty girls' exciting and daring, they honestly believe they can tame them and help them to mend their ways. Nature Children are often the grandchildren of Peacekeeper Children and the offspring of Winter Children, and many will have Warrior Children as aunts and uncles, cousins and, in some cases, siblings (although there are always exceptions).

Despite the fact that Nature Children are typically described as charming, ideals-oriented activists, speakers and romantics, the kind who seem to communicate telepathically with friends and family and those who love nature so much that they openly commune with nature spirits and animals, they also have a shadow side that must be addressed if they are ever to move fully into their positive phase. Although Nature Children work deliberately and consistently, are self-possessed, considerate and satisfied in life, they can also appear aloof, unresponsive, cowardly, languid and stagnant, and as a result, many are prone to or are diagnosed with autism. Enormous and, in some cases, instant success has been witnessed by medical scientists and lay-people alike when observing children suffering from autism who are given the chance to swim with Dolphins. No one knows why for sure, but merely being in close proximity to the marine mammals seems to give the children brief moments of clarity when the 'dome' that isolates them emotionally is temporarily lifted, allowing them a brief chance to express themselves with words, squeals of laughter and tears. Perhaps it is because they understand one another. Animals are similar to autistic people in that they think visually rather than linguistically and perceive the world as a series of unrelated elements rather than a logical whole. Animals (and autistic people) are easily worried by trivial things that non-autistic humans rarely notice. Cattle being ushered up a ramp, for example, or a Horse being ridden through unfamiliar terrain may startle at an unfamiliar sound or sensation, an unexpected colour or a sudden peripheral movement. Other animals display behaviour that can only be described as fixated attention — a trait common in autistic people, like a caged Ferret working their latch over and over until it falls open, setting them free — something I have observed my own pet Ferrets, Rats and Foxes doing on more than one occasion. Even those not identified as autistic, though, all Nature Children 'open up' excitedly when they see Dolphins and Whales in their natural habitat.

To avoid their more negative labels, Nature Children must seek and embrace causes that inspire and energise them; causes that teach them to accept help, acknowledge praise and receive encouragement from others; causes that depend on them learning to communicate and interact with other people and, hopefully, spend quality time in nature surrounded by animals. Not until they are excited by the beauty that surrounds them every day can the Nature Child truly understand and embrace their purpose.

As per the Four Humours: the Phlegmatic

As phlegmatics, Nature Children can be lazy, anxious and apprehensive. They are infamous for being unable to make up their mind, for avoiding responsibility and for their silent resolution. They are often egocentric, introverted and uncommunicative, overly accommodating and, at times, sanctimonious. Hence the need, according to the philosophy advocating the

Four Humours, for the phlegmatic to be given the chance to be 'warmed up and dried out' in order to reach their potential.

When working in their positive phase, anyone who knows a phlegmatic will agree they are modest, tolerant, calm, stable, gentle and droll. They live dependable lives, are compassionate and kind-hearted. They are reserved and private, universal to a fault and prepared to accept and deal with what life dishes out.

Phlegmatics thrive on frequent encouragement and the development of interesting hobbies and personal pursuits. They do best when given confidence to let their imagination run wild and when offered significant opportunity to spend time with animals. For the phlegmatic, Mother Nature in all her glory is both stimulating and refreshing.

As per the Five Esoteric Elements: Water

In accordance with the Five Esoteric Elements, Nature Children correspond vibrationally to the energies of autumn, water and the Undines, the elemental spirits of water.

Water is the element that vibrationally rules autumn, the season of great change, when rain showers the earth. Autumn is a time of contemplation and introspection and of reaching the point in one's life when, as a mother or father, partner or spouse, we ponder the meaning of life by asking ourselves, "Is this it…?" and when all that has been sewn is now ripe for the harvest. Autumn, by its very nature, is flowing, purifying, healing, soothing, nurturing and loving. The goddess is in her mothering phase and the land is readying the fruits of our labour for harvest. It is a time for acknowledging that the end of the cycle of growth is fast approaching and that all that is born must eventually die, to be reborn again in the spring. It is a time of personal growth, realisation and enlightenment in a time of approaching darkness.

During autumn we find ourselves symbolically standing in the west, the place of the setting sun. It is twilight or dusk on an energetic level. While standing in the west we are in the phase of life dedicated to parenthood, the gaining of maturity and the realisation that the wisdom we seek is typically found within. Autumn is feminine, receptive, calming, and introspective. During autumn we are encouraged to explore our emotions, our feelings, and our concepts of love. Evident in the qualities of those born under the zodiacal signs of Cancer, Scorpio and Pisces, autumn embodies the water element, and as such, tests our courage and daring, intuition and the subconscious mind by raising questions of fertility, the womb, of healing, purification, pleasure, friendship, partnership and our immediate happiness.

As autumn is the time when the animals prepare to hibernate, our sleep patterns and the rate at which we dream becomes a factor at this time. Autumn is an excellent period to investigate the psychic planes and to begin communicating with the spirit realms, because at this time, with its association with the west and the moon, the veils between the worlds are rapidly thinning. Autumn is a fine time for the investigation of the inner self, too, as well as inner knowing, self-healing and one's sense of security, sympathy and love.

Water has long been considered a symbol of the emotions, being cleansing and feminine in energy. It has been linked throughout esoteric history with the astral plane and the intangible forces of the universe. As the element that rules the west on the Wheel of Life, water encourages us to quiet the inner chatter, to sit in silent contemplation and to find the answers we seek within the solitude of our subconscious mind. The silence is the key to higher understanding; the key that unlocks the line of communication between our higher self and Spirit.

Water people are soft, gentle and adaptable, empathic and intuitive. They tend to be clear minded, fluid and flowing in nature and so, because water is the element ruling human emotion and feelings, so their natural ability to sense what others are feeling is heightened. They commune readily with nature and animals and have inherently potent 'healing hands'. They are both artistic and creative. Water types are prone to tubbiness (or have noticeably 'rounded bodies'), fluid retention, excess mucus build-up, catarrhal problems, 'wet' forms of asthma, recurring throat, tonsil and ear infections, diarrhoea, lethargy, but, despite all this, tend to move gracefully and flowingly.

Water people are introspective, contemplative and reflective. They are often accused of daydreaming, having slipped into a meditative state to find answers to the questions plaguing their conscious mind. They are romantics and visionaries and the ones most likely to say "I had the weirdest dream last night …"

Willowy, elegant music that inspires a similar style of dance, particularly which incorporates the sounds of Dolphins, Whales, harps, violins and other bowed stringed instruments will connect the Nature Child with the essence of their element, while simultaneously honouring the water spirits, Undines and the Merpeople who protectively watch over them.

A Guided Visualisation that explores the Water Element:

Find yourself a comfy place where you know you will not be interrupted. If possible, find a place in nature. Sit with your back supported by the trunk of a tree, a smooth rock or a mossy log. Sit with the intention of strengthening your bond with Spirit and of remembering your inherent relationship with the Earth Mother. You may want to wrap yourself in a blanket, because it is not uncommon for one's body temperature to drop as you sink deeper and deeper into stillness. Quiet your conscious mind and endeavour to silence your inner chatter. Wait for the moment when you intuitively feel inclined to open your consciousness to the Other Realms. Ensure that your subconscious mind is receptive and alert by speaking to your conscious mind. Allow visions and symbolic images to float through your mind. Keep your focus within yourself. Let any thoughts just go by. When you catch yourself engaged in an external conscious thought, just take a deep breath and bring yourself back to your centre.

You are now ready to begin.

Picture yourself on a great grassy plane, dotted with the most beautifully coloured wild flowers. From where you are standing you can see two very different sights. To your right is a path leading up to a steep mountain peak and to your left is a path leading down into a deep valley. The point at which you are standing is in fact the intersection of time and reality; a mingling point of reality and 'the Other Worlds', of the physical and the mystical. It is where the miraculous can be found.

Visualise yourself taking the left path as it leads down into the deep valley. The path leads you to the west, the place of the setting sun. At this point in your life you have reached a level of maturity that allows you to appreciate things on a much deeper level. You are pondering the question — Is this all there is? Is this my life? Mist is beginning to fill the valley. It is twilight and the sun is sinking. The valley is thick with ferns, moss covered willow trees, roses and gardenias. Carpets of blue flowers and wild lettuce plants line the edge of a great lake, itself dotted with water lilies and lotus flowers. A stream, fed by the lake, leads you further into the forested valley and as you walk you notice the ground becoming sandy and the plant life thinning, until you find yourself standing on a beach with white-capped waves crashing onto the shore. Dolphins and Seals play in the surf, alongside Porpoises and Sea Otters. Seagulls circle overhead as rain begins to fall. It is autumn. It is harvest time and the air is unsettled.

Zephyrus, the West Wind, swirls around your head, kicking up the sand and wrapping you in her arms. Mermaids and Water Nymphs play with pearls, coral and shells at the mouth of the lake fed stream and, as you sit yourself down, you cross your legs and rest your hands gently on your knees. You close your eyes with the thought of meditation. You allow images of self-healing and love to float through your mind and you ask for a sign that will show you how to achieve them. You become aware of the fact that the answers you seek will present themselves in your dreams. While you meditate, spirit animals begin to present themselves to you. A Jaguar appears and begins to explain the art of shape shifting: the ability to change on all levels to better fit any circumstance and environment. To affirm its words, it changes form and becomes a huge Bear. The Bear says that it is time to wake from your hibernation, to take responsibility for your actions and to listen to your heart of hearts in relation to some issue that has been plaguing you for some time. The Bear grows wings and becomes an Albatross, which rises on the wind and hovers above the waves. By doing this, the Albatross symbolically tells you to balance your emotions and to ride things out and see where the winds of change take you. You open your eyes and notice that in the water a whirlpool has begun to develop. You watch in wonder, as the whirlpool begins to rise up, looking more and more like an upside down cone of swirling water. The spiralling liquid moves toward the shore and, on reaching the sand, splits into three separate columns. Gradually, the three writhing watery forms become humanoid in shape, each one showing recognisable features: blue/green eyes, a nose, a mouth and ears.

The three forms are Undines — elemental spirits of the water, sent by angel Gabriel and the king of the water elementals, Necksa. One of the Undines is carrying a black cauldron, another is carrying a translucent blue glass goblet and the third is holding a mirror edged in lapis lazuli. Their world is water, they are at one with the water — they *are* the water. The Undines stand in front of you, their 'feet' licking at the sand-covered ground like an incoming tide petting the shore; their solid form made possible only by joint concentrated effort and the pure intent of the creatures. Water is feminine in nature, receptive, nurturing and cleansing. Theirs is a world of dreams, emotions, feelings, healing and love. Of courage, daring, sorrow and empathy and they are bidding you to join them — to explore their world, to become one with the water that is their consciousness. They take your hand and lead you into the water.

As you walk into the surf, the water laps around your ankles and the further you go, the deeper it gets, until your chin is barely above the surface. In front of you are the 'heads' of the three Undines — formed entirely from the salty water. They begin to circle you and gradually become faster and faster, again creating a whirlpool. The force of the water as it swirls around you generates a wall that rises up and closes over your head making a dome of water that is filled with oxygen like a bubble, enabling you to breathe. You realise that you are now under the water and the bubble enclosing your head is clear like glass allowing you to see clearly the underwater world of the Undines without fear of drowning. Schools of fish swim past — some of them pause to look at you in an inquisitive way. You can make out the Undines in front of you — not in the physical sense, as they are near impossible to detect with the naked eye, but instead you are able to feel them vibrationally. Something is different about the water forming the creatures; it is slightly denser, deeper in colour and 'quivery' to look at. They have changed the structure of the water to allow them to be seen just as they have altered reality to accommodate you and your earthly perceptions. Like Dolphins, the Undines dart off, twisting and turning in a playful manner, communicating with you through sound; simple strings of infrasound squeaks and squeals: an abstract, ancient, low-frequency language, but one that makes sense to you somehow.

The Undines lead you on a fantastic tour of their oceanic world, past shipwrecks and sunken treasure, through beautiful coral reefs, thick kelp forests and brightly coloured seaweed gardens.

You approach the edge of a deep ravine and without hesitation the Undines lead you to its depths. At the bottom of the ravine you meet what appears to be the mouth of a cave, but as you enter, you realise it to be a tunnel, a path that leads to an underwater chamber — a temple; a place of nurturing and spiritual purification. The temple is essentially the womb of the Earth Mother, a sacred place of reflection, regeneration and introspection. At the end of the great temple, seated on huge thrones carved from aquamarine are Aphrodite and Poseidon, the goddess and god of the ocean. The Undines gesture for you to stop and to wait for the water deities to address you. At this point you notice that the floor of the temple is littered with perfectly round pebbles, amethyst points and double-ended rainbow fluorite crystals.

Aphrodite and Poseidon look at you and smile, their stare both soothing and loving, but wild and untamed at the same time. Aphrodite motions for you to approach, her movement fluid, purifying and healing in nature. She shares with you information about dreaming and your ability to find your healing gifts within them, your healing gifts that you are to share with the people and your conscious world. She speaks of fertility, friendship and the emotional pleasures of life — laughter, tears of joy, unconditional love, trust and loyalty. She encourages you to seek spiritual renewal by participating in healing circles, by working with your sense of smell and by questing to balance the active yin and yang aspects of your psyche.

Poseidon now speaks to you, but this time of going within, of seeking your own inner vision and truth, of absorbing shamanic knowledge by journeying with the drum and participating in Vision Quest. He promotes emotional protection and security and the positive aspects of hibernation, of deep contemplation and silencing the inner chatter with the purpose of seeking enlightenment.

The Undines inform you that your audience with Aphrodite and Poseidon is now over and that it is time to return to the beach. They lead you out of the temple and back up the tunnel. As you rise once again toward the surface, a lone Humpback Whale drifts past like a submerged ocean liner. The Whale looks at you as if searching your soul and, through your mind's eye, shares with you a sense of belonging, a promise of personal discovery and a feeling of inner strength. When the time is right, the Whale says, your purpose will be revealed to you, to be eventually shared with the people as a Medicine and a symbol of your personal power. The Whale tells you that she is the spirit guide to the people and the record keeper of the Earth Mother's sacred knowledge, and that she alone holds the key to humanity's past, present and future.

The Undines bring you back to the beach and as you rise to the surface, the bubble of protection around your head slowly becomes thinner, disintegrating, returning to liquid form. For the first time, you feel the water against the skin on your face, seconds before your head pops into the fresh air of night. The full moon shines down, creating an illuminated path back to the shore.

You look to the moon and make a silent prayer to Spirit for a reason sacred to you and to offer thanks, taking three breaths in through your nose and out through your mouth before returning to the physical place in which you are seated.

As per Traditional Chinese Medicine: the Water / Kidney Person

According to the teachings of Traditional Chinese Medicine, Nature Children, as 'kidney people', have their mind, body and energy systems focused on the water element.

The water element, it is said, is the source of life; a strong life-force found energetically in the lower belly. It embodies the essential ingredient that determines the health and wellbeing of our hereditary genes, our DNA, our mental health and our ability to organise our life efficiently in a way that guarantees stability and productivity and, eventually, our chances of finding a viable partner to reproduce with. It also influences our programmed patterns and susceptibilities. As a result, it sanctions the importance of quality rest and rejuvenation, hibernation and contemplation. At a bodily level, when this relationship is understood and the kidney person is working in harmony with his or her element, a greater level of wellbeing for the tissues related to the kidney is achieved, according to the teachings of Traditional Chinese Medicine: a healthier bladder, for example, stronger bones, teeth and nails, more flexible cartilage and joints and a more physically powerful skeletal system overall, thus better structure and support for the body as well as healthier bone marrow, improved hearing and a razor-sharp brain.

In accordance with Traditional Chinese Medicine, the kidney, which is all about safety, structure and stability, is seen as the seat of inherited life-force, with the essential component being kidney Qi ('Qi' referring to life-force). When the kidney Qi of a person is strong, they come across as courageous, resolute, disciplined, focused and enduring. An unyielding willpower is a sign of someone with strong kidney Qi, while a long life is usually put down to healthy kidney Qi, often augured by large, elongated Buddha-like ear lobes.

An obvious lack of mental prowess is often recorded in people with depleted kidney Qi. They tend to have poor concentration, a lower level of intellect, reduced memory and regular moments of confusion. They mentally and physically fatigue quickly, with their ability to recover efficiently left wanting. 'Dryness', weakness and instability are obvious symptoms of kidney deficiency, as is a propensity for fear, uncertainty and apprehension.

They tend to suffer from widespread or shifting aches and pains, vertigo and shakiness. Chronic insomnia and severe constipation are also common. Their joints seem dry, time and again producing audible cracking sounds. Consequently, they may endure arthritis, osteoporosis and similar or related ailments. Kidney people feel best in the mornings — not necessarily when they first wake up, when their body is inflexible and sore, but rather after a warming shower and a bit of exercise. They easily become overly exerted mentally and physically, usually due to a disproportionate reduction in essential bodily fluids, and they suffer terribly when exposed to severe cold, either directly from their environment (they seem to lack natural reserves of essential body heat), or indirectly from an uncomplimentary diet. It is often the case that kidney people are fragile from the onset: overly sensitive and sometimes delicate or weakened from birth. In the severest of cases, some kidney people are so weak and wan it almost appears as if they have gone through life with one foot in the grave. They are often impaired, too, by a history of mental or physical hardship and serious illness. Thus, kidney people tend to worry excessively and suffer from anxiety, usually as a result of consternation regarding their security, safety and stability.

Morning is when the body's 'yang', or masculine energy rises, and it maintains its power until midday, while the evening marks the rising to predominance of the body's 'yin', the essential feminine or visible Qi. An increase in energy around 9 or 10 pm indicates the body's yin being topped up. Yin energy reaches its potential at midnight. Look at your tongue in the mirror. The more cracks on the surface, the more deficient your yin or visible Qi will be. Even little horizontal cracks indicate the onset of a yin deficiency. Old people always have a cracked tongue. Kidney Qi tends to decline with age, heralded by dark circles or pouches under the eyes, diminished hearing or tinnitus (continuous ringing in the ears). When a person's kidney Qi weakens, problems with water metabolism, urination, fertility and sexuality are experienced, with anxiety, fearfulness and introverted traits becoming increasingly evident. In more severe cases, they may even begin to display irrational phobias. It is believed that once the essential kidney Qi is fully expended, life-force leaves and you die, so Traditional Chinese Medicine endorses methods that prolong life by rebuilding the essential kidney Qi.

According to the observations recorded by Traditional Chinese Medicine, kidney Qi is most frequently depleted by a poor or uncomplimentary diet, stress, overwork, intense mental activity / thinking, excessive sensory input, long-term drug use and toxins in the system, a build up of heavy metals, old age, or a sudden or extreme loss of bodily fluids. In men this is usually a result of frequent ejaculation / excess sexual activity (or, alternatively, from too little sex, causing stagnation of sperm). For women it is typically caused by disproportionate menstrual blood loss, heavy frequent periods and from bearing too many children. Imbibing too much alcohol, taking drugs, eating stimulating foods or too much protein or sugar in the diet can go along way to exacerbate kidney Qi depletion.

Symptoms of kidney deficiency include feeling overwhelmingly weak and tired, undue confusion, poor memory and short concentration, wandering pains all over the body, dizziness and vertigo, fainting (also known as 'the vapours'), a bent, almost wasted, skinny body, feeble, flabby muscles, congenital deformities, overworked nervous system, brain related conditions, dry, cracking joints, arthritis, osteoporosis and other problems relating to the bones, skeleton, cartilage and joints, neurasthenia or nervous weakness, fibro myalgia, repetitive stress injury (RSI), chronic fatigue syndrome (CFS), constantly feeling chilly, a coldness in the body's extremities, knees or lower back (especially around the kidneys), chronic insomnia, dryness in the body, chronic constipation, a weakened mind and/ or a weakened body and an overall tendency to complain all the time.

In accordance with Traditional Chinese Medicine, kidney energy may be treated or boosted by eating 'black' foods. Black is the colour that relates to the water element, and as such, is said to restore kidney Qi vitality. To assist the process, therefore, eat dark coloured 'black' root vegetables like beetroot, and try cooking with kidney beans. Eat warming, nourishing foods such as rice congee, root vegetables, potatoes, red meat soups and broths, kidney organ meat, oysters, chicken livers and pork.

Make a point of only eating moderate amounts of dairy products (focusing on un-homogenised milk and yoghurt), and small amounts of added salt. A moderate lifestyle is the key for males, with no drugs, minimal stress and conscious sexual restraint being the rule of thumb. For women, Chinese herbs (such as ginseng) and acupuncture may be considered as a means of equalising periods and regulating menstrual blood loss, while Qigong is an activity that all kidney people should investigate. Qigong refers to the combination of 'Qi' (air, breath, vital energy and life-force) and 'gong', the mastering of self-control and accomplishment. It incorporates meditation, relaxation, physical movement, mind/body integration and various breathing exercises. Dan Tian meditation, too, is advised, an exercise that can be incorporated into the practise of Qigong. It relies on breath and concentration to activate the circulation of Qi and blood through the centre of the forehead, the centre of the chest and the lower abdomen — the three primary centres of power within the body, according to tradition. Acupuncture is deeply rooted in the belief that illness is caused when an imbalance is caused in the body's energy system. It is said to re-establish harmony by balancing the body's yin and yang. Acupuncture involves the painless insertion of fine needles into the body's meridians or energy channels (named after the organs they represent) to clear blocked Qi, releasing energy flow through the body.

As per Ayurveda - (Primary) Earth / Water Energy / Kapha - (Secondary) Air Energy / Vata

In order to reach their potential, Nature Children need to strike a balance between their earth/water energy or, '*Kapha*', and their air energy, or '*Vata*', by becoming fully aware of the seasons that sustain them and those that don't. During the summer and autumn, for example, Nature Children must find ways to appease their Vata energy, while in winter and spring they must do what needs to be done to control their Kapha energy. A very simple way of maintaining this balance is to focus on sour and salty foods during summer and autumn and pungent foods in winter and spring.

Kapha is the balancing force between water and earth. It represents composition and lubrication. It is the blending and binding element that helps keep water and earth from separating. When earth and water are mixed together and then left to their own devices, the earth will gradually sink to the bottom, thus extracting itself from the water. Kapha is the force that prevents this from happening. It binds the elements, thus providing for physical structure and endurance. Water is the main ingredient of Kapha; a vital component physiologically needed to ensure biological power and natural tissue vitality. Vata, on the other hand, (a term that means 'wind, to move, flow, direct the processes of, or command') is drying, cooling and airy, rousing and ever changing in nature. It is a force believed to be composed of the Aether and air elements. The level of Aether (or 'space') affects the degree to which the air may gain momentum. If unbridled, the air element can gather excessively in force and get out of hand, and become a destructive tempest.

The golden rule with Kapha energy is to acknowledge the person's reliability, constancy, empathy and ability to nurture themselves and others. Vary their schedule every so often by changing their routine, especially during winter and spring. Remember, variety is the spice of life. Never allow them to overeat and encourage them to partake in regular exercise (to help control weight, if nothing else) and associate with people, places and things that stimulate their mind. Hobbies are great, especially when they offer a variety of experiences that enhance recreation time. Kapha people tend to have soft hair and skin, large 'soft' eyes and a low, gentle voice. They need to preserve bodily warmth while remaining mindful of their level of 'dryness' and their intake of sweets. Elecampane and wild honey are also known to pacify Kapha energy, while aromatherapy oils believed to soothe excessive Kapha energy include the warm spicy aromas of juniper, eucalyptus, clove and marjoram.

When addressing the diet, focus on bitter, pungent or astringent foods, warm light foods, dry foods and stimulating foods, while avoiding foods cooked in too much water, oily fatty or buttery foods and sugar. Eat plenty of apples, apricots, cranberries, mangoes, peaches, pears and pomegranates, vegetables in general, salads, light, dry foods and herbs and spices, such as black pepper, cardamom, cinnamon, clove, coriander, cumin, garlic, ginger, fennel and nutmeg; raw/natural honey, small amounts of chicken, rabbit, seafood, venison and eggs, goat's milk and ghee and black tea and coffee. Minimise or avoid sweet, sour or salty foods, frozen or fried foods, fatty foods, dairy products, grains, potatoes, tomatoes, water chestnuts, excessively sweet, sour or juicy fruits, red meat, legumes, nuts and seeds, oils and fats, sugar, sweets and salt.

A strict regime is very important when it comes to pacifying Vata energy, as is a quiet, harmonious environment, plenty of warm fluids, ample rest, bodily warmth and a steady supply of nourishment. Vata is a force theoretically made up of the elements of Aether and air. Avoid the risk of becoming over-stimulated by loud, lively music, television and people, excessive sunlight and bright, vibrant colours and cut alcohol, tea, coffee, cigarettes and drugs out of the daily routine.

Summer and autumn are the best times of the year for the Vata person to express and develop their inherent creative artistic selves and to express their imagination in a grounded way. An emphasis on regularity in the daily routine is vital, such as disciplined meal times, bath times and bedtime. Even setting a regular rising time in the morning is important, so the purchasing of an alarm clock is definitely on the agenda. Routine allows the Vata person to become more aware of their strengths and weaknesses; to be alert to when they are becoming agitated or over-stimulated, excited or tired. It gives them the chance to self-regulate and to know when to slow down and find a place of inner calm. Herbs known to pacify Vata include gotu kola and ginseng, while warm, sweet aromas such as basil, orange, rose geranium and clove of aromatherapy are believed to gently pacify excessive Vata energy.

As with everything, the key is to eat in moderation. Avoid excessive eating by only dining in small but regular portions. Include plenty of warm, heavy, oily, moist, foods in the diet: regular servings of meat (in moderate portions) prepared with herbs and spices such as cardamom, cinnamon, clove, coriander, cumin, ginger, fennel and nutmeg. Favour sweet, sour and salty foods, warm foods, moderately heavy textured foods, butter and fat and soothing foods such as warm milk, cream, butter, warm soups and stews, hot cereals and fresh bread.

Eat plenty of rice, oats, rice gruel and cooked vegetables in general: asparagus, beets, carrots, celery, garlic, green beans, okra, onion, parsnips,

KIDS! Indigo Children and Cheeky Monkeys

radish, turnips, sweet potato, and water chestnuts. Most fruits are ideal, if ripe and in season: cooked tomatoes, fresh mangoes and mature apricots are especially good. Meat is beneficial, in regular small portions. Poultry, fresh fish, venison, occasional lamb or beef are great grounding choices, as are eggs, milk and dairy products, legumes, in small portions, especially mung beans, black and red lentils, chickpeas, split peas and lentils cooked or sprouted, nuts and seeds. Pumpkin seeds and peeled almond kernels are perfect. Oils, chiefly sesame oil; honey and sweets, ginger and garlic, small amounts of spices, particularly asafoetida and small amounts of diluted wine may be imbibed, but remain aware of the Vata person's inherent addictive personality.

Minimise or avoid all raw foods, dry foods, leafy vegetables, cold foods and frozen foods. Wheat, bread, spinach, potatoes, raw tomato, eggplant and peppers (actually, all members of the 'nightshade' family) and astringent fruits such as cranberries and pomegranates should be avoided, especially when suffering from sore joints. Drying fruits, such as apples and grapes, dried fruits, safflower oil and sugar should also be shunned.

As per Homeopathy

The homeopathic remedies listed below may be beneficial in helping to balance the Nature Child's constitution:

- Carcinosin
- Nat-murMercurius
- Pulsatilla
- Sepia
- Tuberculinum

For a deeper explanation of these suggested homeopathic remedies, please refer to the section at the rear of this book dedicated entirely to homeopathy and its history, and the chart listing the keynotes of each remedy on page 281.

Other Advice

Herbal remedies known to generally assist the overall wellbeing of the Nature Child include those derived from gotu kola and ginseng and chamomile. Of course, as with all herbal medicines, it is wise to seek advice from your integrative holistic doctor or naturopath before self-prescribing remedies of any sort.

Contemplate the use of aromatherapy, particularly the warm scents of basil, orange, rose geranium and clove, juniper, eucalyptus and marjoram, when addressing the needs of the Nature Child. By gently dispersing their aroma into their space via an electric oil burner or releasing three or four drops directly into their bath, your Nature Child will relish in the healing, calming qualities of the oils. All Nature Children *love* crystals and respond almost right away to their subtle healing energies. Iolite, or water sapphire, for example, is useful for inspiring dreams and revelations and for better understanding the messages hidden within. It also implants the understanding that acknowledgment of responsibility for one's actions and reactions can only lead to brilliance and success in all endeavours, while emeralds help to remove pessimism from one's life. This beautiful stone helps us make positive decisions so that we may remain focused and practical. It removes blockages and things that impede progress. Emeralds enhance memory and are celebrated as the stone of thriving love because they provide familial harmony, compassion and fidelity. Turquoise radiates the consciousness of the Earth Mother's love and wisdom while helping to align all the chakras. It enhances spiritual understanding, is powerfully protective, grounding, healing and cleansing, while aquamarine, the 'stone of courage', enhances the capacity for quick scholarly retort. It instils excellence as a natural quality, while assisting the Nature Child to strengthen their intellectual reasoning and response, learning ability and preparation. Aquamarine is both flowing and structured, providing emotional security and stability to the water-influenced Nature Child. It emits gentleness and empathy in moderation while helping those who tend to be judgemental to be more compassionate and patient. It is very calming and helps those who are stressed to find balance.

Obsidian, a shimmering volcanic glass, candidly reflects the Nature Child's imperfections, while instilling profound understanding of what needs to be done to purge them. It helps them find answers to difficult questions and find the course of action needed to initiate them. Obsidian is powerfully grounding, protective and stabilising. Apache tears, a form of obsidian, are said to have been first created by Native American women whose tears fell in mourning for warriors sent over a precipice by attacking soldiers. Consequently, it comforts in time of grief, is cleansing, healing and comforting, while onyx is useful in the banishing of grief, the enhancing of self-control and the stimulation of wise decision making. It brings happiness and good fortune and is powerfully cleansing. Jet, another stone ideally suited as support for the Nature Child, is in fact a type of fossilised wood. It is said to disperse fearful beliefs and protect against illness and violence. It is calming and useful in combating depression, while sodalite provides for friendship, camaraderie and the unification of a group. It helps one arrive at logical conclusions via rational mental processes, eliminates confusion and builds intellectual prowess. Sodalite enhances acceptance and honesty in our emotions and encourages us to verbalise true feelings — something all Nature Children need help with. Jasper is revered as the 'supreme nurturer'. It reminds us that we are not alone on this planet to live selfishly, that we must consider others and do what we can to make their life better. Jasper provides for the realisation of responsibility and protection. It is a sustaining stone that offers strength and endurance, particularly when energy is low. Carnelian, an inspirational stone, kindles analytical aptitude and precision. It fosters discernment, dexterity and our inherent gifts of power. Carnelian protects against envy, fear, rage and helps banish sorrow. It diffuses laziness, indifference and submissiveness and combats neuralgia.

Rose quartz is better known as 'the stone of unconditional love'. It is excellent for healing emotional wounds and is calming, gentle and peaceful. Tourmaline is motivational, indulgent and promotes self-assurance, while fresh water pearls invite trust, assistance and virtue in the Nature Child's life, while enhancing personal integrity and focusing attention. Blue topaz, a stone of true love and success in all endeavours, provides for clear communication, while lapis lazuli brings about clarity, knowledge, consciousness and greater intellectual capacity. Although already highly intuitive, lapis helps develop the Nature Child's psychic ability, courage and confidence in such matters. Lapis lazuli combats depression by instilling a sense of tranquillity and buoyancy. Aventurine, on the other hand, helps balance one's inherent masculine and feminine energies, while simultaneously enhancing resourcefulness, incentive and an avant-garde attitude to life.

Nature Children are powerfully intuitive. Encourage them to join and participate in a 'spiritual development' group, visit a psychic fair and attend the workshops and seminars being offered, or buy them a deck of faerie or animal oracle cards and teach them how to use them properly. Show your Nature Child how to create a dreamcatcher so that they may harness and better understand their 'good' dreams while banishing their 'bad' dreams and night terrors. Encourage them, too, to call upon the faerie realm, archangel Gabriel and the king of the water elementals, Necksa, for guidance and protection.

Nature Children love and respect animals, so allowing your child to have a pet of their own will offer purpose, immediate love and someone they can tell their secrets to. It will encourage them to take responsibility for something other than themselves, while helping them realise that unless they take responsibility for themselves, no one will be there to care for their pet. Allow your child to choose their own pet as the bond is often forged right there in the pet store, and is always a personal thing. Small, fluffy Dogs, rag-doll Cats, Hares, Guinea pigs, Turtles, Fish, Frogs and Ducks make excellent pets (and companions) for Nature Children. If you are not in the position to have a pet, make regular visits to a local children's farm or petting zoo. There are many children's farms listed in the yellow pages, or organise to have a travelling farm pay a special visit to your child's next birthday party. Nature Children respond amazingly well to the warm, gentle softness of Lambs, baby Deer and Goats, Calves, Rabbits, fluffy Chickens, Ducklings and Piglets. The sight of such animals literally brings both my children to tears, with their soft cooing and giggling melting the hearts of those in attendance.

Tap into this love of animals in a therapeutic way, too, by having them draw a picture of their favourite animal and a picture of the animal they fear the most. Explain that the 'Medicine' or Dreaming of the favourite animal represents their strengths and aspirations while that of the animal they fear represents their vulnerabilities, fears and weaknesses. The animals we fear are equally as important and as valuable to our growth as the animals we love. They represent those aspects of our psyche that we choose to ignore — our fears, our secrets and dark thoughts. They characterise our personal boundaries, our self-imposed limitations and those parts of us that reject spontaneity, risk taking and the development of self-esteem. They also represent our dark side — the shadow aspect of our soul that we tend to ignore or suppress due to the connotations that they represent and the responsibilities that they force upon us. They make us to look at ourselves, to stand before our weaknesses and our frailties and to honour them as lessons and as stepping-stones to power. Nature Children are commonly drawn to Squirrel Monkeys, Serpents, Dolphins, Koalas, Fish, Seals, Sea Birds, Frogs, Turtles, Otters, Platypus, Swans, Crabs, Bears and black Horses as totems or power aspects.

Nature Children love to pretend and make believe. They love to dance, sing and perform little plays for their family. As they grow older, nurture this natural love by inspiring further exploration of the performing arts: drama, dance (particularly classical dance or ballet) and song. Encourage them to learn to play a reed instrument, the harp or some other bowed string instrument, like the cello, violin or viola. Visit a theatre, the Opera House, a museum of performing arts. Alternatively, investigate the fine arts: painting, drawing, sculpture, textiles and fashion design. Visit a gallery, a reputable fashion house or investigate the library, Internet or magazines for inspiration. Take a stroll with your Nature Child along a slow moving stream or river, go on a house boat holiday on a lake or take a trip to the ocean or the beach. Stand atop or beneath a waterfall, drop coins into a well or drink fresh water from a natural spring. All these activities will promote your child's inherent love of nature and their natural creative abilities, as will Qigong (explained above), Hatha yoga and Tai Chi — activities that gently focus the mind while helping to harness self-control. Hatha yoga is all about uniting the mind and body by means of exercise, meditation, focused breathing, healthy attitude and meaningful posture, while Tai Chi is an ancient Chinese art of movement. It was first created as a form of martial art, a form that inspires self-defence by emphasising stillness, inner balance and self-discipline. Today the flowing movements are practised as a holistic form of exercise designed to increase flexibility, body posture and balance and to return us to our innate place of ancient knowing and power.

Nature Children need to be involved in activities that inspire and energise them, and that help them to learn to accept help, praise and encouragement from others; activities that inspire them to communicate and interact with other people. They do best when permitted to spend quality time in nature surrounded by animals. Outdoor activities, such as Whale-watching, swimming with Dolphins, fly-fishing, Horse trail-riding, surfing, hiking, canoeing, kayaking, for example, are so well suited to the Nature Child, it is as if they were created with them in mind, as are white-water rafting, boating, yachting, swimming, scuba-diving, snorkelling, rock-pooling and beachcombing.

Nature Children are predisposed to becoming doctors, nurses and paramedics; people who treat patients at the scene. They are emotionally strong when needed and the best ones equipped when compassion, nurturing and caring are urgently required. Nature Children also tend to become artists, painters, dancers and actors; areas that involve flowing, creative expression. They also make proficient counsellors, due to their caring, intuitive dispositions, and excellent vets, animal/wildlife workers and forestry officers. As spiritual paths, both Wicca and witchcraft are gentle, practical, tangible, nurturing, nature-based and all embracing, and espouse a philosophy aligned with the beliefs and values of teenage and adult Nature Children.

As Janet and Stewart Farrar explain in their book, *Eight Sabbats for Witches* (Robert Hale, London, 1981), *'Wicca is both a religion and a craft. As a religion — like any other religion — its purpose is to put the individual and the group in harmony with the divine creative principal of the cosmos, and its manifestation at all levels. As a craft, its purpose is to achieve practical ends by psychic means, for good, useful and healing purposes. In both aspects, the distinguishing characteristics of Wicca are its nature - based attitudes, its small group autonomy with no gulf between priesthood and 'congregation', and its philosophy of creative polarity at all levels, from goddess and god to priestess and priest.'*

To find out more about witchcraft as a path of ancient wisdom, visit my dear friend Lucy Cavendish at www.lucycavendish.com. You will find that she is a WiseWoman, a powerful teacher and a passionate advocate of the goddess and the old ways.

4

The Ring-Tailed Lemur

Totem of the Peacekeeper Child
Keynotes: Outsider / Witness / Pacifier

Representing the most ancient branch of the order of primates, early ancestors of the Lemur evolved into Apes and Monkeys. Lemurs themselves, however, developed separately into their current forms. Found primarily on Madagascar, the ecological isolation afforded by the island and its wealth of natural habitat has enabled the Lemur to exist with relatively little interference from the outside world. Categorised into three strains (the Dwarf or 'Mouse' Lemurs, the Sportive Lemurs and the True Lemurs) the 43 individual species of Lemur are all native to the island. The most universally recognised is the Ring-tailed Lemur, a true Lemur, which prefers the dry scrub and deciduous forests of Madagascar. The primary predator of the Lemur is the Fossa, a large Civet that fluently chases its prey through the branches of the forest trees.

The word 'Lemur' actually means *ghost*, while the Roman translation *Lemure* refers to 'Ancestral Spirit'. It was thought that, on a set date each year, Ancestral Spirits rose from their resting places to attend The Festival of Lemuria or 'The Festival of the Ghost World' (the term Lemuria literally means 'ghost world'). According to legend, a beautiful continent known as 'Lemuria', or Mu, once thrived in a similar time frame to Atlantis. The two historically overlapped briefly between 30,000 and 25,000 years before the birth of Christ. Lemuria may have been so named because of the controversial claims made by Darwin in association with his theory surrounding the origin of animal species. Apparently zoologists of the time had difficulty explaining the limited distribution of the Lemur, while other animals were found scattered over very large areas. To explain the phenomenon, 19th Century scientists proposed a landmass that may have existed somewhere between Madagascar and India. The continent was named after the Lemur and became known as the 'former land of the Lemur', or *Lemuria*. Legends of Lemuria are alive and well throughout the islands of the Pacific Ocean, with the Polynesian people referring to a mysterious continent that once existed in the Pacific; the Land of Mu, the Motherland of Man and the home of our ancestors. Although psychic mediums claim to channel advanced beings that once inhabited Lemuria, the islander's legend of Mu may tell of a different place entirely — a land riddled with human ancestry.

Ring-tailed Lemur people are charming, appealing and assured. Most are attractive, beautiful and youthful in appearance. They love being the centre of attention and easily draw a crowd. Ring-tailed Lemur people are funny, artistic and demonstrative; someone who will hug, kiss or reach out and hold hands on first meeting. Their positive attitude and child-like personality are both inviting and pleasing. Ring-tailed Lemur people are innocent; they look out at the world in awe and wonder. They are honest, truthful and live in the present. Unpredictable at times, Ring-tailed Lemur people can be candid and blunt. They are family oriented, popular with all ages, supportive, helpful and see only the good in others. They make effective leaders, are inventive and creative.

They are effective networkers, matchmakers and dot-joiners. Ring-tailed Lemur people are profoundly clairvoyant, intuitive and knowledgeable, all carrying an inherent and uniquely personal belief in the spirit world. With the Lemur as their totem (a recognised ambassador of the ghost world) most are profoundly psychic, with 'ghostly visitations' not an uncommon occurrence. As a result, they make powerful mediums, spirit communicators, channels and clairvoyants.

Ring-tailed Lemur people are active, enthusiastic and inspiring; are community oriented, charitable and spontaneous. They love to be complimented, are forgiving and apologise without prompting. They attract friends easily because they seem exciting, privileged and lucky. Ring-tailed Lemur people never 'shut up'. When not of the reserved, watchful type, they can be described as chatterers, gossips, embellishers and storytellers. Ring-tailed Lemur people talk incessantly. They love trivia and can appear frivolous and dizzy because they are forgetful. They forget names, important details and dates. As a result, they can appear self-important and restless. They tend to complain about petty things, are often accused of being lazy and are sometimes loud.

On the other hand, when acting in the negative phase other people can find their ways off-putting. Ring-tailed Lemur people are very naïve to the ways of the world. They are curious and ask a lot of questions, but often don't wait for or listen to the answers offered. Ring-tailed Lemur people can be crass and shallow. They tend to externalise blame, anger easily and be negligent of responsibility. They are also untidy. Very disorganised, Ring-tailed Lemur people are childish, immature and shallow. They are often described as being fake, unsympathetic and forced. Ring-tailed Lemur people suffer from selective hearing, self-doubt and apprehension. They are daydreamers; undisciplined creatures that often don't listen. They sometimes display egocentric qualities, too, while demonstrating uncompromising and sanctimonious attitudes. They strive to bring conversation back to their goings-on whenever possible, and love to offer every little detail when recounting a story (never for one minute considering the possibility that their listeners don't care or that they may be bored to distraction). Inappropriately lenient on one hand and mercilessly strict on another, Ring-tailed Lemur people often make disorganised parents who give their children mixed messages. They can appear unmotivated or disinterested, offering support begrudgingly or when it doesn't interfere with their personal plans. They can also be teasing in their observations. They can be attention seekers, procrastinators and time wasters. They are easily distracted. Ring-tailed Lemur people often confuse their priorities, appear needy and are often unpopular to the majority. They yearn to be popular, successful and wise, but usually fail in their attempts because they interrupt, make excuses and are repetitive and boring (but only when severely expressing their shadow selves).

Individual advice for the Ring-tailed Lemur / Peacekeeper Child

Correspondences:

Esoteric Element: Air
Traditional Chinese Element: Metal
Elemental Instruments: Wind instruments, the didgeridoo, pipes, flutes, bells and wind chimes
Elemental Spirits: Sylphs, Zephyrs and the faeries of the trees, flowers, wind, breezes and the mountains, air or winged Dragons
Direction: East
Directional Colours: Golden yellow
Season: Spring
Time of Power: Morning, dawn, sunrise
Symbolic Phase of Life on the Wheel of Life: The baby, infant, new born child
Power Places: Cliffs, high snow-capped, mist covered mountainous regions, the 'high country', alpine regions, the countryside when it is alive with baby animals, wild flowers and signs of new life
Zodiacs as per the Corresponding Esoteric Element: Gemini, Libra and Aquarius
Organs: Lungs, large intestines
Chakras: Throat (fifth), Thymus or the 'Ananda Khanda' (fourth/fifth)
Chakra Colours: Sky blue, white, turquoise
Crystals: Turquoise, tiger eye, blue lace agate, howlite, sapphire, clear quartz topaz, yellow fluorite, citrine, tin and copper
Totems: Palomino Horse, Ring-tailed Lemur, the Sunbird, the Eagle, Hawk and the Owl
Herbs: Pansies, primroses, vervain, violets, yarrow, dill, wattle blossom and bracken fern, daffodils and lavender

The prime objective of the Peacekeeper Child's journey is to move from a state of detachment and disinterest to a place of illumination and inspiration. Their 'mission' is to breathe the Breath of Life — to not only deliver themselves into a place of understanding and ecstasy, but to instil it in the lives of all they meet. Their tool is the spoken word; its vehicle, Sacred

Breath. Breath is life. Without breath, we are disconnected from each other and ourselves. Without breath we are devoid of Spirit. Attentive and proper breathing is vital for the attainment of higher levels of awareness. Breath is one of the oldest forms of healing, with focused breathing known to harness and manage pain during childbirth, for example. Their true purpose is to bring people together and to encourage good communication between them. It is to build bridges and join the dots; to create a web of sharing. It is to become a messenger: one who spreads the true word and it is to learn to use their intellect in service of their true purpose.

Peacekeeper Children are natural born communicators and networkers. Unlike the animal-loving Warrior and Nature Children, Peacekeeper Children *love* people, mobile phones and email. They enjoy nothing better than linking people up and bringing people together. As adults, they make perfect matchmakers and wedding planners, who thrive on organising blind dates and surprise reunions. If ever anything needs doing, Peacekeeper Children are the best people to ask. They may not offer to help themselves, but they will have a friend or associate trained or experienced in the required field, no matter what that area may be. They will know immediately who to call, when to call and what to ask. If ever you get the chance to be a contestant on *Who Wants to be a Millionaire?*, phone a Peacekeeper Child if you get stuck because if they don't know the answer, they will know someone who does. Peacekeeper Children are able to look at any situation from a detached, unemotional perspective, and immediately determine what needs to be done and why. They make excellent problem solvers, moderators and counsellors because of their ability to remain aloof and disconnected. While focusing much of their attention on the welfare of other people, however, they often forget about their own families. Not overly paternal or maternal in nature, adult Peacekeeper Children typically espouse the 'tough love' approach to raising their children and are often accused of being cold and, at times, heartless when it comes to attending to their emotional needs. In some cases, Peacekeeper Children are seen as being somewhat unbalanced, sardonic, miserly and narcissistic.

Peacekeeper Children are the theory-oriented rationalists. As children they are light-hearted, cheerful, sociable and optimistic. They are the confident, helpful, positive, honest members of the community who hate conflict, fights and disagreements. Instead, they love to talk, laugh, sing and dance, and believe that everything is beautiful and perfect. Growing up, they are the pacifiers, outsiders and the observers, who try to see only the good in others; the gregarious, unpredictable ones, driven by a genuinely benevolent desire to make a difference. As adults, they are the romantic 'new agers'; the rescuers who frequently refer to themselves as 'Light Workers'. Light Workers affectionately sign their emails off with 'in love and light' and candidly sanction the existence of angels and other celestial beings (and rightly so). They are usually the ones endowed with the knowledge to organise and run spiritual development circles and offer tarot readings at spiritual festivals. They are highly intuitive and, in some cases, profoundly psychic, but sometimes fall victim to overblown ego. Despite being driven to spread the word (which they do with style and grace), the wounded do-gooders among them occasionally express their wisdom in sanctimonious, condescending ways, giving the rest a bad reputation for being wacko or 'out there'.

In the severest of cases, Peacekeeper Children carry the 'abandoned child' archetype and tend to adopt the victim mentality. They hate being alone, for example, and blindly jump from one relationship to the next to avoid loneliness, ignoring the safety, wants and needs of others close to them (often their own children). In doing so, they unwittingly repeat their patterns and continue a personal cycle of unrequited or overly possessive love, while losing the respect of those who genuinely adore them. They are likely to fall prey to confusion, denial, disassociation, depersonalisation and even drug-induced psychosis or hebephrenic schizophrenia. When this is the case, they appear outwardly gentle and loving, but when crossed, fire up quickly and react rather than respond. They become angry, resentful and hurtful. They tend to blame circumstance or other people for their misfortunes or shortcomings and would rather wait to be rescued by a knight in shining armour than put effort into improving their own lives. They often conceal a spiteful, jealous nature under a veil of feigned 'love and light'. They are quick to accuse others of being judgemental and egotistical because they know they are very much guilty of those 'sins' themselves, while failing to recognise the law of reflection that clearly states that what bothers you about another is typically your greatest weakness or downfall.

The depersonalisation, paranoia and suppressed fury is often induced by a past riddled with drug or alcohol abuse, or cellular or conscious memory of it happening within their immediate family circle. Like the Warrior Children, many Peacekeeper Children have lived a life of violence, abuse, poor health, uncertainty or unstable foundation, and this is why they hate conflict and respond to it the way they do. It is as if they internally panic; feeling as if they have to do something to prove their worth and resolve the unrest (even when they are not at fault). They feel as if they are being blamed or are somehow responsible and fire up in defence and become quite emotional and irrational when they can't explain or argue their case. As teenagers and adults, they often pair up romantically with fellow Peacekeeper Children because they are drawn to their physicality and dynamic personality. Unless fully balanced and in tune with themselves holistically, however, such a pairing rarely lasts. Peacekeeper Children will generally pair up second time round with Winter Children (but must be careful not to do so in the role of 'rescuer'). They often have Warrior Children as siblings or offspring and are generally the grandparents of Nature Children or Golden Children (although there are always exceptions).

To move to their positive phase or to maintain balance, Peacekeeper Children must be given opportunity to develop belief in their own self-worth, to remain true to themselves and never ever sell themselves short and to speak up and stand their ground, but in an assertive rather than aggressive, resentful way. They must be encouraged to persevere and complete what they set out to do, find what works for them and keep at it, find a career they enjoy doing or that supports their sense of higher purpose, and have fun with people, the whole time being sensitive to their needs, personal beliefs and preferences. Peacekeeper Children achieve more and do best when they can stick to a strict daily routine. They must endeavour to remain grounded at all times (and avoid floating away with the pixies), partake in regular exercise, prayer and meditation and take time out to ponder the deeper, meaningful aspects of life.

And they would do well to remember that things are not always what they seem and to never judge a book by its cover, especially when it comes to affairs of the heart and the spiritual arena. Although it is generally safe to assume that 'if it quacks like a duck, it probably *is* a duck', one should never make assumptions based on appearances or first impressions alone; a realisation that must be integrated into *all* arenas of their life.

Just as there are angelic forces (both cosmic and earthly in form) that yearn to inspire us and see us prosper and heal, for example, there are apposing forces (of equal strength and power) that would happily starve us of purpose and see us shrivel up and die. The light and dark are present in all things, with the word 'light' not always corresponding to what is 'good' or 'positive' and the word 'dark' not always meaning 'bad' or 'negative'. One should never accept or trust without question. Should you ever encounter an 'angel' (either in the tangible world, or in the non-physical realms of meditation, dream or vision), immediately and ruthlessly quiz the entity for proof of its authenticity and integrity. Why? Because, although it is safe and correct to assume that a true 'being of the light' would never betray, forsake or abuse its role as messenger of God, Spirit or 'the light', a true dark-side entity would. If you were to ask "Are you an angel?" an authentic angel (a being of pure energy charged with the role of messenger, healer and bringer of wisdom) would explicitly reply, "Yes". Angels are ambassadors of Spirit, and Spirit never lies, makes mistakes or has accidents. Yes means yes, remaining the only answer that can be absolutely trusted. Should your angel reply with a riddle; an answer hidden behind a question, your angel is not what it seems. If you were to ask your angel: "Are you an angel", and if your 'angel' were to reply with a challenge like: "Why? Do you *need* me to be an angel?" then you can bet your bottom dollar that what you have standing in front of you is in fact a dark-side entity wearing the acceptable and expected garb of an angel. Dark-side entities are driven by one motivation: to confuse, obstruct and dissuade, and they will do whatever it takes to fulfil that goal, even it if it involves 'dressing up' or pretending to be something they aren't. We should endeavour to always walk the fine line of integrity and impeccability, all the while demonstrating full awareness of both the 'light' and 'dark' in all things. To only dance 'in the light' is equally potentially as dangerous as working primarily with the forces of the 'dark-side'. To assume that everything of Spirit is good and beautiful is just as ignorant as assuming that all aspects of the dark are inherently evil. Although it remains a universal truth that the light side will never intentionally betray you, the dark-side will readily permeate the light, negatively affecting all that it encounters like a cancerous tumour. But, while this is the case, the dark-side offers valid lessons and experiences that, although usually devastating in nature, offer opportunities to grow and broaden one's view of life. Therefore, while walking a path of impeccability, it is a wise man that acknowledges the good and bad in all things, but only draws to him those things that promise to benefit him in a balanced way while questioning their authenticity constantly.

As per the Four Humours: the Sanguine

Sanguines are both engaging and charming; the loquacious narrators of truthful anecdotes and exaggerated adventures. They are fun to be around, are exciting and entertaining, with a hilarious sense of humour and a comical outlook on life. Sanguines are demonstrative and affectionate, expressive and friendly, passionate and animated. They are positive about what drives them and fervent about their loves and passions. They are inquisitive, and love to study, find answers and ask questions. They are the performers, comedians and show-offs. Sanguines are present in everything they do. They live in the now.

Although they can be unpredictable at times, they are genuine at heart. They are obsessive chatterers. They love to embellish stories while going into painful detail when relaying their interpretation of accounts, and they often forget important details, like names, dates, and so on. This aspect of their persona can make them sound like 'try-hards' and come across as being a tad off-putting and fake. They often appear fidgety and nervous, over excitable and arrogant. Sanguines tend to protest and grumble, are naïve, gullible and boisterous. Sanguines have a propensity to believe life is best controlled by external force, and when working in their shadow, see it as influenced by negative conditioning and circumstances outside their control. They can be hot-headed, irresponsible and immature. Hence the need, according to the philosophy advocating the Four Humours, for the Sanguine to be given the chance to 'dry out and cool off' in order to reach their potential.

Sanguines need to remember that there is more to life than superficial fun and games if they are to reach their highest potential. They can do this by regularly spending time focused on the spiritual, ethical and benevolent aspects of life. One suggestion worth investigating is to follow the law of true tithing, which espouses giving ten percent of the day to God so that they may be blessed. Meditation and prayer may also help. They must strive to live life in a good way by doing unto others as they would have done unto them. They need to participate in grounding activities and spend time working with the Earth Mother. Sanguines need to structure their day's routine by developing strict timetables and thorough planning and they need to complete what they start, have fun and remain mindful of others.

As per the Five Esoteric Elements: Air

Each morning the sun rises in the east — the direction of the greatest light, wisdom and consciousness. As the Kookaburras' chuckle heralds a new day, the promise of new beginnings is realised by all. As the sun's first rays banish the dark mysteries of night, it simultaneously births a new day. Potential is ripe, the air is crisp and opportunity is there for the taking. The east symbolically embodies the energies generated by spring, the season of new growth and fertility, governed by the element of air. In the spring the countryside is dotted with baby animals, the air is warm and the fields are being sown. It is a time of balance and harmony, when light and dark stand equal. It is a time to celebrate life and what it means to be alive. Spring and its correspondences are masculine in nature, being dry, expansive and active. According to the teachings of the Wheel of Life, during spring we find ourselves symbolically back in infancy, ready to start life over, armed with the innocence of childhood. The gifts of illumination and intuition are ours for the taking. Spring's energies also govern the zodiacal signs of Gemini, Libra and Aquarius, which are all air signs.

Those ruled by the air element are also ruled by their mind, for better or worse. They are typically intuitive, aware, sharp, clear-thinking people who can sometimes appear overloaded, overwhelmed and befuddled, especially when tired or stressed. They are eloquent speakers when roused and, at times, a tad unpredictable. Being an air type is about connecting with people. They are likable and are easy to listen to. They are popular, stimulating and blessed with the 'everyone loves them' gene. When working in their positive phase, they are genuinely angelic in nature, bringing joy and contentment to those they meet. When in this phase, they are whisperers of the Breath of Life and the heavenly realms because they resonate energetically with Mercury, the messenger of the gods. The air element is all about understanding, the mind, communication, truth, composed observation and blowing with the winds of change. Air types are also prone to anorexia, stiff aching cracking joints, insomnia, a racing mind, constipation and a shortness of breath. They are often physically beautiful or handsome, with long, thin, willowy bodies and well defined arms, and they typically move in a fast, abrupt gait.

Intellectual by nature, air types spend too much time in their heads thinking analytically about everything. They mentally pick things to pieces, assessing and reassessing all the time. Air types stress and strain about the simplest of things, often suffering from nervous tension, headaches and anxiety as a result, while occasionally leaning dependently upon cigarettes and alcohol as supportive crutches. They care too much about what other people might think, but are able to blend themselves, chameleon-like, into any situation, environment or setting. Most air types would do well to spend time exploring their polar opposite element: water. The water element invites people to go within, to meditate, quiet the mind-chatter and ponder; to seek answers to their questions within the recesses of their conscious mind and to completely trust the inner guidance they find there.

To appeal to the supportive, constructive qualities of air, dance merrily to the sound of wind instruments, pipes, flutes, bells and wind chimes to invoke the Sylphs; the elemental spirits of the air. Take strolls along mountain paths, practise yoga on a cliff top, go hang-gliding, parasailing, parachuting, hot-air ballooning or try flying a kite on a particularly windy day.

A Guided Visualisation that explores the Air Element:

Find yourself a comfy place where you know you will not be interrupted. If possible, find a place in nature. Sit with your back supported by the trunk of a tree, a smooth rock or a mossy log. Sit with the intention of strengthening your bond with Spirit and of remembering your inherent relationship with the Earth Mother. You may want to wrap yourself in a blanket, because it is not uncommon for one's body temperature to drop as you sink deeper and deeper into stillness. Quiet your conscious mind and endeavour to silence your inner chatter. Wait for the moment when you intuitively feel inclined to open your consciousness to the Other Realms. Ensure that your subconscious mind is receptive and alert by speaking to your conscious mind. Allow visions and symbolic images to float through your mind. Keep your focus within yourself. Let any thoughts just go by. When you catch yourself engaged in an external conscious thought, just take a deep breath and bring yourself back to your centre.

You are now ready to begin.

Picture yourself on a great grassy plane, dotted with the most beautifully coloured wild flowers. From where you are standing you can see two very different sights. To your right is a path leading up to a steep mountain peak and to your left is a path leading down into a deep valley. The point at which you are standing is in fact the intersection of time and reality; a mingling point of reality and 'the Other Worlds', of the physical and the mystical. It is where the miraculous can be found.

Visualise yourself standing on the steep, mountain peak, facing the east watching the sunrise in the direction of the greatest light. The delicate, airy scent of pansies, primroses, violets, yarrow and lavender fill your nostrils and the sound of the leaves rustling on the surrounding aspen trees comfort you. You feel the whispered breath of Eurus, the East Wind stroking your hair. It is spring and the air is fresh. You look to the yellow sky and see symbols forming in the clouds. As if offering a blessing to the new dawn, you begin tossing golden feathers into the air. You watch them drift away, being carried on the light breeze to the mist-covered valley below. You feel positive, alive and strong. You realise that this is a new day and everything you didn't get done yesterday is ready to be tackled today. You are like a child, an infant, waking for the first time in a world filled with promises, wonder and excitement. You hear the sound of a flute, its song carried to you on the gentle breeze.

Suddenly you hear an approaching sound and as you look up, you see a flock of Ravens. Mingled amongst them is a pair of Eagles and several Hawks. You watch them fly and feel an intense desire to join them, but before you get the chance, they are gone – except for a single Eagle, circling above, so high that it is no more than a dot against the now crimson sky. You sit down and close your eyes and in your mind's eye, you picture yourself surrounded by faeries and zephyrs, elemental beings that inhabit windy, magickal places. You open your eyes and to your surprise, standing in front of you are three beings, transparent as glass, yet quite physical. They are each holding something in their hand — one carries a sword, one carries a dagger with an amethyst encrusted handle and the other holds a wand with a clear crystal point. They tell you they are Sylphs — elemental spirits of the air, sent by angel Raphael and the king of the air elementals, Paralda. Their flowing robes look like wisps of smoke or swirls of mist. They appear to be suspended, yet physical enough to stand. They are of this world, but somehow not. They speak, but not with words. It is as if they communicate through thought alone. Their world is governed by the mental and their knowledge is abstract in nature. They travel on the wind, they speak by breathing and their instruction is both telepathic and inspirational.

They invite you to join them. They beckon you to enter their ethereal world, where freedom beyond belief can be found. They inspire you to learn, to know and to understand everything, to unlock secrets and to grow on a psychic level.

The Sylphs bid you to step forward. They ask you to close your eyes and walk. You shut your eyes and take a step. You take another and find that you cannot find a foothold. The Sylphs encourage you to continue, to have trust in their wisdom. You continue and to your surprise, you do not fall. You open your eyes and realise that you are in fact about a metre or so from the edge of the mountain peak and moving further away by the second. You are standing, yet not, on nothing, yet something. You are one with the

Sylph's world. You are suspended as if by invisible threads, yet none exist. The Sylphs have altered you and your perception of reality and in this world you are capable of travelling through their airy terrain on notion alone. You are capable of flight. They laugh and dart off. They look back and call to you to follow. You dive as if falling and then, as if by instinct, you pull yourself up before reaching the valley floor. You follow the Sylphs as they lead you on a flight of fancy across farmlands and forests, through valleys and mountain ranges, great lakes and sandy beaches. You fly for what seems like an eternity, all the time hearing the joyous laughter of the Sylphs — the envoys of the east.

After some time, the Sylphs bring you back to your mountain top retreat and, through the language of thought, reveal a truth to you that only you can relate to. It may be a memory, a new learning; the location of a thing thought lost or a communication with someone in Spirit. They may be telling you to study something new, such as divination, herbal knowledge, a wind instrument, Zen meditation or to make contact with the angelic realm. Whatever they share with you, they remind you to look to the ancient art of prophecy and to always remember the rules of karma.

With that, the Sylphs disappear and leave you on your own. Hearing a gentle flapping sound, you turn to see a string of prayer flags fluttering in the breeze, suspended in the branches of a leafless tree. Realising their significance, you make a silent prayer to Spirit for a reason sacred to you and to offer thanks, taking three breaths in through your nose and out through your mouth before returning to the physical place in which you are seated.

As per Traditional Chinese Medicine: the Metal / Lung Person

According to the teachings of Traditional Chinese Medicine, Peacekeeper Children, as 'lung people', have their mind, body and energy systems focused on the air/metal element; metal in its gaseous form, that is, or when it appears as a vapour. The colour traditionally associated with metal is white, hence the pale complexion of those strongly influenced by this element.

The lung person has their dominant focus on the analytical and intellectual aspects of life; on the power of breath and art of detachment — just as leaves will often detach from the tree and go sailing on the breeze. At a bodily level, when this relationship is understood and the lung person is working in harmony with his or her element, a greater level of wellbeing for the tissues related to the lung is achieved, according to the teachings of Traditional Chinese Medicine: a healthy large intestine and regular bowel, clear, radiant skin and a clear nose, the main appendage used for inhaling air. The lung person who has balanced metal energy is logical, abstemious, and reliable. They crave organisation and regulation, with many choosing to join the police force or the military. They thrive when they know their boundaries and can achieve something by staying within them. Metal Qi (life-force) imparts endurance, stamina and inner strength, like the steel framework that supports a skyscraper.

When out of balance with his or her element, though, the lung person quickly becomes unbalanced, particularly if they insist on participating in excessive sedentary mental work, allowing themselves to become bored, or by not getting enough physical activity. They literally dry out and become noticeably listless and dull, which if not addressed, may lead to apathy and melancholy. A metal Qi imbalance may instil a sense of grief, with the person overwhelmed by depression. They can become snappy, impatient and picky and have trouble leaving well alone. A decline in metal Qi is often signified by illness of the lungs or skin; asthma, for example, allergies and frequent colds, rashes, eczema and excessive perspiration. If left untreated, the unbalanced lung person may become physically thin, anaemic, hunched over and short of breath, developing further into problems such as chronic insomnia and constipation, diarrhoea and other bowel disorders. Metal energy is easily boosted by the lung person being exposed to cool, crisp, clean air and after such a lift, lung people feel so invigorated and inspired they can achieve pretty much anything they put their mind to.

As metal/air people, Peacekeeper Children are prone to lung deficiency, so it is essential they do what they can to boost and maintain their lung Qi. According to Traditional Chinese Medicine, the lung is all about breath and personal advancement through life. Energetic activity in nature, such as a vigorous walk along the beach or a brisk trek through the mountains where there is plenty of fresh, clean air and oxygen will significantly aid in the restoration of depleted lung Qi, with a gradual increase in the daily regime built up over time, as will breathing exercises specifically designed to increase the level of oxygen carried to each of the body's cells (such as the Buteyko Breathing Technique). Public speaking courses (such as Toastmasters — a course that helps to conquer the fear of public speaking) and Hatha yoga will also benefit the process greatly. Hatha yoga rebuilds vitality and endurance, offering strength to get on with life. It reinstates focus by teaching effective breathing techniques and how to work from one's centre, removing that which is unimportant or disruptive.

The Breath of Life is thought to be nourished by the colour white, so boosting and maintaining lung Qi is made easier by wearing white clothing and eating white-coloured foods, especially *pungent* white foods such as onions, garlic, turnips, ginger, horseradishes, cabbages, radishes and white pepper. Moderate amounts of flake (shark meat), mutton, chicken broth, clams, eggs, watermelon, pine nuts, walnuts, peanuts, tangerines, rice, tuna, duck, pork and meat broth and leek soup is also recommended.

No matter how clean we keep our home, our environment nevertheless contains toxins that are normally flushed from our body with each healthy bowel movement. Irregular or unhealthy bowel movements may lead to the retention of these toxins in the body that, if left untreated, may lead to a number of disorders such as chronic constipation, headaches, bloating, bad breath, ulcerative colitis, diverticulosis (the formation of abnormal pouches in the bowel wall), allergies, depleted energy, bowel problems or irregularity, stomach ulcers, body odour, arthritis, irritable bowel syndrome and respiratory problems. Once a year, therefore, (from the age of approximately 18 onwards) lung people should investigate having some form of bowel-cleansing procedure done, such as colonic irrigation, a procedure also known as colonics, colonic lavage, colon irrigation and high colonic or colon hydrotherapy. Colonic Irrigation is a practice that gently cleanses the colon using filtered and temperature regulated water by means of a rectal catheter. Irregular or poor bowel movements may lead to bodily waste building up and compacting the colon, to be re-absorbed into the blood stream resulting in low vitality and disease. Colonic irrigation gently flushes the colon, thus softening and removing excess waste built up over time. It should be noted, however, that people suffering from acute or chronic illness, diarrhoea or immuno-compromising conditions should seek medical advice before carrying out any bowel-cleansing procedures. It is also advised that people who develop unusual infections, experience weakness or show other uncharacteristic symptoms as a result of colonic therapy should stop their treatment immediately, consult their doctor and report their symptoms to the therapist as soon as possible.

Like the Nature Children, Peacekeeper Children can similarly boost their life-force by practising Qigong and Tai Chi, and by embracing the benefits of acupuncture. Qigong refers to the combination of 'Qi' (air, breath, vital energy and life-force) and 'gong', the mastering of self-control and accomplishment. It incorporates meditation, relaxation, physical movement, mind/body integration and various breathing exercises. Acupuncture is deeply rooted in the belief that illness is caused when an imbalance is caused in the body's energy system. It is said to re-establish harmony by balancing the body's yin and yang. Acupuncture involves the painless insertion of fine needles into the body's meridians or energy channels (named after the organs they represent) to clear blocked Qi, releasing energy flow through the body. Tai Chi, on the other hand, is an ancient Chinese art of movement. It was first created as a form of martial art, a form that inspires self-defence by emphasising stillness, inner balance and self-discipline. Today the flowing movements are practised as a holistic form of exercise designed to increase flexibility, body posture and balance and to return us to our innate place of ancient knowing and power. Chinese herbs known to help boost lung Qi are astragalus, ginger and tang-shen, a herb related to ginseng, but milder, often added to meat broth.

As per Ayurveda: Air Energy / Vata

Vata, (a term that means 'wind, to move, flow, direct the processes of, or command') is drying, cooling and airy, rousing and ever-changing in nature. It is a force believed to be composed of the Aether and air elements. The level of Aether (or 'space') affects the degree to which the air may gain momentum. If unbridled, the air element can gather excessively in force and get out of hand, and become a destructive tempest.

Vata people are famous for their superior imaginations and intellectual acumen. They are highly creative and make fast learners. Vata people pick new skills up quickly but tend to forget them equally as fast, especially when they no longer need them. Physically, they tend to be finely built, thin and small with dry skin and hair. They don't seem to perspire very much. Vata people speak and walk in a hurried fashion, and complain constantly about having cold hands and feet. They hate cold weather or spending time in areas of cold climate. Vata people are highly strung and emotional, with vivacious, entertaining personalities. They tend to display unpredictable moods and can be quite unsystematic in their daily routine. They tend to have high levels of energy that only last for short bursts. They tire quickly and generally over do things. Those who know them would probably describe them as being happy, spontaneous and animated when in balance, but stressed, fearful, fretful and nervous when not. Vata people tend to spend money as quickly as they earn it so, as a rule of thumb, rarely have enough to cover the bare essentials.

From an early age, Vata people need to be provided with opportunity to express and develop their inherent creative artistic selves and to convey their imagination in a grounded way. An emphasis on regularity in the daily routine is vital, such as disciplined meal times, bath times and bedtime. Even setting a regular rising time in the morning is important, so the purchasing of an alarm clock is definitely on the agenda. A strict regime is very important when it comes to pacifying Vata energy, as is a quiet, harmonious environment, plenty of warm fluids, ample rest, bodily warmth and a steady supply of nourishment. Vata is a force theoretically made up of the elements of Aether and air. Avoid the risk of becoming over-stimulated by loud, lively music, television and people, excessive sunlight and bright, vibrant colours and cut alcohol, tea, coffee, cigarettes and drugs out of the daily routine. Habit allows the Vata person to become more aware of their strengths and weaknesses; to be alert to when they are becoming agitated or over-stimulated, excited or tired. It gives them the chance to self-regulate and to know when to slow down and find a place of inner calm.

Vata people can suffer from headaches, hypertension, dry coughs, sore throats, earaches, anxiety, irregular heart rhythms, muscle spasms, arthritis, lower back pain, constipation, abdominal gas, diarrhoea, nervous stomach, menstrual cramps, premature ejaculation and other sexual dysfunctions. For the most part, neurological complaints can usually be put down to Vata imbalance.

Vata people often have inconsistent appetites and irregular digestive systems. As with everything, the key to a healthy diet is to eat in moderation. Avoid excessive eating by only dining in small but regular portions. Include plenty of warm, heavy, oily, moist, foods in the diet: regular servings of meat (in moderate portions) prepared with herbs and spices such as cardamom, cinnamon, clove, coriander, cumin, ginger, fennel and nutmeg. Favour sweet, sour and salty foods, warm foods, moderately heavy textured foods, butter and fat and soothing foods such as warm milk, cream, butter, warm soups and stews, hot cereals and fresh bread. Eat plenty of rice, oats, rice gruel and cooked vegetables in general: asparagus, beets, carrots, celery, garlic, green beans, okra, onion, parsnips, radish, turnips, sweet potato, and water chestnuts. Most fruits are ideal, if ripe and in season: cooked tomatoes, fresh mangoes and mature apricots are especially good. Meat is beneficial, in regular small portions. Poultry, fresh fish, venison, occasional lamb or beef are great grounding choices, as are eggs, milk and dairy products. Legumes, in small portions, especially mung beans, black and red lentils, chickpeas, split peas and lentils cooked or sprouted, nuts and seeds. Pumpkin seeds and peeled almond kernels are perfect. Oils, chiefly sesame oil; honey and sweets, ginger and garlic, small amounts of spices, particularly asafoetida and small amounts of diluted wine may be imbibed, but remain aware of the Vata person's somewhat addictive personality. Minimise or avoid all raw foods, dry foods, leafy vegetables, cold foods and frozen foods. Wheat, bread, spinach, potatoes, raw tomato, eggplant and peppers (actually, all members of the 'nightshade' family) and astringent fruits such as cranberries and pomegranates should be avoided, especially when suffering from sore joints. Drying fruits, such as apples and grapes, dried fruits, safflower oil and sugar should also be shunned.

Herbs known to pacify Vata include gotu kola and ginseng, while the warm sweet aromas such as basil, orange, rose geranium and clove of aromatherapy are believed to gently pacify excessive Vata energy.

As per Homeopathy

The homeopathic remedies listed below may be beneficial in helping to balance the Peacekeeper Child's constitution:

- Argentum nitricum
- Cannabis
- Lycopodium
- Mercurius
- Phosphorus
- Tuberculinum

For a deeper explanation of these suggested homeopathic remedies, please refer to the section at the rear of this book dedicated entirely to homeopathy and its history, and the chart listing the keynotes of each remedy on page 281.

Other Advice

Peacekeeper Children are profoundly psychic, so this innate ability must be encouraged and developed at all costs. The fact that Peacekeeper Children have the Ring-tailed Lemur as their primary totem may suggest cellular memory or a possible past life spent on Lemuria; the 'ghost world' – a land long gone but remembered in our dreams. Introduce non-guided meditation to encourage imagination, creativity and inner peace, and later on, integrate guided meditation to instil an awareness of Spirit, guides, ancestors and the higher self.

There is a chance that Peacekeeper Children hold suppressed genetic memory or an unexplainable knowing associated with Lemuria (also known as the 'Land of the Lemur'), indicated by unexpected emotional responses triggered when stories associated with the continent are heard or when reoccurring dreams or visions of the people or landscape are had. They may develop an overwhelming need to research the lost world or feel a need to explore the 'old ways'. A heightened psychic awareness or a sudden sensitivity to subtle energy, an interest in nature-based philosophy, mythology, animal symbology or the healing properties of plants and herbs (among others), are also indicators of a possible link to Lemuria, or Mu. Visitations by passed-over loved ones, 'dead people' and Ancestral Spirits are common occurrences for the average Peacekeeper Child, with many going unnoticed or written off as 'weird' experiences. Rather than ignoring them, though, Peacekeeper Children should be taught to listen to those 'weird' sensations, visions or occurrences as they may very well be indicating the presence of a spirit person bringing messages, confirmation or healing. Peacekeeper Children are naturals in the specialised areas of mediumship, spirit communication and clairvoyance.

Born with an inherent love and understanding of angels, past lives and all things cosmic, Peacekeeper Children should be encouraged to call upon archangel Raphael for help and guidance, be taught how to smudge and shown how to make their own smudging feather (a tradition that honours their connection to the air element). A tradition recognised by many tribal cultures, but made popular by the philosophies of the Native American People, smudging uses the smoke from burning herbs or specially prepared incense to cleanse and strengthen the energy field or aura of a person before they participate in any journey work or spiritual activity. Smoke is an etheric substance capable of penetrating the subtle veils of Creation. Herbs most commonly used in the smudging ceremony are sweet-grass, white sage, cedar and tobacco, although lavender, frankincense, cinnamon and eucalyptus are also occasionally employed as viable alternatives. Smudging draws in positive energy, while banishing negativity and cleansing or purifying the aura on a vibrational level. To smudge, choose one or a combination of the herbs listed above, dry them thoroughly and place them in a heatproof bowl or dish. Take a match and light the crushed herbs until they start to smoulder, keeping in mind that it is the smoke that is ultimately required and not a healthy flame. Brush the smoke, using cupped hands or a feather, so that it surrounds and touches every part of the body, the whole while asking the spirit of the herbs to remove all negative energy. Visualise this energy leaving the aura and returning to the universe via the smoke.

To make a smudge fan, find two Turkey wing or tail feathers (or any feathers of personal choice, so long as they do not come from a native bird protected by law), hot glue and a hot glue gun, a piece of suede leather, four glass jug beads, a jingle bell and two smaller feathers (for decoration). The two feathers should be similar in appearance and colour. Using the hot glue gun, join the two feathers together at the nib end. Hold them until they are dry, ensuring their spacing and placement is even. Cut a length of strapping about 30 cm long from the piece of suede leather. Find the centre of the strapping, and use it to bind the feather nibs in a downward motion, criss-crossing and overlapping the leather suede evenly until the nibs are completely covered. When this is done, there should be two tails of excess leather hanging off the bottom of the feathers. Tie these tails together, and thread two jug beads onto one tail and onto the other, thread the jingle bell (and secure with a knot) and then add the two remaining jug beads. Into each set of jug beads, push one of the smaller feathers, and secure with a dollop of hot glue.

Because of their ability to focus, concentrate, learn and retain knowledge, Peacekeeper Children are almost guaranteed to succeed in their chosen profession when encouraged to embrace advanced education. Because they have a nimble mind and a high level intellect, they should be urged to complete secondary college, and then continue on to gain further qualifications via higher education and/or associate themselves with institutions that fulfil their need for leadership, order and regimentation; establishments that develop their naturally honed 'people skills' and that fortify them intellectually and physically. Peacekeeper Children are the ones most likely to train and become members of the SES, fire brigade, police force or ambulance / mica service. They make profound academic doctors, university lecturers, pathologists, radiologists and medical scientists because of their mental acumen and their ability to assess and analyse. The armed forces, reserves, Cadets, Cubs, Scouts, Brownies or Guides will also appeal. The aim of scouting is to encourage the physical, intellectual, social, emotional and spiritual growth of all people so that they may adopt a constructive place in society as a responsible citizen and member of their local and broader community. Specifically intended for girls, though, Guides was conceived as a means to help young girls grow into confident, responsible, self-respecting women. As a Cadet, however, young people (be they male or female) are able to take part in adventurous, fulfilling and educational activities in a military setting — an ideal that most Peacekeeper Children respond favourably to. Surf Life Saving Australia, as another suggestion, offers 'Nippers', a lifesaving education program designed for seven to thirteen year olds.

More so than any of the other types of children, Peacekeeper Children excel when allowed to participate in competitive team sports: football, soccer or basket ball, for example, netball, volley ball, hockey, rowing, any of form of gymnastic or athletics sports like fly or rock fishing, golf, tennis, squash and badminton. Pilates, or 'the thinking person's work out', is a form of exercise that fortifies the deep abdominal and postural muscles that support and maintain the spine. It relies on six core principles that correspond and compliment perfectly the Peacekeeper Child's intellectual, regimented approach to all things. It relies on concentration, control, focus, flow, meticulousness and breath — factors that almost exactly match the characteristics of the Peacekeeper Child. It has the potential to help them achieve harmony within their mind and body, augment flexibility and improve posture, muscle tone, staying power, circulation and respiration, bone density and vitality. It can reinvigorate the immune system, increase overall wellbeing and reduce stress.

As stated above, the true purpose of the Peacekeeper Child is to bring people together and to encourage good communication between them. Neuro-Linguistic Programming, or NLP, is said to produce permanent and positive change by investigating how language and communication can help fashion our values, beliefs and behaviour. The knowledge gained will, therefore, arm the developing or adult Peacekeeper Child with the power to alter these patterns for themselves (and others) so they may achieve the life they deserve.

Being offered a forum in which to sit still, find the inner silence and still the mind is essential for the rational Peacekeeper Child, so make it a point to find the time for activities that promote the skill, particularly during the formative years. Massage is helpful, particularly after a rough day. Taking your child to a professional masseuse will create a sense of sacredness and importance. They will feel special and will respond well to the anticipation and excitement a treat like that creates. Foot spas, essential oil imbued baths, incense and appropriately coloured candles will also offer a time for stillness. And make a point of reading to your child every day, or listening to them as they read to you, particularly after their evening bath and just before bed (which also helps to develop a set routine). Reading stories to your child will inspire and initiate discussion, emotional response and a sense of excitement. Introduce your child to the stories that inspired you; it will make them feel special, as if you are inviting them into a sacred part of your life. Stories enjoyed by your child will often inspire creative play, so invest in small toys that will support the stories you select and will invite the child to continue the theme of the stories throughout their play.

A child that needs opportunity to learn how to communicate openly and honestly if they are to reach their highest potential, the Peacekeeper Child should be given as much occasion as possible to engage in real and meaningful conversation. Introduce the 'talking stick', an ornamented stick or feather that affords the one holding it a safe forum to speak out about whatever is on their mind without fear of ridicule, being spoken over, ignored or talked down. Encourage your child to start a diary or journal so they may learn to keep a record of their emotions, patterns and cycles, thus strengthening their relationship with themselves and keeping track of their thoughts, inner dialogue, fears and hopes. Initiate sharing time at meal times, role play and prayers of smoke as a means of communicating with living people (without having to directly speak to them), Spirit, angels and guides, passed over loved ones and ancestors. Investigate the benefits of art therapy as a way of getting your child to open up, or set up a letterbox in the home for family members, friends, relatives. Commence communication yourself by sharing something about yourself: a fear, hope or desire and invite your child to respond by sharing one of theirs. Never forget to ask your child how their day was, even if you know what took place and dedicate yourself to spending regular, quality time with your child. Let them have a day off from school occasionally so that you can spend the day together. Go shopping, have special lunch, go see a movie or get your hair/nails done together. This is as much a bonding day as it is a stress-management day. It will effectively boost your child's air / metal / lung energy and release any built up negativity in an enjoyable way, and share with your child the following affirmations as often as you can. They affirm your child's sense of self worth and they open a channel for trust and love to flow between the two of you: "I love you", "You are so special to me" and the most important one; the one all children are waiting to hear: "Being pregnant with you was the best thing that has ever happened to me."

Although they are drawn instinctively to aqua-aura, amethyst and rose quartz, stones and minerals like turquoise, tiger eye, blue lace agate, howlite, sapphire, clear quartz, topaz, yellow fluorite, citrine, tin and copper are imbued with energy perfectly suited to the energies of the Peacekeeper Child. All of them resonate favourably in support of communication, intuition and intellectual endeavour. Encourage your Peacekeeper Child to carry one or a combination of any in a pouch around their neck, in their pocket or alternatively, in their sock or bra. Turquoise radiates the consciousness of the Earth Mother's love and wisdom while helping to align the chakras. It enhances spiritual understanding, is powerfully protective, grounding, healing and cleansing. Tiger eye is great for the development of intuition and is believed to soften stubbornness, while howlite alleviates pain, stress and rage. Clear quartz offers clarity, awareness and spiritual insight and citrine dissipates and transmutes negativity. Otherwise known as 'the merchant's stone', citrine is said to produce greater income for the merchant when placed in the cash register. It is a stone of abundance, used in both the creation and maintenance of wealth. It also stimulates mental clarity, focus and endurance. Topaz, particularly golden topaz, helps one retain information, energy, thoughts and love. It is relaxing in nature as it inspires peace and a lightness of spirit. Blue lace agate promotes open communication, peace, acceptance and trust, while sapphires are known as the 'stones of prosperity'. They help us appreciate and take full advantage of our inherent gifts of power and the abundance of life that is ours for the taking. Yellow fluorite promotes creativity and intellectual pursuits, while both copper and tin afford mental clarity, dispel despondency and help initiate new beginnings. They combat laziness, compliance, impatience, impulsiveness and low self-esteem.

5

The Golden Lion Tamarin

Totem of the Golden (Rainbow) Child
Keynotes: Visionary / Prophet / Intuitive

The *Callitrichid* family contains 26 species of Marmoset and Tamarin. They are only found in the rainforests of Central and South America. Marmosets and Tamarins are among the world's smallest Monkeys, with some species only weighing 100 grams. Adept climbers, Marmosets and Tamarins cling vertically to trees. Their arms are shorter than their hind legs, and they do not have opposable thumbs. Marmosets and Tamarins congregate in family groups with one to three young produced each year. The young travel on the parent's back. Marmosets and Tamarins are primarily insect eaters, but will also eat small birds, fruits and seeds. The name 'Lion Tamarin' was inspired by the handsome mane-like hairs sprouting from the animal's head. Golden Lion Tamarins (so named after their golden orange coat) inhabit lowland tropical forests. Diurnal and arboreal in nature, Golden Lion Tamarins sleep in deserted woodpecker holes drilled into the branches and trunks of old trees. As a subspecies, Golden Lion Tamarins are at serious risk of being lost forever due to deforestation and urban development. Sadly, less than two percent of the Monkey's preferred habitat remains in its natural state today.

Golden Lion Tamarin people make powerful leaders, healers and teachers. They are intuitive, knowing and dreamy; their calm, gentle personas inspire peace and tranquillity. Golden Lion Tamarin people often display advanced spiritual knowing and powerful spiritual gifts: telepathy, for example, and telekinesis. They can communicate readily with animals; are powerfully empathetic and sensitive to the vibrations and energies of plants, places and people. They are sensitive to change and readily champion charitable causes. They carry ancient knowledge and crystal-clear past-life memory (an ability often demonstrated from an early age), are profound healers and are usually described as being 'old souls'.

Golden Lion Tamarin people are dreamers. They have green thumbs, love animals and are at one with nature. Golden Lion Tamarin people are worldly, politically aware, educated and make powerful leaders because they guide by example. Golden Lion Tamarin people are peaceful, tranquil and carry 'old world' charm. They are wise, sensitive, appealing and attractive. They radiate a powerful presence and easily attract a crowd. They make happy, content babies. As children, they are known to stare, sit introspectively and hum quietly to themselves. They are honest, truthful, gentle and kind. Golden Lion Tamarin people are pacifiers. They make excellent teachers; being both inspiring yet firm, quietly spoken and loved by all, but also strong, powerful and assertive.

Golden Lion Tamarin people are idiosyncratic, independent and artistic. Often heralded as eloquent, inspiring and encouraging, Golden Lion Tamarin people are typically groundbreakers in their chosen field, being both innovative and entrepreneurial. Many describe them as being strangely appealing, eerily attractive, and both familiar and exotic. They unapologetically march to the beat of their own drum, and because of this are easily classified as 'weird', eccentric and strange. They are incongruous, both appealing and off-putting. When unhappy, they may appear agitated, insensitive and dull; qualities instantly regarded as tiresome and tactless.

In the shadow phase, Golden Lion Tamarin people can emerge as selfish, critical and emotionally numb. They often embrace the victim mentality; appearing ostensibly unmotivated, boorish and self-centred. They can be incredibly naïve, bordering on stupid. When working from their most extreme dark side, they may present as falsely dumb-witted and feigning ignorance. Some Golden Lion Tamarin people seem to enjoy being stuck in a rut, preferring to complain about their circumstance rather than doing anything about it. When this is true, their lives are chaotic and disorganised, with them coming across as critical, boring, old fashioned and morose. They can also be indifferent, intimidating and irresponsible. They repel others and are often accused of being deceitful, insincere and manipulative. Other times they may be overly demanding, closed-minded and aggressive. They can be troublemakers and attention seekers, opportunists and instigators of peer-group pressure. When working in the negative, Golden Lion Tamarin people are uncouth, controlling, forceful and offensive. They can be closed-minded, destructive and common, displaying bizarre traits, frightening habits and unusual beliefs. When dancing with their shadow self, these people can be pitiless, unsympathetic and will do anything to make a point.

Individual advice for the Golden Lion Tamarin / Golden Child

Correspondences:

Esoteric Element: Spirit, Aether
Beings: Spirit guides, angels, extraterrestrials
Direction: Centre, above
Directional Colours: Clear, gold, silver, rainbow
Season: All or any
Time of Power: Pertinent to the individual, when we feel 'closest' to Spirit or God
Power Places: Pertinent to the individual, any place Spirit or God can be found
Symbolic Phase of Life on the Wheel of Life: That place of contentment, clarity, knowing and understanding that only comes with realisation, acceptance, total surrender, peace and unconditional love. Traditionally, we are said to realise it just before death, when we 'see the light', willingly shed our robes and rejoice in returning to our ancestors.
Zodiacs as per the Corresponding Esoteric Element: All or any
Organs: Heart, small intestines, pericardium
Chakras: Crown (seventh), Transpersonal (eighth)
Chakra Colours: Clear, rainbow, violet, magenta

Crystals: Clear quartz, apophyllite, gold, silver, ametrine, fluorite, peacock ore, aqua aura, rainbow moonstone, clear amethyst, clear prism (not a true crystal)

Totems: Winged Horses, Unicorns, white Doves, Rainbow Lorikeets, Parrots, Golden Lion Tamarins

Herbs : 'Power' or 'master' herbs traditionally used to induce altered states and aromatics used as incense: cedar, sage, sweetgrass, tobacco, psychedelic mushrooms, fly agaric, peyote, datura, morning glory and cannabis.

(NB: It is illegal to own or use many of the above-mentioned plants. It is also dangerous to partake in their use without experienced guidance, so leave them for people who understand their potentially lethal power or use them in a vibrational sense only.)

The principle idea of the Golden Child's journey is to transform passivity and boredom into realising the Spirit and embracing their inherent gifts of power. It is to move away from 'oddness' and 'social marginality' to a state of inner joy and acceptance of their uniqueness, greater inspiration and interrelatedness with the Other Realms. With many Golden Children destined to become spiritual leaders, such a move will see them shift from the 'outsider' to the 'prophet'; a role that will afford them the chance to present their gifts to the world.

Golden Children regularly hear voices, see spirits and/or 'dead people' and, at some point in life, usually find themselves endowed with uncanny healing abilities that prove both effective and unexplainable. They are the dreamers, the feelings-oriented visionaries, intuitives and the mystics who more often than not find themselves denigrated as weirdos and ostracised as freaks and frauds. As a result, many are diagnosed with ADD, depression and autism, or find themselves suffering from hallucinations due to the use and abuse of drugs such as LSD, speed and mescalin, which they take in an attempt to cease the mental chatter and dampen their greater awareness. With this as their cross to bear, Golden Children, when not supported or nurtured adequately, are the most likely to fall prey to psychosis, delusion, schizophrenia or disorientation.

To become the true visionary, healer, teacher and Shaman, facets of their essential nature, it is essential for the Golden Child to identify, develop and share their gifts of power and use it to help others realise and celebrate theirs. To move to their positive phase, Golden Children must accept and honour what makes them different and unique. By making an effort to connect with God, Spirit or the divine, the gods and goddesses, The void, Great Mystery, Mother Earth and the subtle realm of faeries, elementals and nature spirits, the angelic realms or entities and beings otherwise known as extraterrestrials, they will quickly recognise and harness their inherent kinship with the Other Realms and the distinctive gifts of power they awaken.

Not much is known about true Golden Children because they are both 'rare' (the ones that are aware of their gifts of power, at least) and elusive by nature. They tend to keep to themselves, believing themselves to be alone or shunned by their families, friends and their broader community because of their uncanny abilities, bizarre beliefs and the otherworldly knowledge they espouse. They anger quickly and sometimes come across as being unreasonable, stubborn and precious. Golden Children have unusual looking, almond shaped eyes and nervous dispositions. They tend to stare, think deeply before responding and answer questions with questions. They are both appealing and off-putting, captivating people and drawing them in, while simultaneously repelling attention and keeping them at a distance. People want to see them, stand beside them and talk to them, but when they get the chance, they feel compelled to remain at a distance, walk away or avoid eye contact. They exude a deeply spiritual energy, their aura imbued with an almost tangible, audible vibration. As small babies, Golden Children radiate knowing, old soul energy. They are peaceful, calm and sensitive to their surroundings, often lying awake in their crib for hours, smiling and cooing at things invisible to the average person. On stooping to saying "Hello, aren't you beautiful?" to an infant Golden Child propped up in its stroller, a well articulated "Thankyou!" response would not be at all unexpected (albeit a tad unnerving) because they are so present and intense. As adults they usually choose to live solitary (often troubled) lives. They occasionally pair up with Nature Children — but rarely marry. They seldom have children of their own, instead dedicating their lives to people in general or the 'children of the Earth Mother'. They are usually the offspring of Nature Children and grandchildren to Peacekeeper Children (although there are always exceptions). They find Warrior Children interesting and stimulating, with the two types often forging lasting friendships.

Being that they represent the few among us born 'awake' and fully aware, Golden Children need to remain mindful of staying spiritually grounded, practical and 'normal'. It is too easy for the Golden Child to allow the magnitude of their role to go to their head and to suddenly find themselves out of touch with reality. Remember, it is a very fine line that separates what it means to be classified as 'spiritual' and what it means to be diagnosed as 'psychotic'. It is often all too easy to slip from spiritual revelation into insanity, especially when you become arrogant, foolhardy or 'fly too close to the sun'. Psychosis can occur if the person is ungrounded, poorly integrated on a personality/ego level or unable to assimilate their spiritual experiences with their mundane life, while indulging in intoxicants (drugs, psycho-active medications and alcohol) will also quickly shift the balance.

Golden Children must remember to remain grounded at all times so as to avoid allowing their spiritual experiences to go to their head. They must address and surrender feelings (and the belief) that they are better or more spiritual than everyone else. That is just silly. Instead, they must maintain a sense of proportion and nurture a good dose of humility. It may be a hard pill to swallow, but it is highly unlikely that they are special beings, personally handpicked and sent on a wonderful mission by God to save the planet single-handedly — at least no more so than just about everyone else on the planet. They (and everyone else) are and always have been spiritual beings having physical encounters, not the other way around. They are just more aware, that's all, and more inherently in touch with their spiritual aspects than the rest of us.

Golden Children must be afforded time spent in nature, either walking or gardening, especially with good friends who are both sensible and nourishing. Yoga, Tai Chi and Qigong are also encouraged, as is plenty of solid sleep, swimming and taking warming showers both morning and night. Water is symbolic of our feelings, sentiment, cleansing and the feminine creative force. It has long been associated with the astral plane and the inspired power of the universe. Water is a natural conductor of energy. Spiritual energy is sustained and transmitted in a similar fashion to how electricity is carried and supported by water. I don't know if it is just me or not, but I find I get the best messages from Spirit whilst taking a shower. I have always put it down to the fact that water, as a conductor of energy, allows for Spirit's messages to be transmitted (and received) with greater clarity and less effort. When it comes to integrating their 'wow' spiritual experiences, Golden Children must honour the process by running their realisations past others whose opinions on such matters they respect, and then allow themselves plenty of quiet 'inner' time to digest the experience and the feedback they receive.

As per the Five Esoteric Elements: Spirit / Aether / Akasha

I remember when I first discovered Spirit. I was sitting on an old futon mattress in the craft room of a New Zealand born Medicine Woman. I had approached her to teach me how to make dreamcatchers. I had gone to her thinking she could teach me a skill I could share with the kids at the school where I was employed as an art teacher. I was on leave recovering from the shock of a tragic accident and so I thought spending the day weaving a dreamcatcher would be good for me, therapeutically and, looking back, I have never been more right.

When I got out of my car, I noticed a sign that read 'Walk in Beauty' hanging at the gate, and as I entered the Medicine Woman's home, I instantly felt a presence — not a ghostly presence, per se, but a presence nonetheless. The walls were decorated with Medicine tools — smudge fans, drums, pelts and blankets, there was rhythmic music playing and the air was fresh and heady, imbued with the smoke of sage and cedar. She spoke in a soothing, knowing voice and I instantly felt at peace. I felt like I was remembering something that I had not realised I had forgotten. During the workshop, as I sat weaving the web of my first dreamcatcher, a bolt of energy passed through my body. It seemed to last for ages, while in reality it was instantaneous. I felt alive. I felt recharged. And I felt emotional, because as the energy passed through my body, I clearly heard the words 'You are home', and I knew that I was.

She looked at me and smiled, and I started to cry from a very deep, primordial place, and it was quite a while before I was able to stop. When I heard Spirit's words and felt Spirit's presence, I knew I was going to be okay and that all that I had experienced in my life had been for a greater reason. Although I had no idea what that reason was, I was comforted by the knowing that I had never been alone and that despite the fear that I had somehow been forsaken growing up, I was safe now and on my way back to a place of innocence and perfection.

I returned to her home the next day and every day after for twelve months or so, learning the ways of the Earth Mother and 'the people'. She helped me to understand the ways of the ancients and the animal wisdom I inherently carried as my personal Medicine and my gift of power. And she helped me to find Spirit — the life-force that resides within all living things and the energy that binds us together and unites us as a people.

When I wasn't at her house learning, participating in Sweat Lodge, Pipe Prayer and mini impromptu Vision Quests, I was at home strengthening my relationship with Spirit and dedicating myself to my Medicine and growing awareness. Each morning I started my day with a learned prayer, and every night I ended it in the same way. I made my own drum, my own rattle and my own tobacco pouch. I carried a Medicine pouch and I made a Medicine bundle. My walls were decorated with Medicine shields and dreamcatchers; all permeated with symbols that reminded me of my personal connection to Spirit and the place of beauty it had delivered me into.

The point I am trying to make is that, as a Warrior Child, I had to find my way back to Spirit. I had to remember something that had lain dormant inside me since before my conception; something old and forgotten, waiting for the day of my spiritual rebirth. Golden Children, however, are born 'awake'. They are born with their eyes wide open. There is no remembering that needs to be done, no training and no awakening. They are consciously celestial, born joined at the hip with Spirit and its sanctified wisdom.

The relationship we share with Spirit is both personal and sacred, with the bond celebrated by Golden Children being no exception. Golden Children embody the element Spirit, and once this relationship is realised, they are able to access the Spirit *within* and honour it accordingly. It is vital for

Golden Children to acknowledge their elemental force so that they may harness and celebrate their relationship with God or Spirit, those in Spirit and what Spirit means to them *personally*.

Golden Children incarnate what their element represents. They literally act as mediators between the mundane world and that of Spirit, ferrying messages and intent back and forth. Their essence is pure. It is largely untainted by the imperfections and heaviness of the mundane world. Golden Children are born fully switched on to the ways of Spirit and fully aware of their higher purpose. They walk hand in hand with their element, embodying what it represents both consciously and subconsciously each and every day, no matter what. Even though they may occasionally fall prey to the trials and tribulations of everyday life, they are able to remain focused on their spiritual destiny and their higher purpose no matter what may come their way.

Also known as Aether and Akasha, Spirit is all encompassing, embracing the past, present and future, the four seasons, the four directions, and the remaining four elements concurrently, and perplexingly, none of them at all. We witness the seasons but once a year, with the force and glory of each cyclically enjoyed like clockwork. We not only visit them over and over on a physical level, however, but also emotionally and spiritually many times over countless lifetimes, and each time we do, we find greater harmony with ourselves and the world around us. We come to better understand the significance of life, too, and the sacred gifts of power afforded by each; illumination, innocence, introspection and wisdom, with the hope of becoming a more compassionate, prudent, confident, healthy person.

The element 'Spirit' exemplifies all four seasons and their correspondences in chorus, symbolising the qualities of one or more at any given time. It espouses the belief that the universe exists both within and external to all living things. It subsists at the heart of all things, as 'the one', the centre, the outward, inward, above and below. It governs and nurtures the cycles of life, death and rebirth. From the Greek 'aither', the term *Aether* (which means 'upper air') derived from an Indo-European word meaning 'burn' or 'shine', refers to the celestial fire of the gods and the pure essence or 'upper air' they breathed. Aether, as the soul of the Earth, is said to protect the world and fuel all life with its essence. Spirit, as the fifth element, epitomises the universal soul that permeates all things, which, when pictured with the mind's eye, resembles white light or pure energy. It provides space, foundation and equilibrium so that the remaining four elements may exist. It is immaterial and subtle, but tangible and present in all things.

Since the day my spiritual 'apprenticeship' began, Spirit has been the Creator; the one, the source, the keeper of Great Mystery and The Void. It is both the god in his many forms and the goddess in hers. Spirit is all that is known to be unknowable, to be explored but never fully understood. Spirit is magic. It is breath. Spirit represents balance: the fine line that exists between all that is 'light' and all that is 'dark'. Spirit demands that we trust, remember and know. Spirit is both tangible and non-tangible. It is found within all things feminine and all things masculine. It is both physical and non-physical. It is the tilling of the fields, the birthing of the children, the nurturing of the people and the changing of the seasons. It is the power found within one's dreams, intuition and the sacred darkness of the womb. It is war, lightning, sexual energy, passion and sunshine. It is rampant during the hunt and savoured in the kill. Spirit is our link to Creation. Spirit inspired Creation, because the two are separate but the same. It allows the cycles of life to flow in a sacred way, with the inevitable progression of life, death and rebirth to maintain equilibrium. With every death, Spirit ensures there is a birth. Spirit resides within all things of nature. It is life-force. Spirit is neither feminine nor masculine. It is both. It is all encompassing. It is the essence of all life.

Spirit is not something that can be fully explained. It cannot be described or categorised. It represents many things; things sacred to different people in personal ways. It is inherently found in all cultures, but bears different names wherever you go. It is ancient, but ready and waiting to be acknowledged today. Spirit is like the wind: you cannot see it, but you can feel it. You cannot contain it or hold it in the palm of your hand, but at the same time you can and do whenever you embrace your child, pick a flower or pat a Dog. Spirit must be explored directly, on a personal level. It cannot be taught or bought. It must be remembered and, once found, it must be approached with a deep and genuine respect, but treated with the same calm expectation one would normally reserve for family, best friends and soul mates.

For me, Spirit is the joy I feel when my kids call me 'Daddy'. It is the unquestionable love I feel for my wife and the love she feels for me. It is the miracle of watching a Duckling hatch from an egg or to see flowers blooming in my garden. It is the cry of a Peacock, the purr of a Cat or the sound of rain on my roof. For me, Spirit is found in the knowing that I have friends who would do anything for me. It is the surprise seen on a friend's face when you do something unexpected for them, for no other reason but to see that look. Spirit is all these things, as well as the beauty that surrounds me, and when I think of it, I am humbled beyond compare. I am literally brought to tears.

That is what Spirit has come to mean to me. Although Golden Children understand this bond and exude it from every pore, they must be nurtured and afforded time and opportunity to keep the flame that is their connection to the Creator burning in a healthy, vibrant way. They must be encouraged to connect with Great Spirit in ways that are both meaningful and individual to them. Opportunity to uncover and use magickal tools and rituals, for example, research ancient wisdom, engage in esoteric practices and develop a relationship with and request assistance from the Other Realms is of the highest importance. Whether or not they choose a traditional or 'religious' path is unimportant (they may choose to follow an angelic path or one inspired by a fascination with extraterrestrial life, for example), the key to raising a healthy, happy Golden Child is that spirituality (in whatever form it takes) must be seen as the highest priority. Meditation and prayer must be integrated into the Golden Child's daily routine. For their development, both are as vital as taking a bath or getting to bed at a reasonable hour. In the case of the Golden Child, a healthy mind and a healthy body promise to sustain a healthy connection to Spirit. For them, to become a spiritual being, they need to be able to claim it, honour it and live it as part of their normal, everyday life.

As per Traditional Chinese Medicine: the Fire / Heart Person

According to the teachings of Traditional Chinese Medicine, Golden Children, as 'heart people', have their mind, body and energy systems focused on the fire element.

The fire element is indicative of the sun overhead, its rays blazing down at their fullest. It refers to heat, literally, and the danger of getting burnt when arrogance and foolishness are allowed to prevail on both a physical and esoteric level. Consider Icarus, for example, and his wings of wax. Daedalus was an Athenian architect, inventor, and master craftsman who, according to Greek legend, murdered his apprentice for showing skills that surpassed his own. After committing his ghastly crime, Daedalus fled to the island of Crete, during which time he helped the queen satisfy her lustful yearnings for a sacred white Bull by building her a wooden Cow to hide in. The queen soon fell pregnant to the Bull and gave birth to the Minotaur, a creature half man and half Bull. When the Minotaur was born, Daedalus built a labyrinth to contain the brute. Daedalus later unintentionally aided in the killing of the Minotaur and, as punishment, was imprisoned with his son Icarus. The pair escaped, but they knew the only way off Crete was by air. So Daedalus built wings for himself and Icarus; wings fashioned from feathers held together with wax. He warned Icarus not to fly too close to the sun as it would melt the wax, but Icarus became careless and arrogantly flew too close to the sun which, of course, caused the wax to melt. The wings collapsed and Icarus fell to his death, drowning in the sea. The Icarian Sea was named after the boy, forever marking where he fell as a sacred place. The warning here is that if you fly too high, believing yourself untouchable or indestructible, you run the risk of getting burnt. After all, the immortal life was never intended for the common man. A person must be Herculean himself (or else foolhardy) to challenge the gods and expect to win.

The heart person becomes unbalanced with their element when exposed to too much heat in the form of hot weather or when they excessively indulge in hot, spicy food. Heart people cannot afford to let themselves dehydrate, either. Water is the most important nutrient required by the human body. An adult male's body is more than fifty percent water, while an adult female's is nearly sixty percent. The human brain alone is composed of about seventy percent water. We lose two to three litres of water through urination, sweating and breathing each and every day. Dehydration is a grave situation in which the volume of water required by the body to maintain its normal functioning drops to life-threatening levels.

The colour most commonly associated with the heart and its corresponding element is red, the colour typically linked to the emotions: rage, joy and obsession (when taken to the extreme), as well as desire, passion, inspiration, life-force and Creation itself. In its productive phase, it radiates the qualities of the balanced yin and yang; the union of the two opposites that are equal, the feminine and the masculine, night and day, dark and light, without which, life could not exist. It implies the Earth Mother's molten core, the revelries and orgiastic rites of Bacchus (in Roman mythology) and Dionysus (in Greek mythology), the god of wine, intoxication and stupidity, and the unbridled life-force and divine Tantric embrace of the Hindu deities Shiva and Shakti. It is said that only when Shiva is united with Shakti does he have the power to create. Physically it personifies the heart, the tongue, the power of speech (which can become frenzied when out of control) and the 'Wei Qi', or the protective sheath said to surround the body's surface, warding off mania, infection and harmful influence. The colour red is also recognised for its healing potential, and is known to boost heart fire, passion and joy. Eat red-coloured foods, therefore: tomatoes, red onions, peppers and chilli.

According to Traditional Chinese Medicine, excessive heart Qi (life-force) is known as 'mania', while heart Qi deficiency is known as 'ennui', which refers to tedium or monotony. Too much passion or laughter may unhinge heart Qi, as can boredom or a lack of excitement in life. Life for the heart person must involve balance and moderation, with a little of everything and nothing in excess. Symptoms of unbalance include disproportionately fast-talking, non-stop babbling, rapid-fire tangential thinking, mania, hysteria or activity that results in a red face, high blood pressure or, alternatively, a pale complexion, a weak body, listlessness, or lacking 'inner fire'. The heart is about passion to live and the health and wellbeing of the body's inner fire, which burns food and air to produce Qi. The heart is also about inspiration. Traditional Chinese Medicine looks to the heart as the seat of the 'shen', spirit or mind. It is the purest and highest expression of yang or masculine energy, and human consciousness. There is apparently an intimate connection between the heart and the kidney, which houses our essence and the root of our feminine yin. The kidneys, whose water helps keep the heart's yang in balance, deeply influences heart Qi. Kidney 'fire' is said to be the source of the heart 'fire'.

An excess of heart Qi is typically indicated by manic overactivity, rapid thinking and the tendency to go off on a tangent, scattered and confused thinking, pomposity and over-excited, excessive talking. A flushed, red face, red-tipped tongue and high blood pressure are also sure-fire signs of excessive heart energy. People with robust heart fire often appear charming and enigmatic, loquacious and outgoing and excel at inspiring others or calling them to action. When heart fire wanes, however, they quickly become uninspiring and ordinary, suffering from bouts of apprehension, agitation and sleeplessness. Severe cases may see the heart person stammer, talk quickly and excessively and giggle uncertainly. They may over excite easily and become manic or, alternatively, go the other way and appear aloof, selfish and heartless.

Extreme heart energy may be pacified by ensuring one's environment remains restrained, calm and organised; a deliberate slowing of activity will also have a calming and centring affect on the heart person's inner fire. Light fasting, or eating 'cooling' foods like barley, beef broth, celery, asparagus, apple, banana, lettuce, oysters, rice, rosemary, wheat, wheat germ, and mushrooms will lower excess yang and calm the shen (mind). Heart people should eat moderate amounts of tomato and whole, freshly ground, well-cooked wheat-based products, especially when eaten with warming, easily digestible foods such as rice congee, meat broths and soups. They should avoid stimulants and rich, spicy foods, but consider acupuncture and herbs such as valerian, chamomile and catnip as a way of balancing or pacifying excessive heart Qi. Fish rich in omega-3 is also said to benefit the physical health and wellbeing of the heart.

People suffering from heart Qi deficiency are easily identified by obvious boredom and a lack of interest in all things, listlessness, a pale, anaemic complexion, dizziness and low blood pressure, a thin build, pale tongue and the tendency to minimise speech or to speak in a quiet, almost inaudible voice. Physical symptoms may include palpitations, hypertension, heart conditions and sores on the mouth and tongue. Bitter flavours enhance fire Qi. Although coffee, for example, has a bitter flavour, its effects may aggravate the heart Qi. Healthy, bitter flavours are best found in vegetables that have dark green leaves. Their dearth may be treated by engaging themselves in stimulating activities, such as regular aerobic exercise, walking and imbibing warm milk drinks, eating potatoes, rice congee, meat broths, soups, stews and by taking traditional herbs such as ginseng and, again, investigating the fortifying benefits of acupuncture.

As per Ayurveda: Tri-doshic or Sama-dosha -
An equal mix of Vata / Pitta / Kapha Energy

According to Ayurvedic philosophy, the five elements combine (in pairs) to form three dynamic forces known as *doshas*, a term that translates to 'that which changes'. Each dosha constantly moves in balance with the others, with all being necessary for life to exist. It is most common for people to display the qualities of a single dosha, be it Vata, Pitta or Kapha. There are cases of people presenting a combination of two, but it is very rare for people to display a stable combination of all three. A combination of all three is extremely difficult to achieve, let alone balance and maintain, but if this can be done, the results often produce true gurus, great saints and avatars.

In order to reach their potential, therefore, Golden Children need to strike a balance between their earth/water energy or, Kapha, their air/Aether energy, or Vata, and their fire/water energy, or Pitta by becoming aware of the seasons that sustain them and appeasing those that don't. During the summer and autumn, for example, Golden Children must find ways to appease their Vata/Pitta energy, while in winter and spring they must do what they can to control their Vata/Kapha energy. A very simple way of maintaining this balance is to focus on bitter, starchy, sweet foods during summer and autumn and astringent, sour and salty foods in winter and spring. In general, however, they should keep excessively spicy foods to a minimum.

Vata (a term that means 'wind, to move, flow, direct the processes of, or command') is drying, cooling and airy, rousing and ever changing in nature. It is a force believed to be composed of the Aether and air elements. The level of Aether affects the degree to which the air may gain momentum. If unbridled, the air element can gather excessively in force and get out of hand, and become a destructive tempest.

When considering the ideal Vata diet, it is best to avoid excessive eating by only dining in small but regular portions. Include plenty of warm, heavy, oily, moist, foods in the diet: regular servings of meat (in moderate portions) prepared with herbs and spices such as cardamom, cinnamon, clove, coriander, cumin, ginger, fennel and nutmeg. Favour sweet, sour and salty foods, warm foods, moderately heavy textured foods, butter and fat and soothing foods such as warm milk, cream, butter, warm soups and stews, hot cereals and fresh bread. Eat plenty of rice, oats, rice gruel and cooked vegetables in general: asparagus, beets, carrots, celery, garlic, green beans, okra, onion, parsnips, radish, turnips, sweet potato, and water chestnuts. Most fruits are ideal, if ripe and in season: cooked tomatoes, fresh mangoes and mature apricots are especially good. Meat is beneficial, in regular small portions. Poultry, fresh fish, venison, occasional lamb or beef are great grounding choices, as are eggs, milk and dairy products. Legumes, in small portions, especially mung beans, black and red lentils, and chickpeas, especially split peas and lentils cooked or sprouted, nuts and seeds. Pumpkin seeds and peeled almond kernels are perfect. Oils, chiefly sesame oil; honey and sweets, ginger and garlic, small amounts of spices, particularly asafoetida and small amounts of diluted wine may be imbibed, but remain aware of the Vata person's somewhat addictive personality. Minimise or avoid all raw foods, dry foods, leafy vegetables, cold foods and frozen foods. Wheat, bread, spinach, potatoes, raw tomato, eggplant and peppers (actually, all members of the 'nightshade' family) and astringent fruits such as cranberries, pomegranates should be avoided, especially when suffering from sore joints. Drying fruits, such as apples and grapes, dried fruits, safflower oil and sugar should also be shunned.

Pitta is a force created by the dynamic interaction between water and fire. Pitta people must learn to appease their excess fire energy if they are to reach their fullest potential. The golden rule is 'balance and moderation'.

They must find a balance so that their fire does not dry out their water, and so their water does not extinguish their fire.

When considering the Pitta diet, eat plenty of salads, fruit and vegetables (except those listed at the end of this paragraph), barley, wheat, oats, white rice, tofu, soy, chickpeas, mung beans and olive oil, and 'cooling' herbs and spices, such as cardamom, coriander, cinnamon, dill, fennel, mint, saffron and turmeric. Flavours that are bitter, sweet or astringent are okay. Poultry, black pepper, cumin, butter, ice cream and milk should be eaten in moderation, while red meat, chilli, fiery herbs and spices, fat, pickled food, salt, vinegar, yoghurt, sour cream, cheese, coffee, fermented items such as beer and vegemite, fried foods, carrots, eggplant, garlic, hot peppers, onions, radish, spinach, tomato, lentils, apricots, bananas, berries, cherries, peaches and grapefruit should be avoided completely.

Kapha is the balancing force between water and earth. It represents composition and lubrication. It is the blending and binding element that helps keep water and earth from separating. When earth and water are mixed together and then left to their own devices, the earth will gradually sink to the bottom, thus extracting itself from the water. Kapha is the force that prevents this from happening. It binds the elements, thus providing for physical structure and endurance. Water is the main ingredient of Kapha; a vital component physiologically needed to ensure biological power and natural tissue vitality.

When addressing the Kapha diet, focus on bitter, pungent or astringent foods, warm light foods, dry foods and stimulating foods, while avoiding foods cooked in too much water, oily, fatty, or buttery foods and sugar. Eat plenty of apples, apricots, cranberries, mangoes, peaches, pears and pomegranates, vegetables in general, salads, light, dry foods and herbs and spices, such as black pepper, cardamom, cinnamon, clove, coriander, cumin, garlic, ginger, fennel and nutmeg; raw/natural honey, small amounts of chicken, rabbit, seafood, venison and eggs, goat's milk, ghee, black tea and coffee. Minimise or avoid sweet, sour or salty foods, frozen or fried foods, fatty foods, dairy products, grains, potatoes, tomatoes, water chestnuts, excessively sweet, sour or juicy fruits, red meat, legumes, nuts and seeds, oils and fats, sugar, sweets and salt.

As per Homeopathy

The homeopathic remedies listed below may be beneficial in helping to balance the Golden Child's constitution:

- Sulphur
- Causticum
- Phosphoric acid

For a deeper explanation of these suggested homeopathic remedies, please refer to the section at the rear of this book dedicated entirely to homeopathy and its history, and the chart listing the keynotes of each remedy on page 281.

Other Advice

Golden Children *love* crystals, semi-precious stones and minerals. They believe in their vibrational qualities, but also fully understand that without pure, clear intent, their properties mean nothing. Golden Children require stones of high resonance and perfection to both ground them and help them maintain their connection to Spirit. Clear quartz, for example, as a stone that inspires intuition and mental clarity, is ideal, especially when enhanced with rainbow inclusions, 'windows', raised triangles on one or more of its faces or when 'double terminated' with points at both ends, among other things. Clear amethyst, a stone of divine love that aids in the art of clear channelling and aventurine, a crystal that inspires emotional tranquillity, prosperity and independence and smoky quartz, as a tool against depression and a stone used to assist in remembering one's dreams are also excellent rocks the Golden Child could consider carrying or integrating into their work. Apophyllite is a stone used to create a conscious 'bridge' between the mundane world and the spiritual realms, whereas Gold symbolises the sacredness of oneness. It personifies spirituality and helps to develop greater understanding, allowing for the attainment and maintenance of direct communion with Spirit (without having to go through 'middle men' such as guides and angels). It is said to attract marks of respect, prosperity and bliss. Silver begets advantages in life. It enhances speech by affording fluency in conversation, while instilling a sense of 'culture' to one's presence and a state of worldliness. It offers a mirror to the soul, effectively allowing one to view the self from a remote perspective. Silver enhances the powers and qualities of the moon, literally 'drawing down' the lunar energies to aid in menstruation, conception and the cleansing of ritual tools and crystals. Ametrine (a combination of amethyst and citrine) is a stone said to inspire universal symmetry, while providing clear connection between the physical form and the ultimate state of spiritual perfection. It balances the feminine and masculine aspects and wilfully integrates spiritual realisation. Fluorite discourages muddled, unsettling and unsystematic growth, while peacock-ore (or bornite) brings innovation and 'newness' to one's life. It encourages the inner spirit to reach new heights and allows for one to realise true happiness in the moment. Aqua-aura (a favourite among Golden Children) is essentially clear quartz coated in a layer of pure gold, which when considered as one, offers dynamic properties. The gold essentially enhances the qualities of the clear quartz, and the clear quartz magnifies the qualities offered by the gold. Rainbow moonstone is a talisman of good fortune and safe travel. It is a crystal that promises new beginnings, so is a powerful 'wishing stone' for the young Golden Child. Although not a true crystal, hanging a clear prism in the window of your child's bedroom will fill them with delight and their room with hundreds of perfectly clear rainbows. My children believe their rooms to be magical places where faeries and other enchanted beings gather when the sun's first rays hit the clear prisms suspended from their curtain rods.

For the young Golden Child, animated movies like *Balto 2:Wolf Quest*, *Brother Bear* and *Spirit — Stallion of the Cimarron* are excellent because they offer insight into the world of Spirit by addressing topics such as spirit, totems, the cycle of life, death and rebirth, honour, devotion, growth, loyalty and self-worth. For the older Golden Child, movies like *Phenomenon*, *Powder*, *Dragonfly*, *Signs* and *The Sixth Sense* (among others) are perfect for similar reasons. To ensure they reach their potential, suggest your Golden Child visit Mind Body Spirit festivals and attend the workshops and seminars being offered, or attend spiritual developmental circles where they will learn about channelling, astral travel and past-life regression and be taught how to safely access other dimensions and the realms of angels, extraterrestrials and guides.

To help them uncover their gifts of power, Golden Children must be encouraged to explore the plethora of options currently on offer; options never before available to the everyday man, woman or child. The healing work of Dr. Eric Pearl, for example (a Golden Child if ever there was one) is one such opportunity. Dr. Eric Pearl, who was a highly successful chiropractor before deciding to develop and share his gift of power, 'Reconnective Healing', reconnects us through his work to the richness of the universe and the fullness of who and what we are. If that doesn't appeal, then consider Reiki. Reiki is a system of healing created by Mikao Usui in Japan in the early 1900s. Reiki was originally created to support people on their spiritual journey toward enlightenment, drawing on elements borrowed from an esoteric form of Tendai Buddhism and Japanese culture and philosophy. The word 'Reiki' translates from a Japanese word meaning 'spiritual energy'; the concept of energy thought to be harnessed in its practice; the 'energy of everything', itself fuelled by the belief that everything contains spiritual energy. Reiki helps us expand our own energy so that it might flow more freely through us, reminding us of our original nature. It supports us as we become more balanced, healthier and happier and eventually realise enlightenment. For more information visit my friends Frans and Bronwen at the International House of Reiki (www.reiki.net. au). Another healing modality worth considering is Pranic Healing. Pranic Healing is an energy-based healing technique that utilises 'prana' or life-force to balance, harmonise and transform the body's energy processes. 'Prana' or 'Qi' is vital life energy that helps the body maintain a state of wellness. Golden Children must be afforded quality time to engage in daily meditation and Vision Quest. It is a recognised fact that we can surpass all limitations, fears and illness when we master meditation and celebrate it as the vital link between mind and body, the spiritual and the mundane. The key to manifesting health, wealth and happiness lies in the remembering of the inner spirit and the ancient bond we share with Great Spirit; a remembering best achieved via disciplined daily meditation. For centuries, young men and women have sought the experience of Vision Quest in order to discover their purpose, their Medicine and to better understand their connection to Spirit and their sacred gift of power. They may return as an adult when seeking confirmation or generic guidance regarding life. Vision Quest typically lasts one day and one night, but may extend over two, three or even four days. During Vision Quest, the seeker prays to Spirit and the world around him or her, in the belief that signs and messages will be offered by Spirit, usually symbolically in the form of an animal or bird or through a vision or dream. A token of the vision (a feather, stone or herb) is often found and placed in a Medicine pouch and worn around the neck as a way of physically harnessing the power of the quest, as an anchor or reminder, as protection or when further guidance is sought.

Natural dreamers, Golden Children would do well to pay attention to both their daydreams and their sleep-time dreams. Dream journals should be considered vital aspects of the Golden Child's night-time routine, as should dream-circle in the morning. During dream-circle, members of the family are encouraged to share the dreams they had the night before and discuss or interpret their possible meaning. Dreams are Spirit's way of allowing us to intuitively check in and consult with our higher selves. Many of us live our lives innocent to the presence of Spirit, assuming that what we have within our physical existence is all that life has to offer. It is very difficult for Spirit to inspire us when we are ignorant to the presence of the Other Realms. Spirit can send all the signs and omens in the world, but if we are blind to their presence we are not going to notice them. By allowing ourselves to awaken to the power of our dreams, and by realising the potential they hold as portents and signs, we are able to embrace Spirit without having to invest great effort or excess time into the process. Our dreams offer opportunity to overcome hesitation and fear that hampers spiritual growth. As we dream, our astral body leaves its physical confines, allowing us to journey to the Other Realms. Our astral body is connected to our physical body by means of an energetic thread. At the slightest disturbance, the astral body can be drawn back to the physical body by this thread. Some believe that as we dream, the spirit of the Eagle, as the emissary of Spirit, protects the energetic thread and ensures that it remains intact. As we journey through the dreamscape, we are simultaneously bridging the worlds, walking in both the ordinary world and the non-ordinary world of Spirit.

When we daydream we are energetically checking out our potential future selves. While physically doing something mundane or routine, our mind wanders, allowing for our conscious mind to leave the physical confines of our body (on an astral level), to wander out and explore future aspects of our life. When our conscious mind realises that we have been daydreaming, we snap back and instantly forget what we have just witnessed, with the body of the daydream expelled from our mind forever. Daydreams are Spirit's way of allowing us to consciously explore our future while remaining corporeally alert. Daydreaming can be compared to the taking of a walkabout or Medicine-walk, but instead of strolling through the woods, for example, daydreaming encourages us to stroll through the realms of Spirit. To receive a daydream that suggests healing or progress is to know that Spirit is guiding you to a place of greatness. It is like being shown a blueprint of your intended future and a map that leads the way to discovering your purpose. Instead of brushing off your daydreams in future as being idle moments of fancy, record them in a journal. See this as an occasion as important as your child's first words or your wedding day. Your daydreams can be recorded in point form if you wish, so long as you can recall the body of the dream on later reflection. About a week or two after having your daydream, you may be sitting in a café somewhere and suddenly get the uncanny feeling that you have been there before. Even though the conscious mind disagrees, the subconscious mind remembers visiting the café during a daydream. When this happens, reach for your journal and you will find that an entry recites the fact that you placed yourself in the café astrally weeks before, with the subliminal intention of remembering the fact on your actual arrival. The café is the wakeup call in this case, meant to trigger a realisation that something in or around the café offers a window of opportunity, that once acknowledged will initiate a great change of fortune in your life. While looking back in your journal, you may find an entry about a hotel with a green door visible from your café vantage point. Look for the green door, and when you have located it, put down your coffee, march over to the hotel and ask for a job. Promise yourself that no matter what happens from this moment on, you will take it as it comes. The hotel will have a job of course, and you will take it, despite the fact that it involves cleaning the lavatories. Spirit would not have presented this opportunity if you were not going to achieve greatness from embracing it. Find solace in the knowledge that after a period of time, you will move from cleaning the toilets, to sweeping the halls, to reception, to manager, until one day you are offered the chance to buy the hotel. You visioned it in your daydream. Spirit offered you the map, and you followed it with inherent clarity. Spirit never makes a mistake. The Spirits around you can inspire you, but only the Spirit within you can physically help you. When we listen to the inspiration offered by Spirit, and we do what needs to be done to physically affirm its potency, we, too, will never make mistakes again.

According to Native American folklore, it was Grandmother Spider who sang the universe into being by weaving the Web of Life. Grandmother Spider wove the first dreamcatcher, a beautiful and protective web woven within a ring of willow wood. In the centre she placed a single turquoise stone, a symbol of connection to the Creative Force, clarity, peace, communication and protection. It is said that with the aid of a dreamcatcher, our dreams can be harnessed and brought to fruition.

Legend has it that one day Grandmother Weaving Woman looked down from her place in the Great Mystery, The Void in which Spirit beings like herself live. She saw, to her dismay, that the human children she had dreamed into existence generations before were sad and afraid. They had lost sight of the path and were wandering aimlessly through life. Grandmother Weaving Woman knew she had to do something to help her children so, using great power and concentration, she dreamed herself into reality among the people. After many days of recovery, Grandmother Weaving Woman went to the Great Willow Tree and asked her for one of her finest branches. After receiving and giving thanks for the branch, she bent and bound it until she shaped it into a perfect circle. This circle, which had no beginning and no end, symbolised the continuous cycle of life, death and rebirth, a concept forgotten by the children of Grandmother Weaving Woman. Grandmother Weaving Woman then went to the mighty Eagle and requested a wing feather. She humbly gave thanks and suspended the feather from the powerful circle, binding it in place with red twine. The feather, gifted by the majestic Eagle, would teach the children to have courage and belief in their abilities and to find strength in their convictions. Grandmother Weaving Woman wanted her children to know no boundaries to how high they could soar and to know no limit to the great things they could achieve. She wanted them to believe in themselves the way she believed in them. Grandmother Weaving Woman also wanted her children to remember their connection to Spirit, Great Mystery and Creation.

Soon after, Grandmother Weaving Woman transformed herself into the Wise Woman known as Grandmother Spider Woman. It was as Grandmother Spider Woman that she dreamed the universe into being at the beginning of time. Grandmother Spider Woman wove the Web of Fate and now she wove the web of the first dreamcatcher. After Grandmother Spider Woman had completed spinning the beautiful and protective web in the centre of the willow circle, she placed a single turquoise stone in the very middle. Turquoise is said to represent our connection to the Creative Force. It offers clarity, peace, communication and protection to those who wear it or carry it in a sacred way. Grandmother Weaving Woman looked at the dreamcatcher and was pleased. She pondered on it for a moment and in her mind's eye pictured the benefits it would help bring to the people. On taking it to her children, Grandmother Weaving Woman explained its sacred significance. She told them that as they slept, as their subconscious mind woke and actively participated in a life unknown to them, sometimes its adventures are good; promising and even prophetic in nature, but sometimes its adventures are bad; dark, threatening and foreboding. On waking, glimpses of these adventures remain in the conscious memory and can excite us with their possibilities, or fill our heart with dread. The fear can prevent us from going back to sleep, leading to fatigue. Fatigue leads to mistakes, and mistakes lead to wastefulness.

By hanging a dreamcatcher above where we sleep, either from the ceiling or on a wall, our dreams are inherently protected from all negativity. Our dreams are drawn to the web, like bees to honey. Our positive dreams will be allowed to pass through the web to be enjoyed as we sleep. Negative dreams, or nightmares, however become trapped in the web and are destroyed by Grandfather Sun's first rays in the morning. They are believed to turn to dew and trickle down the feather of the majestic Eagle. Eagle's Spirit, which is still alive in the feather, cleanses the dream of negativity so that when it finally drips off the tip of the feather as the first jewel of the morning, it returns to Mother Earth to be absorbed, never to haunt our sleep again. Dreamcatchers were traditionally made by the grandmothers of a tribe, and were given to the children when they were born. From a young age, the people were taught to listen to and respect their dreams. Dreams were considered to be as equally as powerful and truthful as visions and omens. As the children grew, they were taught how to interpret and work with their dreams. The dream catcher was, therefore, a very sacred item and a strong link to Spirit.

To make a dreamcatcher, collect together a metal ring (available from any craft supply store), a piece of leather or suede, wax coated, nylon 'sinew', crystal chip beads, eight 'crow' beads, a selection of assorted feathers (of non-protected species), sharp scissors, hot glue and a hot glue gun. Round each corner of the leather with the scissors, and proceed to cut (in coil fashion) a long strip of leather approximately 1cm wide. Place a dab of glue on one end of the leather and secure it to the metal ring. Wrap the ring in a clockwise direction, overlapping the leather with each rotation slightly until the ring is completely bound. Use the glue to secure the end and trim off any excess. Tie the sinew onto the ring and, working in a clockwise direction of about 3cm each, tie the sinew to the ring in half knots. This is done by taking the sinew over the ring and bringing it back through the loop just formed. It is important that the knots are tight and that good tension is maintained throughout the construction of the webbing. Continue around the ring until the last half knot is made (about 1.5cm or half the normal spacing) from the starting point. Even spacing will ensure a neat central hole at the end and maintaining tight tension will prevent a sagging web. The second and following rows need to be executed in the same fashion, but instead of the half knot being tied to the ring (as it was before), it now must be secured to the sinew itself, approximately half way between the first and second knots, second and third, third and fourth, and so on. You will notice that triangular shaped holes are beginning to form in the webbing. As the web develops, thread a crystal chip bead on to the sinew and push it down to the last knot and continue weaving the web as before. There is no limit to the number of beads that can be added to the web. When it becomes evident that the web is complete (when the central hole becomes too small to work) tie the sinew off on the last loop and cut away any excess. Note: do not cut the excess off too close to the final knot, for the knot will surely come undone, and the web will collapse. The sinew is wax coated, so it is easy enough to squash the ends together to disguise them. It is now time to decorate the dreamcatcher. Cut a length of leather strap of about 20cm in length. Using the larks knot technique, create a loop at the top of the web so that it may be suspended over the bed. Cut three further lengths, about 30cm long, and using the larks head knot again, attach the straps, in even distance to one another, to the underside of the ring. These are the dreamcatcher's tails, and should be decorated with the feathers and beads. The feathers should be glued in place, to prevent them falling out.

Although naturally inclined to explore the traditional and the more obscure religions and spiritual paths guiding the people of the world (Christianity, Paganism, the Kabala, Tao, Hinduism, Buddhism and the Baha'i Faith, for example), Golden Children are unlikely to embrace any one of them as the only truth. Instead, Golden Children tend to go 'the way of the Horse' and explore all cultures, beliefs and traditions. They pick out what makes sense to them and dump the rest, uniting what they have learned and what nurtures their soul to formulate their own sound, spiritual philosophy. They dare to challenge the establishment by asking questions and arguing their opinion. They research the origins and the basis of religion, and love going back to the roots to discover why, when and how religions are followed today. Golden Children understand the Dreamtime, for example, a sacred time for the indigenous people of Australia; the time before time, when the world was new and the Ancestor Spirits wandered the Earth helping to shape the land, the plants and the animals. They almost remember this sacred time, and feel an ancient calling to return to it, or to honour it in some way. The Dreamtime was when everything on the horizon was being created and when everything was getting used to being. Some indigenous people refer to this time as The Dreaming while others refer to their personal spiritual connection to the ancients as The Dreaming. As the Ancestor Spirits wandered the Earth they set about forming links between groups and individuals and some of these were human and some were not. As they travelled they shaped the horizon by creating mountains and valleys, rivers and streams. Places marked by the ancestors held great spiritual significance to the people with stories and legends related to their Dreaming emerging as a way of explaining this sacred time of Creation. After the ancestors had finished shaping the land, some returned to the stars or the land, while others became animals and other things. This was a sacred time, alive with the magic of Creation; a time now gone, but still imbued with great power for the people who continue to believe that the spirits are still here, disguised in the forms they took when the Earth was new.

Shamanism is a path that pays tribute to this ancient time. It is also a universal path ideally suited to the Golden Child and their inherent spiritual outlook, their level of awareness and their individual (activated from birth) gifts of power. Shamanism is the oldest known practiced faith; the foundation of many of the world's most respected religions. It refers to a range of traditional beliefs and practices that claim the ability to diagnose and cure human suffering by forming a special relationship with 'spirits' and the spiritual realm. Shamans (those who practise Shamanism) are believed to control the weather, exercise divinatory arts, interpret dreams, astral travel and drift between the upper and lower worlds. Shamanism, as a tradition, has existed since prehistoric times. Shamans are said to form a bridge between the natural and spiritual worlds and to travel between worlds in a trance state where they call upon the spirits to help with healing and hunting. Shamanism champions the belief that the tangible world is infused with invisible forces or spirits that influence the lives of the living. Unlike Animism (a path that espouses the belief that all objects and living things are permeated with wisdom, insight and choice that preside over their reality), Shamanism requires specialised training, initiation, knowledge and ability. Shamans, it could be said, are the 'experts' employed by Animists to instigate necessary and beneficial change on behalf of the wider community.

Golden Children enjoy low impact and recreational sports and activities like inland fishing, walking and cycling and, as adults, generally seek out occupations where they feel safe and free to develop their radical skills and unique knowledge. When all is said and done, however, they are probably best left to work on their own. Many Golden Children excel at university, so long as their chosen field of study does not suppress them or dampen their eccentricities or oddities. Golden Children do well in any career where their unique slant on things and special skills are valued. Some forms of cutting edge science and mathematics would suit their needs and requirements; work in the aerospace industry, for example, or the IT industry, while others become nuns, priests and spiritual leaders. Career options must offer high-level work where effort is employed in brainstorming new paradigms. Golden Children (no matter how old they are) need to be allowed to follow their instincts as to what work they do; they have a direct hotline to Spirit, after all, which allows them to get all the guidance they need directly from the source.

PART THREE

Integrated Healthcare for the Five Little Monkeys

As we have established, it is important to look at all children as being wonderfully alive and radiant, each blessed with special skills and contributions. Gifted with 'extra sensory perception', many of today's children are fully aware of the Other Realms, angels and nature spirits. They can easily see to the heart of things, quickly discerning truth from deception. Despite this uncanny ability, however, many find themselves overwhelmed and confused by dishonesty.

All children have an inherent ability to share their gifts and 'shine their light', but only when opportunity is afforded them. They are well equipped to make a great contribution to the changes developing in our society at present. No one can deny that the world is becoming increasingly polarised with divisions between what is deemed 'good' and 'evil'. Never assume, though, that children cannot see the illusions and deceit presently rampant in society — because they can. They are far more aware of what is happening than we give them credit for. It is vital, therefore, for our children to be supported on all levels so as to allow them the strength and endurance to contribute positively to the development of a new and healthy direction for the world to head in.

As with everyone, it is wise to keep in mind that today's children easily become 'messed up', especially when feeling confused, angry, resentful and defiant. This largely happens due to the negative impact the problems, complexities and falsehoods of society have on our children. In addition, many seem to have experienced difficult births, thorny childhoods and poor family or school experiences.

So as a general rule, the aim must be to help our children:

- Firmly establish themselves and get well grounded in the world.
- Teach them the rules of living safely and effectively in our society.
- Treat any disturbances they have acquired from difficult birth or childhood experiences.
- Learn to handle their emotions effectively.
- Learn how to achieve effective relationships.

If left unaddressed for an extended period of time, it is not unusual for the difficulties experienced by our children to eventually lead to actual illnesses, either physically or emotionally. Of course, illness can also arise for no obvious reason. In these cases specific treatment is required, but do not discount the more subtle types of healing which are better suited to the developing, sensitive and highly aware people today's children are. Subtle forms of therapy may include integrative medicine, good counselling, family therapy, naturopathy, cranial osteopathy, acupuncture, kinesiology, homeopathy, intuitive healing and Reiki.

An Overall Integrated Approach to Helping your Child

The first thing one must do is to consider the option that your child is fine. Perhaps your child simply needs a different approach as far as their parenting and schooling goes. If so, then it is probably safe to assume that it is you (and not your child) who would benefit from some assistance. That is to say, you would probably benefit from discovering some more productive ways of supporting and raising your child. But if your child is experiencing residual difficulty or illness beyond what might be deemed environmental, it is advised that you seek suitable therapy to help your child function more efficiently so that they may reach their potential.

A sensible approach to getting good integrated healthcare may include:

1. Assessment by:
   • An integrative holistic medical doctor
   • A specialist paediatrician
   • A naturopath
   • A cranial osteopath
   • A counsellor
   • A remedial teacher

2. Live Blood Analysis
   • This is a simple test performed on a single drop of blood that gives a lot of information about your child's metabolism. It is used by integrative holistic doctors and by naturopaths.

3. Hair Analysis
   • A test that checks for possible heavy metal toxicity and for mineral levels. This test is used by integrative holistic doctors and by naturopaths.

4. Specific therapies — usually carried out by integrative doctors and naturopaths:
   • Dietary modification.
   • Nutritional supplements.
   • Restoration of proper function of the liver and digestive system.
   • Cranial osteopathy.
   • Diagnosis and treatment of any chronic infections, including otitis media, sinusitis, bronchitis, enteritis, parasites, worms, candidiasis.
   • Treatment of any allergies, including asthma, eczema, hay fever.
   • Chelation for heavy metal toxicity — if found to be present.
   • Laser acupuncture — a gentle form of acupuncture which is safe, effective and painless, and uses no needles.
   • Homeopathy.
   • Flower essences.
   • Colour therapy.

5. Special schooling.

6. Family therapy.
7. Consider other approaches.

Remember the aim is to help your child lead a full, happy, well-rounded life, to develop their many abilities and to fulfil their potential so that they may play their part in making the world a better place. And remember, too, that there is assistance available for parents living with today's often challenging children.

For those looking for more specific or detailed information, consider the following points:

Diet

When it comes to healthy eating, the entire family needs to get involved. Here is a practical regime for the whole family to follow; a diet plan recognised as being helpful for children suffering from conditions such as allergies, ADD / ADHD and the milder cases of autism.

1. Avoid or minimise:
    *   All food colourings and preservatives
    *   All chemicals
    *   Refined sugar (white sugar)
    *   Sweets
    *   Added salt
    *   Pastries, cakes and biscuits
    *   Fizzy drinks
    *   Processed foods
    *   Preserved foods
    *   'Fast' or 'Junk' food

2. Eat plenty of:
    *   Fresh foods
    *   Fresh water
    *   Fresh fruit and vegetables

- Free range chicken
- Fish — fresh or canned in spring water, oil or brine
- Red meat — preferably organic, or at least lean meat (lamb is best as it doesn't involve the high levels of steroids, antibiotics or hormones in its production as other red meat)

A few children benefit from more intensive dietary therapy and this is best done under the guidance of an integrative holistic doctor, naturopath or expert nutritionist.

Further specialised diet changes can include:

- Avoidance of dairy food. Some children can be allergic to casein protein in milk.
- Avoidance of wheat products. Gluten in wheat can cause allergic reactions or induce Leaky Gut Syndrome.
- With any dietary change, it is worth trialling for two months to see if it is going to help. If there are no real benefits within that time, you can go back to your old diet and perhaps then try a different dietary change after that. Be aware, however, that sometimes symptoms get worse before they improve; the body has to adjust to the new way of eating.
- If you are concerned about diet or about responses to dietary changes, please consult a suitable health practitioner.

Useful Therapies in General

- Homeopathy: uses very small doses of extracts from plants or minerals to stimulate the body's own healing response.

- Flower essences: special extracts from flowers, which can have a useful balancing effect on the emotions.

- Kinesiology: a system derived from both movement analysis of the human body and from acupuncture. It can help repair or rebalance disturbed function of the brain and nervous system, and to correct problems with balance, co-ordination and motor function.

• Laser acupuncture: a gentle, safe and painless way of doing acupuncture. University research has confirmed its safety and efficacy. Acupuncture can help many problems with motor function, neurological and brain function, allergies, and emotional problems.

• Colour therapy: appeals to sensitive children, and can have a powerful effect on how the brain, emotions, chakra system and aura function.

• Crystal therapy: affords similar effects to colour therapy, but in a tangible way. Besides, some children relate better to crystals.

• Aromatherapy: uses scents from various essential oils to help balance the emotions.

• Healing: refers to such approaches as Reiki and other forms of gentle 'hands-on healing', and also spiritual or channelled healing. These approaches work on the subtle levels of the human being such as the aura and chakra system.

• 'Re-training of parents': Many parents benefit from specific instruction in how best to handle these children.

• Total honesty and integrity, respect for all parties and effective boundary setting are essential living plans for all family members to follow.

• Learn effective grounding: which often helps both the child and the parents to learn effective ways to settle themselves down and to regain physical and emotional equilibrium. Typically it involves practices based around conscious awareness of self and of the surrounding world. This is called 'grounding'.

Main Potential Problems Requiring Treatment

Birth trauma

Difficulties can occur leading up to, during and after the birthing process, due to:

- Infections – both within the womb and in early infancy
- Precipitate labour
- Premature labour
- Delayed or ineffectual labour and the use of labour-inducing drugs
- Impaired oxygen supply during birth
- Forceps birth

These difficulties may leave ongoing problems for the child as far as their growth and development goes. Problems such as:

- Distortion of the skull bones
- Subsequent irritant effects on the brain from this skull distortion
- Recurring headaches
- Learning problems
- Developmental delay
- Hyperactivity
- Mild brain damage
- Poor drainage of the middle ear, sinuses and nose with resultant chronic recurring middle ear infections or tonsillitis
- Weakened immune system with recurring infections
- Low vitality and susceptibility to illness in general – the so-called 'sickly child'

These problems can often be helped by methods such as cranial osteopathy, cranio-sacral therapy and Reiki (among other gentle forms of hands-on healing).

Vaccination trauma

Homeopathy teaches that in some constitutionally vulnerable children, any type of vaccine <u>may</u> cause illness by depleting the child's vitality and unmasking latent susceptibilities to illness. The use of 'one shot' multiple vaccines may worsen this problem. This is called a grafted sycotic layer. Homeopathy and naturopathy can help many of these problems.

Heavy Metal Toxicity

We are frequently exposed to heavy metals as pollutants in our environment, which can accumulate in the human body, especially in our bones, teeth, hair, brain, nervous system and bone marrow. In some cases, the heavy metals can cause significant toxic effects such as fatigue, gut disturbances, anaemia, low white cell count, intellectual impairment, emotional disturbance or aggravation of pre-existing illnesses.

For example, the heavy metal mercury can accumulate in the body from:
* Preservative in some paediatric vaccines (Thimerosal)
* Ingestion by the child or by the mother as a result of eating large amounts of 'contaminated' fish. Mercury is known to cross from the mother to the child via the placenta's blood circulation or after birth via her breast milk.

Mercury is known to be toxic to the brain, nervous system, digestive system and bone marrow, causing or aggravating learning problems, motor development problems, autism and malabsorption of nutrients, immune system weakness and recurring or chronic infections. These problems can often be treated with diet, supplements and chelation therapy to remove the heavy metals from the body. This is treatment is done by some specialised integrative doctors and naturopaths. See the advice on the Autism Research Institute website: www.autism.com

Leaky Gut Syndrome

Poor digestion often leads to impaired function of the wall of the gut. As a result large protein chains and other poorly digested food molecules can enter the bloodstream from the gut by literally leaking through the gut wall. These molecules have an irritant effect on many body tissues (known as 'free radical overload'), triggering allergies or toxic effects. This digestive problem can also be associated with an overgrowth of candida or other parasites / microbes in the gut. Treatment is usually handled by addressing the diet, probiotics (healthy digestive bacteria) and certain herbs, which greatly alleviates the problem. This treatment is offered by many integrative holistic doctors and naturopaths.

Liver Toxicity

The liver forms a crucial aspect in the processing and binding of toxins in the bloodstream (free radicals), transmuting them so they can be safely eliminated from the body via the urine, faeces, sweat and breath. When the liver's inactivating function is defective (a condition known as impaired conjugation), excess toxins are allowed to accumulate in the body, thus damaging various tissues. This so-called free radical disease is the basis of many of the chronic degenerative illnesses witnessed in today's society. The tendency for impaired liver conjugation and resultant liver toxicity is often inherited. Signs of it in the family include recurring fatigue, migraines, allergies, asthma, eczema, hay fever, period problems, poor alcohol tolerance and depression that is suffered by a number of family members.

Treatment is best tackled via the diet, anti-oxidants, herbs, homeopathy, and acupuncture; approaches that all help to greatly improve this condition. Once again consult a naturopath or integrative medicine doctor.

Microbe overgrowth and immune system overload

Microbe overgrowth and immune system overload are often indicated by problems with candidiasis, bowel parasites, and recurring respiratory or gut infections. The immune system can become weakened by Leaky Gut Syndrome, liver toxicity or by the effects of stress, and this can allow infections to take hold. In addition microbes, which are normally present (in healthy levels), can sometimes overgrow to such a level they begin to cause significant problems themselves. This is often the situation with organisms such as candida and some normal bowel microbes. All this can occur because of a possible weakness in the immune system. Such infections can be contained with various natural therapy approaches, including certain herbs, homeopathy and acupuncture, especially when attention is given to any underlying problems. In resistant cases, intensive medical anti-microbial therapy is needed.

All these therapies are typically administered by integrative medicine doctors and naturopaths.

Food and chemical sensitivities

Due to the combined effects of excess sensitivity to the environment, immune system weakness and liver toxicity (remember: the liver is the key organ for processing chemicals), people sometimes develop sensitivities or allergies to certain foods or substances. This sometimes leads to the development of other complaints, such as asthma, eczema, hay fever, hyperactivity, chronic fatigue syndrome, and a range of more serious autoimmune disorders.

These severe allergic problems can be treated by various natural therapy approaches employed by integrative medicine doctors and naturopaths. These therapies include exclusion diets, nutritional supplements, laser acupuncture and constitutional homeopathy.

Delayed fine motor skill development

Excessive clumsiness, poor co-ordination and dyslexia are often indicators of problems affecting the development of some children's fine motor skills. These conditions affect the function of the physical body, which can seem heavy and awkward to a sensitive individual. The problems are sometimes the result of an isolated neurological delay in development, which often sees the child growing out of the problem at a particular age and then experiencing a catch up growth spurt. At other times these problems can be due to difficult circumstances in the environment, either at home or at school. And of course, sometimes there is no obvious reason at all.

Approaches that encourage the child to remain fully 'in the body' can help, such as 'grounding' therapies like kinesiology, acupuncture, yoga, tai chi or gentle forms of martial arts. In addition, motor re-patterning exercises, Brain Gym and sensory integration, drama classes or dance therapy can be useful.

Parenting problems

Unconvincing or half-hearted parenting techniques will, in time, lead to major problems for a lot of children. Excessively strict parenting, denial of the child's own knowing, lying, denial of true reality, inconsistency of standards and poor boundary setting are common examples of poor parenting skills. Restrictive or distorted parenting gives the wrong message, not to mention how it inhibits, confuses and disturbs our children.

Consistent, honest parenting, total integrity in all dealings with the child, the establishment of clear, consistent boundaries and rules, affirming the child in their experiences, offering experiences that foster a fulfilled, competent, integrated and effective happy adult, and lots of expressed unconditional love are vitally important, as are (where necessary) parental education and re-training.

Sensory overload

There are, and always have been, cases of highly sensitive children. Unanticipated or excessive stimulation from the external world can easily overwhelm such children and send them into a spin, or even into a numb dissociative state. Bright or flickering lights, loud noise, overpowering smells, too much contact with other people, places with 'bad vibes', or unhappy, unsettled people, all contribute to a negative experience for highly sensitive children. These children are so aware of external force that they are easily influenced by negative surroundings or unexpected stimuli. Such stressors must be removed from the child's environment and their impact cleared from the child. The child must also be made aware of and taught how to defend themselves against these triggers in the future.

With assistance, these children can learn to handle these prompts and learn to integrate them into their lives. Physical aides designed to reduce intense input, such as sunglasses, earplugs, iPod music earphones, or aromatherapy on their clothing, are common ones. Useful therapies include Tomatis sound therapy, sensory integration therapy, homeopathy, laser acupuncture, kinesiology, healing or Reiki. These approaches help to reduce irritation from excessive sensitivity while helping the child integrate unfamiliar sensory inputs. These treatments are best performed by specifically trained health professionals.

Withdrawal and isolation

When left to their own devices, the sensitive child may withdraw deep into their own selves as a way of coping with the overwhelming stimuli and demands of living in today's world. This can lead to depression, social isolation and some forms of autism.

The obvious and necessary step is to somehow 'reach' the child and gently guide them back out to celebrate their place in the world. Therapists trained in helping autistic children (such as specially trained counsellors, psychologists, occupational therapists and teachers) may be helpful. Computers and other forms of technology are tools frequently used to reach the withdrawn child and establish a productive line of communication between them and the 'outside world'.

Some subtle forms of therapy may also have their place: sensory stimulation programs, for example, constitutional homeopathy, flower essences, colour therapy, Reiki or spiritual healing. These therapies must be delivered by appropriately trained health professionals to avoid complications.

'Wiring problems'

Some children experience any one of a number of disturbances in the function of the brain, nervous system or the subtle energy fields that control the physical body; conditions best described as a result of 'miswiring' in the central nervous system or the body's electro-magnetic and energy fields.

Acupuncture, kinesiology, homeopathy and intuitive healing can all help.

Alcohol and drug abuse

Problems arising from substance abuse often begin as a result of peer group pressure. Sometimes, however, children are predisposed to substance abuse because of family history or poor role modelling. There are several reasons why the sensitive child may turn to substance abuse. For one, they may be trying to pacify excess sensitivity by 'anaesthetising' their system with drugs or alcohol. Sometimes a bored unfulfilled child will seek perceived excitement or stimulation through drugs to try to fill their inner emptiness. Other children may lean on drugs in an attempt to numb themselves from negative life experiences such as abuse (in its countless forms), the memory of which being too painful to bear. And of course there are the ones who use drugs as a way of rebelling against their parents or the system as a whole.

Some of these children may need professional help: time spent in a drug detoxification unit followed by extensive counselling, for example. Professional help can be gleaned by exploring the youth support programs and facilities listed in the resource section of this book.

Self-violence

In the more extreme cases, some children engage themselves in self-violence such as head-banging, deliberate self-mutilation, anorexia nervosa or bulimia. This behaviour is often a cry for help, an attempt to release the pain of being overwhelmed, a way to bring some sense of control and safety into the situation, or a dramatic way to attain attention and a sense of reality. These are extreme cases demonstrating behaviour triggered by situations where the child's growth and learning have been seriously hampered by adverse external circumstance.

Obviously this is a grave situation demanding serious attention and professional help over an extended period of time. This can involve psychiatric inpatient treatment (in acute cases), extensive counselling and, in the case of all multi-level problems, ongoing monitoring and appropriate maintenance-style treatment.

Treatment Issues

Any one of the above-mentioned conditions and situations may lead to the diagnosis of disorders such as ADD, ADHD, Asperger's Syndrome, multiple food and chemical sensitivities or autism. It is important to understand that although these disorders are fundamentally products of a troubled society and not necessarily intrinsic to any one particular 'type' of children, with many ending up being misdiagnosed with medical disorders they simply do not have, it is a fact that some of these children do genuinely have significant illnesses that affect their view of the world and the world's view of them. Simply put, many children do not actually suffer from ADD / ADHD or autism. Many are just different (often as a result of environmental, domestic or personal influences) and so demand particularised handling. However, some children do genuinely suffer from disorders such as autism or Attention Deficit Disorder, and so benefit from proper specialised medical and ancillary treatment.

Children identified as having ADD, ADHD or autism are sometimes burdened with their diagnoses because they simply do not fit in. We expect them to fit in, which is something they just can't do. They see things differently to most; they make a fuss and rock the boat and are generally a pain in the neck. In most cases, it is easier to label them as 'sick' or disturbed and trust the first prescribed medication.

Many of these children have a clearer view of the world and of life than we do. It makes sense to assume, therefore, that if we let them, they may be able to help us live better lives. By listening to what they have to say, they may be able to knock some sense into the way things are currently done and, with their motivation to inspire us, we may be driven to take a good hard look at ourselves and make some positive changes on all levels. Today's children are not sick or disturbed. Instead, many are sensitive, honest people with empathy for the natural and spiritual worlds; people who have trouble living in an aggressive, false-hearted world.

As a result, most of these children do not require conventional or mainstream medication. They rarely benefit from heavy medical treatments such as sedation with Ritalin and drugs of similar ilk. Rather, they respond better when offered meaningful assistance and alternative remedies and handling.

At the time of writing this book, stories began to appear in the Australian media (around March 2006) highlighting some 400 new cases of children experiencing documented contrary side-effects to their ADD and ADHD medication (namely Ritalin), including insomnia, irritability, drowsiness, headaches, loss of weight, depression, attempted suicide, hallucinations, heart arrhythmias and stroke. This was reported on the March 28, 2006 edition of the Australian television current affairs program *Today Tonight*, as quoted on their website http://seven.com.au/todaytonight.

Previously the May 4, 2005 episode of *Today Tonight* reported on their website, that in 1995 some 46,000 Australian children were being prescribed dexamphetamines (such as Ritalin). However by May 2005 this figure had risen to a staggering 246,000 children, with a similar rise reported regarding children being given anti-depressants as a way of treating their conditions.

The *Today Tonight* report (4 May, 2005) went on to include comments from specialist child psychiatrists and psychologists dealing with children with ADD / ADHD; comments like:

"If our first line of treatment is to give the kids medication that is probably, in many cases, unnecessary then … we are overmedicating."

"Many families are not prepared to look at their own dynamics or how they interact with the child for the benefit of the child. Instead, it's easier to blame it on the child and go to the doctor and get some medication for it."

"They should look at their family situation, look at their child and the development of the child, look at themselves and the daily wear and tear, the stresses, and then they should listen to the child. Maybe the child's communicating something about what is actually going on, that mums and dads might be too busy to notice."

"Once we look at the seriousness of the generational effects of prescribing drugs – mind-altering, mood-altering drugs – to ever-younger children and see the consequences ... the first issue is to recognise that this is a problem. This is not normal; this is a historical fashion statement. Fashion statements fortunately eventually change. Unfortunately perhaps, not before a lot of damage is done on the way."

"Any medications for children should be prescribed with great caution – this is a basic principle of medical practice. Where there are significant side effects, as with Ritalin, such medications should only be prescribed in extreme situations – such as when life is endangered or when normal development and schooling is impossible, that is after more conservative approaches have been tried and failed."

Even 'Novartis', the distributing company for Ritalin (www.novartis.com. au), advise that Ritalin should be used as part of a comprehensive treatment program that typically includes other remedial measures (psychological, educational, social). The prescribing information notes that appropriate educational placement is essential and psychosocial is generally necessary, and that Ritalin should only be prescribed when remedial measures alone are insufficient.

But on a positive note, there is always the odd case where conventional medication does help the individual to grow and live a fulfilling life, as well as being of true benefit to the family and school. This is particularly the case if the child is out of control, or is a serious threat to themselves or others. It must be remembered, however, that in general most children respond favourably to the subtle or energetic therapies and certain gentle natural remedies, especially those supported by conscious parenting.

Choosing Effective Practitioners

When it comes to finding a practitioner, it is vital to find one that is effective enough to assist you and your child on all levels, whether they are medical doctors, natural therapists, counsellors or healers. The rules and expectations should be the same for all. A practitioner who will work with you and your child is preferred — one that can be seen as a team player, or as a consultant to your team. Your relationship with your child's practitioner should be viewed as being a team effort. One wise patient (who came from a managerial background) once described it as interviewing the practitioner to see if they fitted the job description and were good enough to join the treatment team. You want to find practitioners who have sound qualifications and who are skilled and experienced in what they do. Obviously you want practitioners who are practised at helping children, particularly children experiencing similar conditions to those hampering your child's development. They must demonstrate age-appropriate communication skills, honesty, respect and integrity. You want to find a practitioner you can get along well with, and who has the skills you need to help your child. In turn, the practitioner must be able to trust they will receive your honesty, co-operation and candid communication, as well as a willingness to follow through with any recommended treatment regimes you have jointly decided on.

Choose your treatment team mindfully, with due regard to the sort of approaches you would prefer for your child. And, of course, do your homework to determine what approaches are most likely to benefit your child. Look for qualified scientific data or well-documented testimonials that certify the approach works. Then see which of these promising approaches appeal to you and your child. Finally look for suitable practitioners to help you with your chosen modality — those with promising (and eligible) practitioner skills, availability, accessibility and reasonable cost. Finally seek out the individual practitioner you wish to work with and interview them for the job. Not until they measure up should you recruit them for your team.

Word-of-mouth endorsement or contacting professional organisations that cover the modality you want are probably the best ways to determine what practitioner is ideal for you and your child. Such organisations usually have a referral list of qualified members that they readily make available to members of the general public. Some of these organisations are listed at the resource section of this book.

Homeopathy

Homeopathy is a treatment system well suited to most people, especially those on the sensitive side. You may notice that it has been recommended throughout this book.

Homeopathy is as much an excellent first-aid tool for home use as it is a viable treatment for a number of severe diseases. Before self-medication is considered, however, it is recommended that individual advice from a professional homeopath or naturopath who uses homeopathic remedies be sought.

Overview of Homeopathy

Homeopathy is a specific system of medicine developed about 200 years ago in Germany by a leading medical physician, Dr. Samuel Hahnemann (1755 – 1834). This system was based on extensive clinical observation and experimental trials of therapeutic compounds. Eventually two fundamental 'Laws of Cure' were developed:

- The Law of Similars (which says that a disease can be cured by a substance that causes <u>similar</u> symptoms to the actual disease symptoms)

- The Law of the Minimum Dose (which says that the smallest dose that has an effect, has the <u>maximum effect</u>)

Hippocrates first described the 'Law of Similars' when he recommended that an effective treatment for recurrent vomiting was ipecacuanha which would normally induce vomiting. Hippocrates observed that the remedy actually reduced the vomiting instead of making it worse. In the late 1700s,

Dr. Hahnemann was researching the mechanisms of action of quinine in the treatment of malaria and decided to take some quinine himself in order to experience its effects first-hand. He was surprised to find that the quinine produced in him all the symptoms of malaria. When he stopped taking the drug the malaria symptoms went away and, whenever he resumed the quinine doses, the symptoms returned.

Dr. Hahnemann then went on to test what happened when a large range of therapeutic substances were taken by healthy volunteers. He gathered a vast array of symptom patterns produced from these experimental tests or 'provings' and recorded them in a large volume of 'Materia Medica'. These substances were then given as remedies to patients suffering with diseases producing the same symptom patterns. It was found repeatedly that these remedies greatly relieved the patient's suffering and that the disease process often healed much more quickly. A theory came to be developed saying that the symptoms of the disease are not the actual disease itself, but are the body's *response* to the underlying disease process. It would therefore be helpful to give a remedy that would strengthen the body's specific fight and so help it drive off the illness. This became known as The Law of Similars; 'let like be cured by like'.

Dr. Hahnemann then developed The Law of the Minimum Dose in response to a problem. Some patients would experience a severe aggravation of their symptoms when these remedies were first taken. They would then gain relief after a period of intense discomfort. In order to reduce this, Hahnemann tried diluting the remedies along with giving them a good shake, and called this process 'potentising'. These diluted remedies did in fact significantly reduce the treatment aggravations, and to his surprise Hahnemann found that the more he diluted his remedies the more effective they became in treating the disease process. Dr. Hahnemann came to understand that the body response is subtle and so all you need to do is to give just enough to trigger a healing response. Any more than this can overstimulate the body and so produce problem reactions, or even reduce the benefit of the remedy. This realisation became known as The Law of the Minimum Dose.

Another way of understanding how homeopathy works is to consider that the human organism has a specific frequency that it vibrates to in health. The body also has its own self-healing capacity linked in with its fundamental life energy — called the Vital Force. Each person has their own unique vibrational signature. Then if a disease force invades the body it pushes the Vital Force away from its fundamental health frequency. If this is not quickly corrected by the Vital Force, the resulting disturbance can in time translate to illness on the mental and eventually the physical level. However if a suitable remedy is supplied that is primarily vibrational and so acts on the Vital Force, it can stimulate and strengthen the Vital Force so that it now becomes active enough to throw off the disease force, and so restores health to the mind and the body.

Scientific studies

Over the last 25 years there have been a number of scientific studies carried out on homeopathy, but many have been of variable quality with conflicting results. Several high quality studies have been carried out in recent years that demonstrate a definite positive effect to homeopathy in such conditions as hay fever, allergic asthma, fibromyalgia and rheumatoid arthritis.

How Homeopathy works

No one really knows how homeopathic remedies work but there are a few theories around with some supporting evidence.

The most plausible theory is that in the preparation process of the remedies (which involves dilution and vigorous shaking of the original substance), information or energy is imparted to the water molecules in the solution. This energy is then stored by changes in the molecular bonds and structures formed by the water molecules. The energy is then released when the remedy is taken into the human body, and it perhaps rebalances the subtle electromagnetic fields that control function of the mind and body. Work by Dr. Paul Callinan at Southern Cross University, Lismore in New South Wales supports this idea. In addition, the work of Dr. Masaru Emoto (as seen on the film *What The Bleep Do We Know*), backs this up by demonstrating that water has memory and responds to the influences around it — whether from physical effects such as pollution, or from people's attitudes and emotions.

Visit Dr. Emoto here: http://www.masaru-emoto.net/english/entop. html

Scientific References

- 'Homeopathic Therapy in Rheumatoid Arthritis: Evaluation by Double-Blind Clinical Therapeutic Trial' by Gibson et al, Br. J. Clin. Pharmac., 1980; 9:453-459.
- 'Is Homeopathy a Placebo Response? Controlled Trial of Homeopathic Potency, with Pollen in Hay Fever as Model' by Reilly et al, The Lancet, Oct.18th, 1986; 881-885.
- 'Human Basophil Degranulation by Dilute Antiserum against IgE' by Davenas, Benveniste et al, Nature, 30 June 1988; 333: 816-818.
- 'Effect of Homeopathic Treatment on Fibrositis (primary fibromyalgia)' by Fisher at al, BMJ, 5 August 1989; 299: 365-366.
- 'Clinical Trials of Homeopathy' by Kleijnen et al, BMJ, 9 Feb. 1991; 302: 316-322.
- 'Evidence of Clinical Efficacy of Homeopathy: A Meta-Analysis of Clinical Trials' by Cucherat et al, Eur. J. Clin. Pharmacol., April 2000; 56; 1:27-33.

Some useful First Aid Homeopathic Remedies

General principles:

- Consult a qualified therapist trained in Homeopathy before self-prescribing in case of serious or acute situations
- Consult the list of keynotes (below) when considering the situation
- Choose the most appropriate remedy as set by the keynote

Dosage:

- In acute illness, give the indicated remedy in a medium potency (such as 6c or 30c) every 15 to 30 minutes until the symptoms are subsiding.

- In general, the more active the symptoms, the more frequently you give the remedy.
- Once the illness symptoms are coming under control, continue the remedy at the same potency every four hours until the patient is fully recovered.

How to give the remedy:

- Be aware that the remedy is on the surface of the homeopathic pilules, which are made of milk sugar.
- It is important to avoid contact with your hands. If you touch the pilules the sweat from your hands can neutralise the remedy, and the remedy may even come off onto your palms.
- The pilules are dissolved in the mouth via large blood vessels under the tongue, and generally throughout the lining of the mouth.
- Do <u>not</u> try to wash the pills down with any liquids.
- It is important to avoid any food or persisting tastes in the mouth (such as spices, mint or strong toothpaste) otherwise this can inactivate the remedy.
- In some susceptible people certain things will inactivate the remedy — coffee, mothballs (camphor) and chilli.
- Store the remedy bottle in a dry situation out of direct sunlight, away from strong smells, and at least one metre away from any electronic equipment such as microwaves. Keep out of reach of children. They often think of the remedies as sweet lollies, and so love to sneak extra pills. Storage inside a high cupboard is usually best.

Simple dosage instructions:

- Tip two to three pilules out of the bottle into the bottle cap.
- Then tip these pilules directly onto your tongue.
- Dissolve the pilules on, or preferably under, your tongue. It is like sucking a lolly.
- If you are using drops, allow two to three drops of the remedy to drip onto your tongue. Let the drops sit on your tongue for at least one

minute so the remedy can be absorbed.
• Nothing to eat or drink, nothing in the mouth, and no teeth cleaning for at least 15 minutes before or after the remedy dose.

When to see the Medical Doctor:

Always consult a medical doctor <u>immediately</u> if there is:
• Severe trauma
• A high uncontrolled fever
• The patient is delirious
• Severe pain
• The patient has a convulsion
• The patient is unconscious or nearly so
• Breathing difficulty
• The patient is in any way seriously ill

In general, get medical advice from the doctor if:
• You are unsure how serious the patient's condition is
• To discover what the diagnosis is
• The illness is not settling well within 12 hours of beginning homeopathic treatment

A well-trained natural therapist may also be able to offer advice if the condition is not severe but is taking some time to settle, or if you want additional complementary treatment in conjunction with medical treatment.

Homeopathic Remedy Keynotes

For First Aid:

• Remember the Bach Flower Remedy called Rescue Remedy is often helpful for any sort of physical or emotional distress or trauma. Take two drops on the tongue every 15 minutes until the patient is settling, then continue every four hours until the patient is back to normal.

Cuts:

- Arnica (mountain daisy) — Major remedy for cuts in general, especially if there is bruising and a feeling of soreness or lameness.
- Calendula — Topical application to damaged skin. Do not put directly onto an open wound. Promoted skin healing in general.
- Ledum (marsh tea) — For deep puncture wounds.

Sprains, Strains and Bruises:

- Arnica (mountain daisy) — Major remedy. For bruising and sensations of feeling bruised, lame or sore.
- Ruta (rye) — For bruised pains in tendons. For tendon or ligament trauma.
- Symphytum (comfrey) — For sore bones with pricking pains. For bone or periosteal trauma, including assisting broken bones to heal after they have been set by a doctor.

Minor Burns:

- Calendula – Apply regularly as a lotion. Promotes rapid wound healing and clears up skin discharges.
- Cantheris (Spanish fly) — For severe burning pains. When the skin is red, blistered and peeling. More severe burns.
- Urtica (stinging nettle) – For swelling and bruising of the skin. Can be taken internally as pilules and also applied externally as a lotion.

Stings and Bites:

- Apis (bee sting) — For redness, soreness and severe swelling after a bite or sting.
- Ledum (marsh tea) — For deep puncture wounds and deep bites.
- Urtica (stinging nettle) — For itchy blotches around bite.

Hives and Urticaria:

- Apis (bee sting) — Swollen red stinging spots
- Rhus tox (poison ivy) — Intensely itchy red raised blotches.
- Urtica urens (stinging nettle) — Stinging itchy spots. Very itchy. Burning heat in the spots, which is worse from touch and from water application. The patient is agitated.

Fevers:

- Aconite — Feverish but pale and chilled. Started from getting chilled.
- Belladonna — Feverish, hot, red and flushed face. May be a little delirious.
- Chamomile — Feverish, hot, irritable and clingy. Better for being cuddled.

Colds:

- Nat mur — Profuse sneezing. Nose running like a tap.
- Pulsatilla — Thick congestion with stuffiness and copious greenish mucus discharge.

Tonsillitis, Otitis Media and Ear Infections:

- Mercurius — Pain on swallowing with pus on the tonsils. Ear pain worse in bed. May be yellow discharge from the ears.
- Lachesis — Swollen purplish tonsils especially on the left side

Minor Indigestion and Belly Pains:

- Arsenicum album — Burning pains in the stomach. Irritable and restless.
- Colocynthis — Cramping pains in the belly. Pains eased by bending double.

- Mag phos — Cramping pains eased by a hot water bottle or gentle massage.
- Nux vomica — Feels as if food is sitting like a brick in the stomach. Chilled and nauseated.

Nausea and Vomiting:

- Ipecac — For nausea and vomiting in general.
- Nux vomica — For nausea and vomiting if the patient is pale and feels very chilled.

Diarrhoea:

- Arsenicum album — Much urging to empty the bowels but only passes small amounts. Burning pain in the rectum.
- Podophyllum — For profuse 'gushing', watery diarrhoea with a very offensive smell.
- Phosphorus — Painless diarrhoea. Feels chilled and weakened after each bowel motion.

Constipation:

- Alumina – No desire at all to pass a stool for days at a time, followed by violent ineffectual urging to pass the motion. Totally unable to expel the stool. Eventually may pass marble-like masses, but the rectum still feels full. Anus may itch, especially after passing a stool.
- Bryonia — Constipation with hard <u>dry</u> stool. Seems as if the stool is too large to be passed.
- Sepia — Constipation with large hard stools. Feeling as if a ball is in the rectum. May be much urging with pains shooting upward from rectum.

Emotional Upset:

- These remedies can be used on their own for temporary minor emotional problems.

- For more severe and long-term problems the patient should also see an experienced counsellor, psychologist or psychiatrist.
- Remember the Bach Flower Remedy called Rescue Remedy is often helpful for any sort of physical or emotional distress or trauma. Take two drops on the tongue every 15 minutes until the patient is settling, then continue it every four hours until the patient is back to normal.
- Rescue Remedy can also be taken as two drops on the tongue every four hours, plus an extra dose as needed, on stressful or disturbed days.

Anxiety and Worry:

- Aconite — Panicky feelings. Patient fears that they will die or that something terrible will happen. Feels chilled. May begin from getting chilled. Pale.
- Argentum nitricum — Anxious and trembling. Craves sugar. Impulsive and irritable. Jerky movements. Thoughts jump all over the place. Anticipatory anxiety. Pre-exam nerves. Jittery before an important event.
- Arsenicum album — Restless and anxious. Paces about. Worries about security and about their health. Fussy. Feels chilled. Despairing.
- Gelsemium —Weak and trembling. Dizzy. Stage fright.
- Nux vomica —Restless, irritable and driven.

The relationship between the Five Monkey Types and Homeopathic Constitutional Remedies

Monkey	Child	Keynotes	Four Humours	Five Elements	TCM	Ayureveda	Typical Homeo-pathic Rememdies
Capuchin	Indigo Child	Militant Achiever Warrior Action-oriented Artisan	Choleric	Fire	Wood Liver	Pitta	Lachesis Sulphur Med. Ferrum met. Nux vomica Arsenicum album
Colobus	Winter Child	Guardian Fact-oriented Martyr Logician Problem solver	Melan-cholic	Earth	Earth Spleen	Kapha	Calc-carb Calc-phos Carcinosn Thuja Syph. Baryta-carb. Ferrum met. Arsenicum album Nat-mur
Lemur	Peace-keeper Child	Rationalist Theory-oriented Loner Witness Pacifier	Sanguine	Air	Metal Lung	Vata	Mercurius Arg-nit. Tub. Phosphorus Cannabis Lyco-podium

Monkey	Child	Keynotes	Four Humours	Five Elements	TCM	Ayureveda	Typical Homeopathic Rememdie
Squirrel Monkey	Nature Child	Idealist Ideals-oriented Activist Speaker Romantic	Phlegm-atic	Water	Water Kidney	Kapha-Vata Mix	Pulsatilla Carcinosin healthy Nat-mur healthy Sepia Mercurius Tub.
Golden Lion Tamarin	Golden Child	Dreamer Feelings-oriented Prophet Intuitive		Spirit	Fire Heart	Tri-doshic: Vatta-Pitta-Kapha Mix	Sulphur Causticum Med - healthy

Homeopathic constitutional remedies are very deep acting and should only be used by trained homeopaths.

These remedies can help to boost health on all levels of mind and body. They can even help to minimise the expression of inherited patterns of illness. Even for the relatively healthy person, constitutional remedies can be used to enhance vitality and good health and to reduce the chances of becoming sick in general.

These remedies can therefore be very helpful because they tend to be well received by the more sensitive children, and they are usually free of side effects. If adverse effects do occur, they tend to be minor and self-limiting. In fact, any such reactions are likely to be a temporary 'healing-crisis' as the body rids itself of toxins and rebalances itself, leading to improved health.

These constitutional remedies are prescribed on the basis of both physical and mental symptoms — particularly symptoms that give a clue to the unique nature of the person.

Many of these remedies are derived from poisons or damaging substances, even from disease products. This gives them the power to act on the deepest inner levels of the human being, based on the belief that what can destroy can also heal. Think of the very small doses of the poison arsenic, for example, which trainers give to racehorses to help them run faster.

The following is a list of some of the more important remedies that relate to each of the five Monkey types (as listed in each of their individual chapters earlier in the book). This list is more for interest's sake than anything else; examining it will afford a deeper sense of what each Monkey type is about. Of course, the correlation with each type is not exact so, in the final analysis, be guided by the key individual symptoms displayed by the person so as to choose the most suitable remedy.

Remedy	Origin of Remedy	Keynotes
Lachesis	Snake Venom	Driven. Restless. Talkative. Cannot bear tight clothing. Jealousy. Sadness. Lustful / sexual excitement and tension. Haemorrhage. Septic states. Delirium tremens. Swollen purplish tonsils – especially on left side. Hot flushes. **Positive aspect**: Passion for life. Raw sexuality.
Sulphur	Mineral Sulphur	Ragged philosopher type. Forgetful. Scruffy. Dirty. Lazy. Selfish. Irritable. Heat, itching and burning in various parts of the body and skin – worsened by washing and by warmth. Eczema. Recurring illness. Craves sweets. Becomes faint around 11am – must eat and feels better for it. **Positive aspect**: The inspired ego. God in action. The Eagle totem. Spirit. The Sun god.

Remedy	Origin of Remedy	Keynotes
Medorrhinum	Gonorrhoea	Extrovert. The ultimate party animal. Emotional roller coaster – up and down all the time. Sex, drugs and rock 'n' roll type. Weak memory. Fear of going insane. Catarrh. Excess mucus. Wet asthma. Moles and warts. Benign growths. Heavy periods. Endometriosis. Ovarian cysts. Chronic rheumatism. Craves oranges and orange juice. **Positive aspect**: Great appreciation of the pleasures life has to offer. Sensuality in its pure sense. Passionate adventurer in life.
Nux vomica	Poison nut	Fiery temperament. Stressed businessman type. Thin, irritable, nervous, quick, peevish. Ill effects of indulging in stimulants, alcohol and rich food – which he craves. Over sensitive to all external input. Thick head, hangover, heartburn, bad temper. **Positive aspect**: The archetypal conqueror.
Arsenicum album	White arsenic	Very restless. Despairing. Feels frail and that his health will fail. Fear of getting sick. Miserly and selfish. Burning pains – relieved by heat. Great exhaustion even after minimal exertion. **Positive aspect:** Polite and courteous. Old world charm and manners. Fastidious. Attentive to health. Sentimental. Devoted to the family.
Calc carb	Calcium Carbonate	Fears misfortune. Apprehensive. Forgetful. Obstinate. Averse to work. Swollen glands. Catarrh. Perspires easily. Slow recovery from illness. Craves eggs. Averse to fat and milk. Very sensitive to cold. Physical insecurity. **Positive aspect**: Placid and content. Enjoys people yet self-reliant.

Remedy	Origin of Remedy	Keynotes
Carcinosin	Cancer tissue	Deep survival level fears. Feels numb, or very deeply depressed. Feels crushed. No sense of self. Damaged by past abuse or rape. Weird eyes. Moles. Can have very low vitality. Fear of cancer. Prone to severe illness including cancer sometimes. Severe insomnia with night terrors. **Positive aspect**: Excellent counsellors and healers – sympathetic, understanding and experienced. Wise through suffering. Animal workers. Good carers.
Thuja	Thuja plant- the Tree Of Life	Introvert. Strange fixed ideas. Sexual guilt. Deep hidden dirty secret – feels unclean. Feels ugly and deformed. Can feel as if another entity is living inside her body. Suppressed illness from previous vaccination – causes more severe illness. Large moist fleshy warts. Polyps. Genital and reproductive diseases or rheumatism from suppressed gonorrhoea. Emaciated. Chronic insomnia. **Positive aspect**: Sensitive and psychic. Can feel what others feel. Caring and serious.
Nat mur	Rock salt	Depressed and irritable. Introvert. Locks emotions in – bottles them up. Suppressed emotional pain. Tension in mind and body due to held emotion. Illness due to suppressed or chronic grief and sadness. Wants to be alone so they can cry on their own. Loner. Stiff upper lip. Sensitive to noise. Aggravated by talking about their problems and by sympathy – counselling worsens them. Control freaks. Music makes them weep and soothes them. Craves salt. Weakened by hot weather. Body is always cold. Anaemia. Dry mucous membranes. Nose runs like a tap – hay fever with much sneezing. Blinding headache after menstruation. **Positive aspect**: Practical organisers. Discreet stable affectionate empathic ethical people.

Remedy	Origin of Remedy	Keynotes
Mercurius	Mercury	Weak mind – slow in answering questions – dull and confused. Or quick mind. Racing thoughts. Fast talker. Glib. Ever youthful - Peter Pan. Puerile. Charming. Mercurial personality. Fool and trickster. Detached. Always changing. Can never find stability. Aggravated by extremes of temperature. Sweats easily but it makes them feel worse. Easily aggravated by many things but few things relieve them. Tonsillitis with much saliva, metallic taste in mouth and severe halitosis. Tremors. Worse at night. Foul breath, excretions and body smell. Tends to form thin green putrid pus. **Positive aspect**: Great speaker and communicator. Loves words – a real wordsmith. Excellent actor and mimic. In touch with the communications from Spirit. Divine inspiration. The medium. Like Mercury — messenger of the gods. Chameleon – can adapt to any situation.
Arg nit	Silver nitrate	Fearful and nervous. Jumpy. Anxious. Erratic. Twitchy. Trembling. Impulsive. Wants to do things in a hurry. Strange impulses – such as a strong irrational desire to jump out of the window. Poor co-ordination and clumsy. Anticipatory anxiety. Craves sweets. Gets irritable, light-headed and confused if misses a meal – relieved by eating. Severe inflammation of mucous membranes. Headache with coldness and trembling. Brain fog. When swallowing feels as if a splinter is stuck in the throat. **Positive aspect**: Innocent child-like curiosity. Independent free thinker.

Remedy	Origin of Remedy	Keynotes
Tuberculinum	Tuberculosis	Restlessness. Weakened and emaciated. Nervous weakness. Alternates between irritable peevishness and sweet angelic disposition. Melancholy and listless depression. Easily catches colds and chest infections. Prone to severe asthma and pneumonia. Head banging. Very sensitive physically and mentally. Extreme temper tantrums in children. Bright but easily bored. Nasty and vindictive. Romantic and sentimental. Strong creative artistic impulses. Feels better in the open air – loves walking in the mountains. Long thin bones with pigeon chest. **Positive aspect**: The classic intellectual with a strong mind and excellent powers of reason.
Phosphorus	Mineral Phosphorus	Dreamy. Space cadet. Little sense of personal boundaries. Over sensitive to external impressions. Dread of being alone – fears she might die. Vertigo – especially of standing up. Tall and slender with pale complexion and white transparent skin. Haemorrhages. Coughs up blood. Weakened by severe diseases. Inflamed mucous membranes. Asthma from cold air and from talking too much. Brittle bones. Many body tissues are inflamed and damaged. **Positive aspect**: Adventurous carefree lover of life.
Pulsatilla	Anemone – the wind flower	Mild gentle yielding female type. Weeps easily. Likes sympathy. Timid and indecisive. Easily discouraged. Changeable and contradictory emotions. Very emotional. Can be superficial, trivial and peevish or charming and lights up the room. Craves fresh open air – even on a cold day. Catarrh. Mucous membrane discharges which are profuse, thick and greenish. Glue ear. **Positive aspect**: The archetypal soft feminine woman – the full expression of yin and the feminine principle.

Remedy	Origin of Remedy	Keynotes
Sepia	Cuttlefish ink	Irritable, cranky and easily offended. Pushes people away yet dreads to be alone. Averse to loved ones. Chilly with hot flushes. Cold stagnant body fluids. Bearing down or dragging sensations in the body. Feels as if a ball is lodged in the body. Feels as if the womb is so heavy it will drop out. Better for dancing. **Positive aspect**: The archetypal independent woman and earth mother – courtesan, Wise Woman, witch and crone.
Causticum	Caustic soda	Very sad and feels hopeless. Cries easily. Does not want to go to bed alone. Aggravated by thinking about his complaints. Feels as if there is an empty space between the forehead and the brain. Tearing arthritic pains. Restless at night with severe joint pains. Feels faint and as if sinking. May progress to paralysis of parts of the body. **Positive aspect**: A practical idealist.

Afterword

On August 20, 1994, on a ranch in Janesville, USA, a single pure white Buffalo calf was born into the world. They named her 'Miracle', for this animal was no ordinary Buffalo calf. Being that she was born white marked her as a creature of Lakota prophecy, with her birth heralding the return to a time of peace and beauty; a time of purification and renewal for the children of Mother Earth.

The Buffalo calf was not an albino, but an animal exhibiting *leucism*; a form of albinism where the individual lacks melanin skin pigmentation, but has blue eyes instead of the familiar pink. Such a trait is relatively atypical among wild animals (although common and, in some cases, encouraged in domestic breeds). It presents a very real disadvantage to creatures in their natural habitat, limiting camouflage potential, ability to successfully stalk prey and to absorb both heat and required levels of UV rays. Thus, animals exhibiting either albinism (from Latin *albus*, meaning 'white') or leucism rarely survive to adulthood.

The Lakota, Dakota and Nakota clans are collectively referred to as the Sioux. The Sioux nation is one of warriors; a noble and proud people. The White Buffalo Calf Woman sits at the heart of the Sioux nation and offers beauty and conviction to their legends. In keeping with belief, The White Buffalo Calf Woman presented the sacred Buffalo Calf Pipe to the Sioux people. She offered them the pipe as a form of reconnection to Spirit.

Many believe that the white Buffalo calf named *Miracle* and every other white Buffalo calf born since (approximately 16 in total), collectively herald the re-uniting of humanity and the reawakening of oneness: the state of mind, body and spirit that rejects solitude, fear and abandonment and re-establishes sacred connection to Spirit, the Earth Mother and the people. The white Buffalo symbolises hope and renewal, harmony among all people and a joining of all races of man so that we may walk together and unify.

Apart from the prophesised white Buffalos (which are among the most sacred animals a person could ever encounter), other rare and beautiful white animals have begun to appear the world over: Lions, Servals, Giraffes, Zebras and Gorillas; Robins, Foxes, Sparrows, Bats and Hedgehogs; Tigers, Elephants, Raccoon Dogs, Pythons, Cobras, Monkeys, Leopards and Peacocks; Kangaroos, Wallabies, Kookaburras, Koalas, Possums, Emus, Echidna and Kiwi; Ravens, Crows, Deer, Black Bear, Skunks, Moose, Squirrels, Pronghorns, Coyotes, Horned Owls, Hummingbirds, Rheas, Pumas, Rattlesnakes, Alligators and Lynx; Whales, Penguins, Fur Seals, Dolphins and Sea Turtles, with many appearing in the last four years, or directly before, during or after world events that call for peace and global unity.

According to Chief Arvol Looking Horse, traditional leader of the Lakota clan of the Sioux nation and 19th generation Keeper of the White Buffalo Calf Bundle, the appearance of these white animals heralds a time of great urgency for the Earth and humanity as a whole. It is said that the appearance of such unusually coloured animals is a sign; an omen calling for us to unite as a people and walk as one; to see past the colour of our neighbour's skin or the ancestry of their people and to come together and embrace them as brothers, sisters and all-related children of the Earth Mother.

Despite the fact that animals exhibiting albinism or leucism are far more vulnerable than their naturally coloured kin, we are seeing an increase in these creatures developing into healthy adults with many going unnoticed by man until fully mature and quite certain of unaided survival in the wild. It is said that the lesson behind the emergence of these rare white animals is one that must be acknowledged by every man, woman and child if we are to bring healing to the Earth Mother and humanity. We are being reminded to be ever mindful of our actions and reactions, to be more accepting of others, their beliefs, orientations and customs and to be more respectful of the animals and the Earth Mother herself.

Chief Arvol Looking Horse believes that we are now deep in a time of prophecy, when animals are choosing to be born as head-turning anomalies; white ambassadors of their species with messages that double as both blessings and warnings. He endorses the idea that the animals are being born white to attract our attention, as embodiments of a universal need for humanity to unite in the name of peace so that our children and their children will be ensured a future on Mother Earth. He says 'all nations, all faiths' must unite 'in one prayer' no matter how we believe in the Creator Spirit, if we are to acknowledge and honour the birth of these sacred animals and heed their message.

Albino animals have been revered in most cultures for centuries; venerated as omens of good fortune, fertility, plentiful rain and bountiful harvest. Some even describe them as being imbued with supernatural or magical powers, usually charged with extraordinary strength, speed, shape and size. In medieval Europe, for example, it was believed that white Mice personified the souls of departed children, while the appearance of a white Elephant was said to have proclaimed the birth of Gautama Buddha. As a result, the white Elephant has become a sacred symbol of appreciation in Hindu tradition. The white Elephant (and the Hindu elephant god, Ganesha) are both said to offer deliverance from the obstacles created by the mundane influences of life, aspects such as embarrassment and limiting circumstance. In Thailand, the people believe that white Elephants may very well contain the souls of people who have crossed over to the spirit world.

White animals appear regularly in Welsh and Celtic mythology, too, as creatures of the Otherworld, often sporting red ears, pink eyes and rosy snouts. In these stories, brave warriors and noblemen more often than not pursued them when they ventured into the ordinary world.

Again, according to Chief Arvol Looking Horse, the appearance of the white Buffalo calf and the plethora of other white animals come as both a good omen and a forewarning of powerful but necessary change. The animals have been trying to warn humanity for ages of the inevitable changes the

Earth Mother has in store for us. We have witnessed countless mudslides, earthquakes, floods, droughts and strong winds over the centuries, but in recent years there have been an increased number of occurrences, with each event proving more devastating than the one prior. The people who survived the Asian tsunami on Boxing Day, 2004, for example, say the wave seemingly came out of nowhere. Thousands of people died that day ... but not one single wild animal was lost. Why?

Many animals rely on atmospheric pressure to navigate their path and use infrasound (the ability to hear sounds and make noises of very low frequency that are inaudible to the human ear) in order to communicate with members of their herd or flock, and because of this, they received advance warning of the approaching wave. They, unlike us, have never lost their ability to communicate directly with the Earth Mother, nor have they forgotten their inherent relationship with the forces of nature or to trust what they feel intuitively and 'know' rather than what they physically see. The ancient cultures had it, but we, as 'modern civilised beings', have long forgotten ours.

I believe the arrival of the white animals (not to mention the synchronistic 'emergence' of Indigo Children), may be seen as a warning, urging us to take the time to better understand and accept each other's differences and to be less fearful of not being the most powerful force or the biggest and the best. They are trying to tell us that if we don't stop calling in our worst fears by worrying about the 'what ifs' or believing all the 'she said, he said' half truths infiltrating our written and electronic media, relationships and minds; if we don't stop criticising and punishing our brothers and sisters because of petty differences generally created and maintained by fear and a desire for control and if we don't stop blaming or judging our neighbours by their nationality, the colour of their skin, their beliefs, behaviour and customs instead of loving them for their differences and treating them as friends and equals; if we don't embrace our children as being fine as they are instead of trying to silence them and make them comply to a system that doesn't support them (or us), then we will soon be living in a time of great darkness. I believe the white animals are offering themselves as beacons of hope, spiritual yet tangible guides driven by one goal — to inspire us to follow and trust only in the 'light' that is the heart of the Creator Spirit and life in chorus. A light guaranteed to lead us away from the confusion caused by true darkness into greater awareness, clarity and unified abundance as a people.

They are inviting us to partake in the sacred 'hunt' – a hunt for what this light might mean for each of us on a personal level; a thrilling adventure emblematic of the search for the sacred self or a quest for a deeper understanding of our very soul. In the stories of old, the soul was more often than not depicted as an elusive and magical white beast, while the hunt itself symbolically introduced us to our Sacred Self by leading us deep into a 'dark, ominous forest'.

The white animals, I believe, are here to fulfil an ancient prophecy: to invite us to follow them into that forest now — into an unfamiliar place of deep healing and personal acceptance so that we might finally emerge on the other side as rebirthed, reformed individuals; whole and healthy beings in an interrelated world. They are reminding us to reclaim our beauty, our soul-essence and our personal power; to find a place of trust and acceptance within ourselves, to know our Sacred Self and to systematically forever banish the world of 'evil' in its limitless guises. They want us to strip away our personal facades and drop our excuses, to unite as one, no matter what colour we are, from what country we hail or what deity we worship, and to celebrate each other as equals and as members of the same global family. They want us to realise that only as a united people can we hope to bring about a change potent enough to heal our planet, and that simply being someone with an indigo aura makes little difference to the greater scheme of things if no one is there to support you.

It's a valid thought worth considering further … don't you think?

Scott Alexander King

"You are home ..."These are the words I heard in my heart as I sat cross-legged on an old futon mattress weaving the web of my very first dreamcatcher in a workshop run by an experienced and well-learned Medicine Woman. The voice, clear and precise, was coupled with a dynamic bolt of energy: a flash of consciousness that illuminated my otherwise dark spirit and travelled through my stomach and heart. Magick touched my very being. I knew something wonderful had just happened, but I was more aware that something lay in promise for me. My journey had begun. I had found the path at last, even though until that moment, I had been unaware of my search.

Scott Alexander King is an animal spirit intuitive, psychic, teacher and practitioner of Earth Medicine, and holds a diploma in primary school education. After graduating from Victoria College, Toorak Campus on May 5, 1990, Scott realised his powerful ability to help children discover and harness their personal power and genuine nature. His commitment has led many children to overcome hardship and adversity, not only on an academic level but also on a physical, emotional and spiritual level. Today he is better known for his work with (among others) Warrior Children. He believes the empowerment of these young people is integral to healing our fractured community and his work now merges his two greatest passions: Earth Medicine and the enhancement of our children.

Scott's unique ability to communicate with the animal spirit realm and the energies of the Earth began when he was just eight years old. As a child, Scott realised he could see animal spirits (not 'dead' pets, but the inherent power of animals that walk with us: the power that was once incorporated into tribal lore and labelled as 'totem' energy). Although Australian by birth, Scott looks to the animals from a global perspective: his knowledge is not limited to the teachings of Australia's Indigenous culture or Australian geography. He seems to have an inherent understanding of all animals – no matter which continent they inhabit. As a child, Scott relied heavily on his 'feelings' when it came to meeting new people. This energy warned him of deceit, rewarded him with promise and allowed him to successfully navigate his way through a very confusing childhood. As he grew this 'energy' took form until he began to recognise it as being 'animal-like' in vibration – energy that he felt a natural bond with, energy that has never let him down.

With years of study and practice, Scott has refined his abilities and is today Australia's foremost Animal Spirit Intuitive, Psychic and Earth Medicine teacher. He currently lectures and offers experiential workshops Australia wide. His work not only broadens awareness of humanity's ancient relationship with the Earth and the animals, it also offers a voice to the voiceless – namely our children and the endangered and threatened animals of the world. Scott's work includes: the wisdom of the animals, Earth Medicine, reading signs, omens and portents, psychic protection, divination, moon lore, natural magick, mediumship, meditation, genetic memory, soul purpose, personal power, the web of life and other spiritual topics. Those who participate in Scott's workshops and seminars come from all walks of life. Although most are everyday members of the general public, many are professionally trained in the areas of veterinary science, zoology, natural therapy (naturopathy, homeopathy, traditional herbal medicine etc), conventional medicine, psychology, child and adult education, social work and law.

Visit Scott at: www.animaldreaming.com

Dr. Ralph Ballard

M.B.B.S., F.A.M.A.C., Dip. Clin. Hypnosis., Dip Hom.

Dr. Ralph Ballard lives near Warburton, Victoria with his wife Sushie and their two Cats. They share a lovely property near the head of the Yarra River with all sorts of wildlife – Kookaburras, Parrots, Possums, the occasional Eagle and the Wombat who lives in the gully. There they grow a lot of their own food and live a more relaxed lifestyle away from the busyness of city life. Ralph has been on the spiritual journey for much of his life — from self-examination, inner exploration and meditation through to yoga and Qigong to various forms of healing. He very much honours Mother Earth and fosters conscious, ethical living with everyone he meets.

Ralph is a qualified medical doctor. He obtained his medical degree from Melbourne University in 1982 and then went on to hospital work for four years. Subsequently he spent a further four years in general practice before moving into holistic integrative medical practice. Over the years he has done a lot of work with children diagnosed with ADD / ADHD and autism. He has also worked with many adults suffering from a range of chronic degenerative or auto-immune conditions such as rheumatoid arthritis, Chronic Fatigue Syndrome, HIV / AIDS, and cancer. In addition, Ralph has trained in a range of natural therapies, counselling, aspects of psychotherapy, meditation and hypnotherapy. He has also studied nutritional medicine, acupuncture, homeopathy, flower essences, Ayurvedic medicine, colour therapy, Reiki and intuitive healing.

Ralph has done a lot of teaching, lecturing to medical students and doctors at university level, and to naturopaths. These days Ralph has largely left these intensive activities, and is now primarily engaged in writing and teaching about healthcare from a 'mind-body-spirit' perspective. He is particularly interested in exploring how conventional scientific medicine and the natural therapies meet. For Ralph, the influences of mind, spirit and consciousness in harmony with Mother Nature are paramount in the life journey.

FOOD

King Island Beef Producers Group Inc: NATURAL BEEF
The King Island brand has the best brand image of all red meat products in Australia, with a reputation for excellence throughout the world. Visit: www.kingislandbeef.com.au

La Ionica Chicken: ALL NATURAL CHICKEN
La Ionica Chickens are free roaming chickens that are processed chemically free without hormonal additives so we can enjoy their natural colour, flavour and texture. Visit: www.laionica.com.au

Nutritional Recommendations (based on blood type) the Blood Type Diet:
www.dadamo.com

Organics4U: GOOD HEALTH BEGINS @ HOME
Wouldn't you prefer that everything you put in and on your body was healthy, was produced and grown in a natural, environmentally friendly way, whilst conserving natural resources? Organic products are all this and more. They contain no toxic chemical pesticides or fertilizers, Genetically Modified Organisms, artificial ingredients or preservatives. Visit Organics4U at: www.organics4u.com.au

Otway Pork™ – Bred Free-range: RSPCA ACCREDITED
Otway Pork™ Pigs are born and bred outdoors where they are free to play, forage and do what all Pigs like to do best: socialise, sleep in straw, eat a healthy diet and drink fresh clean water freely. They are reared in large straw-based shelters where they are free to move about, play and exercise and are fed a natural grain-based diet free of added growth hormones. Most importantly, Otway Pork™ Pigs are grown to exacting standards of leanness and health before meeting the stringent quality standards. Visit the farm at www.otwaypork.com.au

Permaculture: GARDENING IN HARMONY WITH THE EARTH
Permaculture describes the mindful planning of one's garden or land so that it works in harmony with the cycles and interactions demonstrated by nature. In doing so, we can produce a cornucopia of foodstuffs, yarn, fabric and renewable

energy in an interconnected way. To find out more, visit:

www.permacultureinternational.org

www.permaculture.org.au

NB: When establishing your permaculture garden, contact your local council and ask them to send you a list of the weeds and noxious plants that should be removed or avoided before you prepare your land for planting.

ALTERNATIVE SCHOOLING - THE OPTIONS

Sathya Sai Schools:

www.sathyasaischoolaust.org

The Sathya Sai philosophy hinges on five prime values — Love, Truth, Peace, Right Conduct and Non-Violence, which are taught through sub-values such as caring, sharing, honesty, helpfulness, justice, fairness, self esteem, responsibility, reliability and democracy.

Montessori Schools:

www.montessori.edu.au

The Montessori philosophy is based on the belief that children hold within them something so special that it could be the key to changing the world. It espouses that all children are inherently good and that, if allowed to develop freely, feel connected to everything and are naturally caring toward each other and the world around them. It endorses the belief that children have precise inner 'guides' and that it is the responsibility of adults to help them be all that they are meant to be. It is the spiritual nature of children that has been forgotten and denied, according to Montessori philosophy and so when celebrated, children hold within them the potential to show adults how to return to a more meaningful, holistic way of living.

Steiner (Waldorf) Schools:

www.steiner-australia.org

The aim of Waldorf schooling is to educate the whole child, 'head, heart and hands'. The curriculum is broad and balances academics subjects with artistic and practical activities. The Waldorf curriculum is designed to be responsive to the various phases of a child's development. For example, pre-class one, children are presented with fairy stories matching their dreamy state of consciousness, class four study the Vikings and Norse mythology which suit their war-like feelings, class five learn of the Greeks at the time their intellect is awakening and their sense of fair play is becoming obvious, and so on.

Victorian College of the Arts Secondary School:

www.vcass.vic.edu.au

The aim of the school is to identify and assist children with exceptional potential (regardless of personal circumstance) by offering world-class specialist training and a balanced education so that they may someday realise a self-sustaining career in music and dance. Regarding Higher Education, visit the Victorian College of the Arts website: www.vca.unimelb.edu.au

Home Schooling

www.homeschooling.com.au

When you educate your children at home you can choose who they mix with. School is the only place that people are forced to mix with other people they have nothing in common with and the only place they are put together with people all the same age as themselves. The truth is that we learn best when we are allowed to interact with older people and get the opportunity to teach those younger than ourselves – which, when you think about it, perfectly describes the family unit.

Other Independent and Community Schools:

www.ncisa.edu.au

Independent schools are non-government schools. They are a diverse group of schools serving a range of different communities. Many independent schools provide a religious or values based education. Others promote a particular education philosophy or interpretation of mainstream education. Independent schools include small and large day schools, boarding schools, co-educational and single-sex schools.

MEDICAL HEALTHCARE

Chelation therapy and treatment for leaky gut syndrome / impaired liver conjugation and for integrative medical help

Autism Research Institute: https://www.autism.com

Centre for the Study of Autism (CSI): www.autism.org

Doctors - Holistic integrative medical practitioners:
www.aima.net.au

Doctors - Nutritional and allergy doctors:
www.acnem.org
Search under 'referrals' by state

Laser and Needle Medical Acupuncture:
Australian Medical Acupuncture College
www.acupunctureaustralia.org

Nutritional therapy:
www.acnem.org

ADD, ADHD, AND AUTISM RESOURCES

ADD / ADHD:
www.add.org
www.newideas.net
www.chadd.org
www.adhdfraud.org

Autism Behavioural Intervention, Queensland (ABIQ):
www.abiq.org

Autism Research Institute (ARI):
www.autism.com
www.autism.org

Autism support groups and counselling and behavioural programs:
www.abia.net.au
www.autismvictoria.org.au
www.fightautismnow.com
www.autismuk.com
www.acd.org.au

Doman-Delacato Motor Repatterning:
www.delacato.net

Homeopathic / Natural alternatives to Ritalin, etc:
ATTEND: www.vaxa.com
FOCUS: www.nativeremedies.com

NATURAL THERAPIES

Acupuncture:
www.acupuncture.com
www.acupuncture.org.au

Aromatherapy:
www.ifa.org.au

Art Therapy:
www.anata.org.au
Cornelia Elbrecht's Apollo Bay Centre:
www.claerwen.com.au/host/Claerwen.nsf/art_therapy

Aura Soma Colour Therapy:
www.aura-soma.com.au
www.aurasoma.com
www.aura-soma.net
www.asiact.org

Bioenergetic Balancing Technique™:
Melissa Hocking
www.melissahocking.com

Buteyko Breathing:
A self generating way of optimising the body's oxygenation
www.buteyko.com.au

Chakra health and vitality with Anita Ryan:
www.goddess.com.au

Colour Therapy with Judith Garrecht
Women's medicine, colour therapy and hot stone therapy
www.womenofchange.com.au

Counselling:
www.psychotherapy.com.au
Search under the relevant locality and practitioner type

Cranial osteopathy:
www.osteopathy4u.com
www.cranial.org.uk
www.osteopathiccenter.org
www.cranialacademy.com

Crystal Essences:
The Liquid Crystals – 'Earth Medicine'
www.theliquidcrystals.com

Crystal Therapy:
With Maria Elita: creator of the world's only Crystal Energy Bed
www.mariaelita.com

Dance Therapy with Susan:
Sensory Integration for Children with ADD, ADHD or Autism
snuzan@aapt.net.au

Drama Therapy:
Bright Lights is a performance school that was started in the Byron Bay area, New South Wales by Brian Dale and Lee Purdie. We have seen the results of providing opportunities and working with creative and talented performers. We have shared the group dynamic, the individual personalities and the trials and tribulations of performance. We have been rewarded with personal growth. We have shared the joy of our performers maturing through their formative years, giving so much enjoyment to children and adults alike. Imagine the importance of participating in and achieving the group goals of a professional performance. What a pleasure it is to see one of our performers, totally focused and controlled, delivering a comedy routine that has other members of our drama group rolling around on the floor in fits of laughter with tears of joy streaming down their faces. Contact Bright Lights Performance School by email: robynfdale@optusnet.com.au or by phone: (+612) 6684 1932

Educational Kinesiology:
www.aka-oz.org

Flower Essences:
www.naturaltherapypages.com.au/therapy/Flower_Remedies

Holistic Beauty Therapy and Massage:
S.O.S. (Save Our Skin)
Email for a brochure
tinkabell3@bigpond.com
(+61) 0423 167613

Holistic Kinesiology:
May Clarke – a unique holistic Kinesiology practitioner who is warm and caring in nature. Her passion is to assist individual people to connect with their true self by sharing her skills and wisdom in holistic health and spiritual healing. Her mission is to touch the lives of many individuals with the aim of making a real difference to people's wellbeing and enabling them to gain a deeper sense of fulfillment and inner peace. For more information regarding May's clinic (located at 196 Buckley St, Essendon), or her retreat in the suburbs (located at 119 Union Rd, Ascot Vale), email her at may.hk@bigpond.net.au, or call her on 0409 231 364

Homeopathy:
www.homeopathyoz.org

Music Therapy:
www.austmta.org.au

Natural Health:
A list of time-honoured alternative remedies:
www.swedishbitters.com
www.spirulina.com.au
www.stevia.com

NLP – Neuro-Linguistic Programming:
www.nlpcoaching.com
www.tadjames.com
www.australiannlpcentre.com.au
www.impeccable.com

Reconnective Healing:
Dr. Eric Pearl
www.thereconnection.com

Reiki:
The International House of Reiki (in my opinion, one of the best Reiki schools in existence)
Bronwen and Frans Stiene
www.Reiki.net.au

Spirale Colour Therapy with Pascale Osanz:
www.spirale.com.au

Natural Therapies:
Australia's #1 Natural Therapies Website
Including yoga, Reiki, Qigong, Tai Chi, NLP, Bowen, colonic irrigation, etc.
www.naturaltherapypages.com.au

Naturopathy:
www.atms.com.au
www.anta.com.au

Qigong with Grand Master Jack Lim:
www.relaxationmusic.com.au

Sensory Integration Therapy:
www.sensoryint.com

Sound therapy:
Tomatis Method
www.tomatis.com.au

Transpersonal Counselling:
www.phoenixinstitute.com.au

Yoga
Iyengar Yoga:
Iyengar yoga is a scientific, disciplined and deeply researched system developed over 70 years by Yogacharya BKS Iyengar. It emphasises the integration of body, mind and spirit. www.iyengaryoga.asn.au

Hatha Yoga:
www.yogateachers.asn.au
www.gita.com.au

YOUTH ACTIVITIES

Flames of Change: FIREWALK TO FREEDOM

By walking over hot coals, firewalking offers a rare opportunity to create for yourself a new reality free from limitation. Contact Peter Roden, 'Sundoor Firewalk' Instructor and Flames of Change founder, to find out more. Visit him at www.flamesofchange.com

Gatherings and Festivals: ACCEPTANCE FOR THE SELF AND OTHERS

- ConFest (Conference/Festival) is a gathering of people wishing to share talents, skills, ideas, concerns and philosophies in a caring, fun-loving and tolerant atmosphere. The presentation of workshops, demonstrations, entertainments and the maintenance of site facilities are all performed by volunteers. Monetary payment is neither accepted nor made. Visit: www.dte.org.au
- Spiritual Unity of the Tribes is an annual event that sees Elders and Grandmothers from all over the world unite to share their sacred wisdom. Visit: http://users. netconnect.com.au/~sueandon/sut/current.html
- The Rainbow Serpent Festival is a summer outdoor event offering music, dance, arts, camping and more. Visit: www.vapourspace.com.au/rainbow

Department of Defence: RESERVES and CADETS

Visit: www.defence.gov.au/reserves

- Air Force Reserve: There is a diverse range of jobs available in the Air Force Reserve ranging from Administration Officer to Aerospace Engineering Officer or Plumber to Electrician.
- Navy Reserve: A career in the Navy Reserve is exciting and challenging with opportunities to serve at sea in any of the Navy's high-tech frigates, submarines, amphibious support ships, patrol boats, support craft, mine warfare and hydrographic vessels. Ashore, Reserves serve in each State and Territory, wherever there is a naval presence. However, being in the NR means you don't have to live near a Navy base to serve. Regardless of where you live you can still be in the NR as the ability exists to transport you to the Navy base or ship where your

training or job is located.

- Army Reserve: The Army Reserve is amongst the most technically advanced organisations in the country and widely recognised as providing excellent skills, training and qualifications.
- Cadets: As a Cadet, young Australians are able to take part in adventurous, fulfilling and educational activities in a military setting. Visit: www.cadetnet. gov.au

Horses:

- *The Tao of Equus: a woman's journey of healing and transformation through the way of the horse* by Linda Kohanov
- Meredith Torpey. Meredith runs 'Running Horse Equestrian Services': an organisation dedicated to personal and community empowerment through unique educational programs with Horses. Email Meredith at spikesfarm@ hotmail.com
- When considering purchasing a horse, contact the Code of Practice for the Welfare of Horses in order to find out how to care properly for your newest member of the family. Visit: www.dpi.gov.au/animalwelfare
- Or the Victorian Horse Council Inc: PO Box 680, Hurstbridge, Victoria, Australia, 3099. For more information, phone: (03) 9714 8689

Scouts and Guides:
SCOUTING

- The aim of Scouting is to encourage the physical, intellectual, social, emotional and spiritual development of young people so that they take a constructive place in society as responsible citizens, and as a member of their local, national and international communities Visit: www.scouts.com.au or www.scouts.com

GUIDES

- Helping girls and young women grow into confident, self-respecting, responsible community members. Visit: www.guidesaus.org.au, www.girlguiding.org.uk or www.girlguides.ca

Sports sites

www.footballaustralia.com.au

www.soccer.com.au

www.basketball.net.au

www.netball.asn.au

www.hockey.org.au

www.athletics.org.au

www.gymnastics.org.au

Surf Life Saving Australia: NIPPERS
The Surf Education Program is a lifesaving education program designed for 7 to13 year olds. This education program provides young members of Surf Life Saving with developmental lessons that provide an introduction into the surf awareness and surf safety aspects of the Surf Rescue Certificate (SRC). The SRC is the introductory award for a patrolling surf lifesaver (13 to15).
Visit: www.slsa.asn.au

Swimming with the Dolphins: TANGALOOMA
The only Island Resort in the world where ALL Resort Guests booked on a Dolphin Accommodation Package can hand-feed a pod of wild Dolphins and benefit from their healing energy. Check out the Dolphins at: www.tangalooma.com

The Gould League of Australia:
For all your required pond-dipping, bug-catching and bird-watching 'how-to' information, visit: www.gould.edu.au

The Gould League of Bird Lovers:
http://www.amonline.net.au/exhibitions/gould/naturalist/gould_league.htm

Toastmasters:
Making effective communication an Australian reality
www.toastmasters.org.au

Tracking: WILDERNESS SURVIVAL
Tom Brown Jr.'s Tracking School (US): Founded in 1978 by Tom Brown Jr., America's most renowned wilderness survival expert, the Tracker School has been educating people on the ancient skills of tracking, wilderness awareness, and survival for over 25 years. Visit Tom Brown Jr. here: www.trackerschool.com

---

COMMUNITY SUPPORT SERVICES

Support and Recovery: SUPPORTING YOUTH AT RISK
- **Appin Hall** (Tasmania, Australia) is dedicated to the future generations who will intuitively understand our planetary need for peace and harmony if the human race is to survive as a species. "We must protect our children and their

future."To learn more about Appin Hall (the work of Ronnie and Maggie Burns), visit: www.appinhall.com

- **Challenge** is an Australian Cancer Support Network and Victoria's major provider of support services for children and families living with cancer and other life-threatening blood disorders. Challenge members are aged from birth to 18 years and begin receiving support at the time of diagnosis, which continues throughout treatment and beyond. Visit: www.challenge.org.au
- **Les Twentyman** has been working with young people in Melbourne, Australia for 25 years. He was awarded the Order of Australia Medal in 1994, and his work has been recognised through a number of other awards. His early life shaped his time on the streets advocating for others. He has a strong passion for football and for getting the education system to better protect young people. http://www.australianoftheyear.gov.au/bio.asp?pID=94
- **New River Cove** blends traditional 12-step based treatment with progressive and holistic program components. A systemic approach is used to assess and define the clinical, physical, and nutritional goals for each resident. Individual treatment plans are developed to help each resident achieve mental, emotional, and physical harmony. Visit: www.newrivercove.com
- **Outward Bound** run personal development courses for anyone aged 12 years and up. Using the outdoors as a classroom for teaching people about themselves and their potential, an Outward Bound course is an experience for a lifetime. Visit: www.outwardbound.com.au
- **REACH** gives young people the confidence to take extraordinary journeys. Reach encourages young people to be inspired by their dreams and to get out there and have a go. Reach encourages young people to follow their heart and keep moving forward even when they doubt themselves. They run programs, camps, workshops and major events that ignite a passion for life. Visit: www.reach.org.au
- **Sober Recovery** lists hundreds of addiction treatment and alcoholism treatment resources in the US, Canada, and overseas. Visit: www.soberrecovery.com
- **The Koori Youth Healing Service** (as part of Ngwala Willumbong Co-operative Ltd) provides services aimed at creating environments that sustain positive change for Aboriginal people whose lives have been affected by alcohol and drugs. Visit: www.ngwala.org
- **The Ted Noffs Foundation** today continues the legacy of Ted Noffs by providing essential services for young people and their families who are experiencing drug and alcohol problems and related trauma. Its range of programs for young people is based on leading research, continually evaluated and is government endorsed. Visit: www.noffs.org.au

- A list of other services targeted toward supporting our youth:
http://www.community.gov.au/Internet/MFMC/community.nsf/pages/sectio
  n?opendocumentandSection=Outreach

Challenge: SUPPORTING KIDS WITH CANCER
Challenge is a cancer support network and Victoria's major provider of support services for children and families living with cancer and other life-threatening blood disorders. Challenge members are aged from birth to 18 years and begin receiving support at the time of diagnosis, which continues throughout treatment and beyond. Visit: www.challenge.org.au

INDIGO CHILDREN

Lee Carroll and Jan Tober: www.indigochild.com
Doreen Virtue: www.angeltherapy.com
James Twyman: www.emissaryoflight.com
Children of the New Earth Online Magazine:
  www.childrenofthenewearth.com

GENERAL INTEREST

Animal Communicators: HUMAN / ANIMAL COMMUNICATION
Visit the sites of Billie, Dawn and Tera (three of the world's leading Animal Communicators) to learn what animal communication is, why it is essential we all strive to understand it and how we may learn to do it ourselves. If you have, or are yourself a Nature Child, visiting these sites is a must:
Billie Dean - www.billiedean.com (Australia)
Dawn Baumann Brunke - www.animalvoices.net (Alaska)
Tera Thomas - www.hummingbirdfarm.org (US)

Archetypes:
Archetypes are personifications of universal energy patterns. Brian Dale is a

primary school teacher, librarian, storyteller and drama teacher. He is also an archetype consultant, trained with the Caroline Myss Institute of Australia. Email him at: robynfdale@optusnet.com.au or by phone: (+612) 6684 1932

Belly Dance:
www.zaarbellydance.com

Blessed Earth: ORGANIC COTTON
Chemical free, low allergenic, organic cotton underwear, sleepwear, sheets and linen
www.blessedearth.com.au

'Chakra Dance' with Natalie Southgate and Douglas Channing:
www.chakradance.com

Chief Arvol Looking Horse: World Peace and Prayer Day and the Wolakota Foundation
www.wolakota.org

Holistic Marriage Celebrant
'Sacred Ceremonies'
www.beyondblueprint.com

Shamanism/Animism: The Worlds Oldest Healing Tradition
www.shamanism.org
www.sacredhoop.org
www.shamansdrum.org

Tao Te Ching: THE HUMAN CONDITION
Written in China centuries before the birth of Christ, the Tao Te Ching offers incredible insight into the human condition. Originally the work of Lao Tsu, this text has been translated more frequently than any other work (except the Bible).
http://www.nokama.com/tao/

The Four Humours:
www.oneishy.com

Wicca / Witchcraft: EMBRACING THE GODDESS
www.paganawareness.net.au
www.esotericbookshop.com.au

www.lucycavendish.com
www.spellcraft.com.au
www.pangaia.com
www.witchvox.com
www.whitemagic.com.au
www.goddess.com.au

FURTHER READING

Antara Amaa-Ra, Solara, *Star-borne: A Remembrance for the Awakened Ones*; Star-Borne Unlimited: Montana, USA, 1989

Aron, Elaine, *The Highly Sensitive Person: How To Thrive When The World Overwhelms You*; Element; Harper Collins: London, 1999

Bailey MD, Philip M, *Carcinosinum: a clinical materia medica*; P.M. Bailey, Australia, 1998

Bailey MD, Philip M, *Homeopathic Psychology – Personality Profiles of the Major Constitutional Remedies*; North Atlantic Books: USA, 1995

Bailey MD, Philip M, *'The Mentals': personality profiles of the homeopathic constitutional types*; P.M. Bailey, Australia, 1998

Baker MD, Sidney, Pangborn PhD, Jon, *Autism: Effective Biomedical Treatments (Have We Done Everything We Can For This Child? Individuality in an Epidemic)*; Autism Research Institute: USA, 2005

Bartlett, J.V, *Handy Farm and Home Devices*; Cornstalk Publishing: Australia, 1980

Baughman Jr., MD, Fred A, *ADHD: TOTAL, 100% FRAUD;* 1992 http://psychrights.org/Research/Digest/ADHD/DHD100percentfraud.htm

Baughman Jr., MD, Fred A, *The ADHD Fraud: How Psychiatry Makes 'Patients' of Normal Children*; Trafford Publishing: USA

Beyerl, Paul, *The Master Book of Herbalism*; Phoenix Publishing: Washington, 1996

Bushby, Tony, *The Bible Fraud*; Joshua Books: Australia, 2001

Callinan, Paul, *Australian Family Homeopathy*; Lifetime Distributors, Australia, 1995

Childress, David Hatcher, *Lost Cities of Ancient Lemuria and the Pacific*; Adventures Unlimited Press: Illinois, 1988

Chopra, Deepak, MD, *Perfect Health: the complete Mind/Body guide*; Harmony, NY, 1990

Cleary, Thomas, (translated by) *Buddhist Yoga*; Shambhala: Boston and London, 1995

Cunningham, Scott, *Encyclopedia of Magical Herbs*; Llewellyn: St. Paul, 1997

Eisner, Elliot, W, *Educating Artistic Vision*; Macmillan Publishing: NY, 1972

Farrar, Janet and Stewart, *Eight Sabbats for Witches*; Robert Hale: London, 1981

Flaws, Bob, *Keeping Your Child Healthy with Chinese Medicine: A Parent's Guide to the Care and Prevention of Common Childhood Diseases*; Blue Poppy Press: USA, 1999

Grandin, Temple, *Animals in Translation: Using the Mysteries of Autism to Decode Animal Behaviour*; Scribner - an imprint of Simon and Schuster: UK, 2004

Howarth, Tony, *Twentieth Century History*; Longman Group: UK, 1979

King, Scott Alexander, *Animal Dreaming*; Circle of Stones: Australia, 2003

King, Scott Alexander, *Animal Messenger*; New Holland Publishers: Australia, 2006

Kohanov, Linda. 'The Tao of Equus: *a woman's journey of healing and transformation through the way of the horse*'

Kusack, James, *A Treasury of Natural First Aid Remedies from A-Z*; Parker Publishing Company: NY, 1995

Littauer, Florence, *Personality Plus*; Fleming H. Revell: Michigan, 2005

Lowenfeld, Viktor and Brittain, W. Lambert, *Creative and Mental Growth* (sixth ed.); Macmillan Publishers: NY, 1975

Mares, Theun, *The Quest for Maleness*; Lionheart Publishing: Sth. Africa, 1999

Mares, Theun, *Unveil the Mysteries of the Feminine*; Lionheart Publishing: Sth. Africa, 1999

McGraw, Dr. Phil, *Family First: Your Step-by-Step Plan for Creating a Phenomenal Family*; Free Press: US, 2004

Melody, *Love is in the Earth: a kaleidoscope of crystals*; Earth-Love Publishing: US, 1991

Mollison, Bill, *Introduction to Permaculture*; Tagari Publications: Australia, 1991

Morrison, Judith, *The Book Of Ayurveda – A Guide To Personal Wellbeing*; Gaia Books: London, 1995

Null, Gary, *The Drugging of our Children*; a Gary Null Production (DVD) www.garynull.com: 2005

Oliver, Susan, *Hunting for Power*; Fire Dragon: Australia, 2005

Pitchford, Paul, *Healing with Whole Foods: Asian Traditions and Modern Nutrition*; North Atlantic Books: USA, 2002

Requena, Yves, *Character and Health*; Paradigm Publications: Massachusetts, 1989

Richards, P.D and English, F.W, *Out of the Dark: a history of Medieval Europe*; Thomas Nelson Australia: Australia, 1985

Ryan, Anita, The Goddess Guide to Chakra Vitality; www.goddess.com.au Australia, 2006

Seymour, John, *The Complete Book of Self-Sufficiency*; Corgi Books: Great Britain, 1981

Speight, Phyllis, *A Study Course In Homeopathy*; C.W. Daniel: USA, 2004

Svoboda, Robert, *Prakruti —Your Ayurvedic Constitution*; Geocom: USA, 1998

Virtue, Doreen, *The Crystal Children*; Hay House Australia: Australia, 2003

Vithoulkas, George, *Homeopathy — Medicine of the New Man*; Fireside: USA, 1985

Williamson, Larry, *A short history of Lemuria*; http://homepages.hawaiian.net/larryw/html/lemuria.html, 1997

Animal Dreaming
The Symbolic and Spiritual Language of the Australian Animals
by Scott Alexander King

Paperback / 336 pages / ISBN: 978-0-9803983-0-4

The understanding that animals can be spiritually called upon to assist us in almost every aspect of our lives is a realisation that opens a floodgate of knowledge and power to those who seek their counsel. Ancient teachings suggest that we are capable of communing with the forces of nature and speaking readily to the animals, birds, reptiles, fish and even the insects. Each animal offers its own sacred teachings. When we take the time to learn the symbolic language of the animals and listen carefully to what they have to say, we can use the knowledge gained to manifest their qualities and wisdom into our own lives.

Featuring an in-depth exploration of the Dreamtime and of Australia's seasonal wheel of the year, as well as a guide to finding your own Australian animal totem, 'Animal Dreaming' explores the spiritual and symbolic interpretations of over 200 native, domesticated and introduced animals, birds, reptiles and fish in Australia. Renowned author and acclaimed Animal Psychic, Scott Alexander King presents these animals to his readers as totems, teachers, healers and spiritual allies, offering a wealth of ancient knowledge and spiritual insight into the ways of the animals. 'Animal Dreaming' is an Australian first and an invaluable resource for anyone with an interest in the animal kingdom, sacred Earth Wisdom and Shamanic Lore.

"Every day, I reach for my copy of this rich and fascinating treasury of the spirit meaning of our sacred animals. I believe Scott Alexander King's 'Animal Dreaming' is destined to be a classic spiritual text, and I feel everyone should own a copy of this beautiful, ground-breaking book."
Lucy Cavendish, Author of 'White Magic' & 'Oracle of the Dragonfae'

Generation Intuitive
A Guide to Nurturing Your Child's
Infinite Potential
by Julie Hamilton

Paperback / 168 pages / ISBN: 978-0-9803983-3-5

The world is changing. Children, more than ever before, are highly sensitive to subtle energies through which they are intuitively and naturally connected to an infinite source of inner wisdom and creativity.

Our children are the pioneers of a new way of living. They have a vastly different perception and experience of the world around them. They see a world full of possibility and endless potential. 'Generation Intuitive' is upon us and it demands a whole new paradigm of parenting.

Now, in this straightforward and down-to-earth guide to nurturing and developing your child's natural intuitive gifts, Julie Hamilton explores the significance of intuition in the modern age, highlighting it as one of the most powerful tools for our children to live empowered and successful lives. Generation Intuitive looks at all the different intuitive 'super-senses' available to our kids, exploring each one individually and providing parents with insights into how they work, and how to nurture and manage them best.

Offering practical tools and advice, 'Generation Intuitive' also features a range of entertaining visualisations, games and exercises to help children tap into their intuition and explore all its wondrous possibilities.

'Generation Intuitive' equips parents with everything they need to know about caring for an emerging new generation of intuitive kids. As you learn to recognise, understand and nurture your children's unique intuitive gifts, you'll be helping them build their self-esteem, confidence and creativity, guiding them to make fantastic choices in life and ensuring they reach their full potential and shine!

Meditations for Kids by Kids
by Jarrah, Tahnaya, Ky & Jessica Wynne
ISBN: 978-0-9757683-6-5

In this touching collection of meditations, the Wynne children - Jessi (age 11), Ky (age 9), Tahnaya (age 7) and Jarrah (age 4) - have created a book to uplift, inspire and nurture kids of all ages! Beautifully illustrated by the Wynne children and presented in full-colour, this is a book you and your children will treasure!

"These words and pictures will take children away from the rush, bustle and harsh realities of the world, opening up a world full of imagination that is endless, safe and full of love. It will encourage them to connect with their feelings, release their fears and worries and provide them with some coping strategies in these days where beauty and innocence are so often forgotten."
- Helen Schweiger, Pre-school Teacher

Meditations for Children CD
by Elizabeth Beyer & Toni Carmine Salerno

Help your children to enter the world of their imagination through these inspiring creative visualisations. Designed for primary school aged children, these guided meditations will help kids tap into the magic world of their creativity and spirit. For use during the day or at night, this series of meditations will calm and relax as Elizabeth and Toni's gentle and reassuring voices take them into their imaginations- where all is possible!   (7 tracks. Running time: 48 mins)

Books

Lady of the Lamp by Caiseal Mór
ISBN: 978-0-9803983-1-1

Mercurius: The Marriage of Heaven & Earth by Patrick Harpur
ISBN: 978-0-9802865-8-8

The Secret Language Of Your Body by Inna Segal
ISBN: 978-0-9802865-5-7

Beyond The Emotional Roller Coaster by Anthony Salerno
ISBN: 978-0-9802865-1-9

Angelic Inspirations by Toni Carmine Salerno
ISBN: 978-0-9757683-5-8

Goddess by Toni Carmine Salerno
ISBN: 978-0-9757683-8-9

The Philosophers' Secret Fire by Patrick Harpur
ISBN: 978-0-9802865-2-6

Gaia: Body and Soul by Toni Carmine Salerno
ISBN: 978-0-9802865-4-0

Oracle Card Sets

Oracle of the Dragonfae by Lucy Cavendish
ISBN: 978-0-9803983-4-2

Ask An Angel Oracle by Toni Carmine Salerno & Carisa Mellado
ISBN: 978-0-9757683-2-7

Animal Dreaming Oracle by Scott Alexander King
ISBN: 978-0-9802865-3-3

Angels, Gods and Goddesses by Toni Carmine Salerno
ISBN: 978-0-9579149-6-4

Crystal Oracle by Toni Carmine Salerno
ISBN: 978-0-9579149-8-8

Guardian Angel Cards by Toni Carmine Salerno
ISBN: 978-0-9579149-7-1

Praise for 'KIDS!'

"Welcome to *KIDS!* - An exciting groundbreaking guide for our new paradigm children. Updated guidance is needed to understand these children and raise them to be happy, healthy and well-adjusted adults. This wonderfully refreshing and very unique approach contains a wealth of information using multiple perspectives with the intent of giving our children every opportunity to actualise their potential. In other words, to be all that they came here to be! Each category explored offers many different ways of understanding the child's makeup and how best to support the child on a physical, emotional and spiritual level. There is a rich reference and resources guide that parents will find a great blessing. An area discussed in great detail and that requires our urgent attention is the labelling and treatment of so-called ADD/ADHD children. Symptoms are a cry for help and are indicative of an imbalance within. Underlying emotional disturbances are usually at the core of the problem. A quick-fix approach via medication can mask the core issue and potentially cut off the child's spirit and creative potential. The *KIDS!* perspective will bring much relief and hope for parents as they discover that these children are gifts and not burdens. Scott brings forth abundance of information, writing with passion about his own childhood, his experiences as a primary school teacher, his knowledge of earth based traditions and as an animal wisdom messenger. Ralph's expertise in the fields of medicine, complementary treatment modalities and esoteric wisdom completes the mix. *KIDS!* is essential reading for parents, children, educators, therapists and anyone interested in the future of the planet. Read this book with an open heart and an open mind. You will be richly rewarded."

- Dr. Hanna Cyncynatus MB BS FAMAS

NOTES

NOTES

NOTES

NOTES

NOTES

NOTES

For more information
on any Blue Angel Gallery release,
please visit our website at:

www.blueangelonline.com